E·D·Brown, Cloverlea, Ellon, 2004

GRAMPIAN BATTLEFIELDS

Other titles by AUP

CROMARTIE: HIGHLAND LIFE 1650–1914
Eric Richards and Monica Clough

THE SHAPING OF SCOTLAND
18th century patterns of land use and settlement
R J Brien

FIT FOR HEROES?
Land Settlement in Scotland after World War I
Leah Leneman

PERSPECTIVES IN SCOTTISH SOCIAL HISTORY
essays in honour of Rosalind Mitchison
editor Leah Leneman

EMIGRATION FROM NORTH-EAST SCOTLAND
Marjory Harper
Vol One: Willing Exiles
Vol Two: Beyond the Broad Atlantic

THE CITY THAT REFUSED TO DIE
Glasgow: the Politics of Urban Regeneration
Michael Keating

GRAMPIAN BATTLEFIELDS

The Historic Battles of North East Scotland from AD84 to 1745

PETER MARREN

ABERDEEN UNIVERSITY PRESS
Member of Maxwell Macmillan Pergamon Publishing Corporation

First published 1990
Aberdeen University Press
© Peter Marren 1990

The publisher acknowledges subsidy from the Scottish Arts Council towards the publication of this volume.

British Library Cataloguing in Publication Data

Marren, Peter
  Grampian battlefields: battles in north-east Scotland.
  1. Scotland. Battles, history
  I. Title
  941.1

ISBN 0 08 036598 1

Typeset and printed by AUP Glasgow/Aberdeen—a member of BPCC Ltd.

To my parents

FOREWORD

By the late CUTHBERT GRAHAM

The knowledge of 'battles long ago' lights up in our consciousness a sequence of sparks and flares to illumine the mirk of our human past. The school children of my generation heard in the main of the nationally decisive battles: Mons Graupius (maybe), Hastings (certainly), Bannockburn, Flodden and Culloden. From the predominantly English history on which we were reared, there were Crecy, Agincourt, Bosworth Field and perhaps, because of the Scottish involvement, the ballad-famed battle of Otterburn. From the seventeenth century we learned of Marston Moor, Inverlochy, Worcester. The point was that they were on the whole rather special and distant places, far from our own doorstep.

It was quite a thrill to discover in due course that there had been momentous clashes in my home town—the city of Aberdeen: the battle of the Crabstane, the battle of the Bridge of Dee and, most horrendous of all, prelude to the gory Sack of Aberdeen, the battle of the Justice Mills. Country bairns might also hear of Barra, close to Old Meldrum, of Fyvie, of Harlaw on its hill just outside Inverurie, Corrichie on the Hill of Fare, Culblean on the slope above Loch Davan, Alford on the road to the bridge.

There were 'doorstep' battles too for the children of the Mearns, Banffshire and Moray. The fortunes of war swayed back and forth around Dunnottar. Farmers' and fishermens' children in Gamrie Bay intoned the infectious rhetoric of Sir William Geddes' ballad:

> Over brine, over faem,
> Thorough flood, thorough flame,
> The ravenous hordes of the Norsemen came
> To ravage our fatherland.

In Moray the spectacular elevated cape at Burghead looked out over the Firth and cherished not merely memories of the time-hallowed Burning of the Clavie, but also of a Scandinavian occupation. Further inland, in the sweet vale of the Dullan Water, the Battle Stone stood guard by the venerable

vii

Kirk of Mortlach. What matter if it long pre-dated a conflict with Danish invaders in the eleventh century?

A world of popular balladry often stands between us and a genuinely historical appreciation of battles like 'Reid Harlaw'. As Ramsay's 'Evergreen' put it:

> Frae Dunideir as I cam through
> Doun by the Hill of Banochie
> Alangst the lands of Garioch;
> Grit pitie was to heir and se
> The Nays and dolesum Hermonie,
> That evir that dreiry Day did daw,
> Cryand the Corynoch on hie
> Alas! Alas! for the Harlaw.

Fantastic numbers of casualties are to be found in the sixteen differing versions of the ballad of Harlaw in the Greig-Duncan folk song collection. There was obviously a competition between singers to multiply the statistics, so we need not take too seriously the most popular version of all:

> As I cam in by Dunideir
> An doun by Netherha,
> There was fifty thousand Heilanmen
> A-marching to Harlaw,
> Wi a dree, dree dradie druntie dree.

The awkward questions one is bound to ask about the highly picturesque traditions which abound in this and so many other localities in the North East of Scotland only emphasise the crying need for the serious survey of the Grampian battles which Peter Marren has undertaken. The battles lose none of their interest when truth rather than romance is the aim of the investigator. We may abandon some highly-coloured fairy tales only to discover that the reality was even more strange and wonderful than the legend.

This book covers a time-span of 1,661 years—from Tacitus' eloquent account in *The Agricola* of the Roman victory at Mons Graupius to the 'unlucky disaster' for the loyalist forces at Inverurie, on 23 December 1745. Taken as a whole, it forms a striking exercise in historical reasoning and historical imagination. Each battle site has been explored on the ground, the contemporary or near contemporary sources have been listed and sifted; where differing accounts and interpretations have come down to us they have been scrutinised with masterly acuteness.

I sincerely hope that Mr Marren's book will find an audience among the young people of the North East. Its educational value is considerable and it fulfils the modern ideal of illuminating the drama of one's immediate environment. His book is an invitation to independent reading and research, to enjoyable and instructive exploration of the countryside. How beautiful are so many of the battle sites—Durno and the north-facing slopes of Bennachie, Culblean and the Burn o' the Vat, Corrichie and the Hill of Fare. Even the suggestion that Bon-Accord Crescent and Terrace in Aberdeen were the actual sites of the action lights up the grim scuffle at the Crab Stane. Beautiful, but so often changed out of recognition, as the scene of the Battle of Alford must be, with the modern village, cultivated fields and cemetery replacing the much wilder landscape of 1645. Perhaps Mr Marren's book will encourage others to share our enthusiasm for the Grampian Battles.

CONTENTS

ILLUSTRATIONS

MAPS

PREFACE

Having written a book, an author then has to get it published. Often the process presents no difficulties, but sometimes events seem to conspire to hinder publication. In such cases the author is left to reflect wryly that writing a book may be a satisfying task, but seeing it published can be a nightmare. Peter Marren's *Grampian Battlefields* is a case in point, with a former publisher going out of business half way through production, leaving the original printer with proofs of part of the book and an unpaid bill, and a tangle of complications which it took several years to sort out. However, all is now well, publication achieved with the help of a much appreciated grant from the Scottish Arts Council and a new publisher, Aberdeen University Press. And the delay has had one positive consequence: it has enabled the author to update his text to take into account the results of research completed since the book was first written—some of which was presented in the papers given to the conference (to which Mr Marren himself contributed a paper) on 'When the Battle's Lost and Won—Military Milestones in the History of North East Scotland' organised jointly by the Centre for Scottish Studies and the Department of Adult Education and Extra Mural Studies of the University of Aberdeen, and held on 8 November 1986. Thus Mr Marren can at least console himself that in this sense the book is the better for the delay in publication.

DAVID STEVENSON
Director
Centre for Scottish Studies
University of Aberdeen

ACKNOWLEDGEMENTS

The bulk of this book was written as long ago as 1981–3 and parts of this draft were published in a series of articles in *Leopard* magazine. I thank the editor, Diane Morgan, for permission to republish this material. The text has since been extensively revised, and three new chapters added. The late Cuthbert Graham read an earlier version of the text and contributed a foreword as well as much encouragement: it is a matter of personal sadness to me that he did not live to see the book published. I have gained from discussing battlefield matters with various friends and acquaintances, among them Robin Callander, John Finnie, John Forster, Marcus Humphrey, Douglas and Anne Riach and Ian Sheppard. I am grateful to Maureen Beaton, who typed the original text, and to Mrs Margaret Croll, the secretary of the Centre for Scottish Studies, for transferring the text to floppy disc. The staff of Aberdeen University Library were most helpful. A generous grant in aid of publication from the Scottish Arts Council is gratefully acknowledged.

David Stevenson, the Director of the Centre for Scottish Studies, has read the entire text and has been responsible for many improvements to it, not least of them a major overhaul of the lists of sources and references. He has also guided the book towards publication, and without his aid it would probably have remained a dusty pile of paper in an attic. Dr John Smith, the Assistant Director of the Centre, has my thanks for his work in assembling the illustrations. Acknowledgements for all the illustrations are due to Gordon Stables, Department of Geography, University of Aberdeen, with the following four exceptions: Burghead and Aberdeen (Aberdeen University Library); Huntly (Scottish National Portrait Gallery); Montrose (David Stevenson). Don Wells of DW Graphics was responsible for production of the maps. The responsibility for any errors of fact remains, of course, my own.

PETER MARREN

INTRODUCTION

This is a book about the battlefields of north-eastern Scotland. Nearly seventeen hundred years separate our earliest battle, the Roman victory at Mons Graupius, from the last, a moonlit skirmish at Inverurie during the 'Forty-Five. This is the longest period of recorded warfare of any province in Britain. These years saw the hill-forts and chariots of the distant past, the longships and raiding parties of Scandinavian marauders, the clash of armoured knights in the high Middle Ages, the religious strife of the Reformation and the Highlander armies of Montrose and Bonnie Prince Charlie. They included the ballad-famed battle of Harlaw, encounters on remote hillsides like Culblean, Glen Livet and Corrichie, tragi-comic incidents like the battle of the Brig o' Dee and murderous feuds like the Bruce-Comyn struggle in the early 1300s and the Gordon-Forbes disputes of later years.

Compared with the well-known tourist attractions of Culloden, Bannockburn and Killiecrankie, however, the north-eastern battlefields are curiously little known. Harlaw, it is true, has an elaborate modern monument and the Deeside Field Club has marked the sites of two other battlefields, but most are unmarked and almost forgotten. Old tracks have been obliterated, burial cairns dismantled as sources of dyking stone and whole battlefields planted with coniferous crop-trees. The only monument to the battle of Alford, in which two thousand Scots are said to have died in the service of their country, lies buried beneath a rubbish dump. The camp of Robert the Bruce at Slioch has been smoothed by the plough and planted with barley. Insensitive planting of trees at Bennachie continues to mar the probable site of Mons Graupius. The battles of the North East are best known not from their location nor even from their impact on the course of history but from the ballads and songs which were composed about them long after the event. In the ballads, stories about 'old, unhappy, far-off things, and battles long ago' live on, and in some cases were perhaps passed down orally from one generation to the next before they were written down. Hence the subject has acquired a strong romantic tinge, with undertones of nostalgia. Many of us can sing or recite 'Harlaw' or 'Corrichie', but how many of us have actually stood on the land where those bloody events took place? Yet battlefields still contain many features which can bring the subject to life and illuminate the

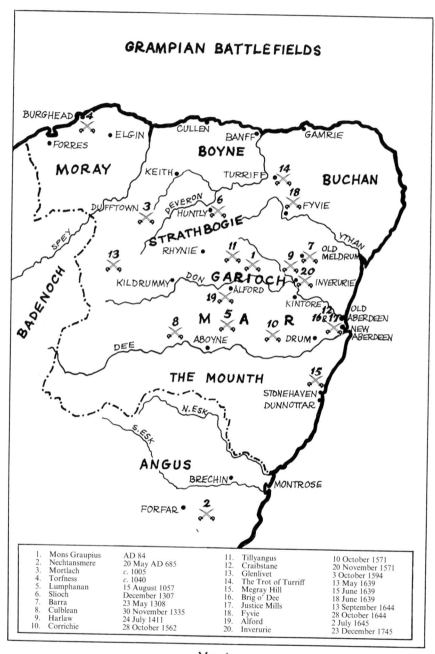

GRAMPIAN BATTLEFIELDS

1.	Mons Graupius	AD 84	11.	Tillyangus	10 October 1571
2.	Nechtansmere	20 May AD 685	12.	Craibstane	20 November 1571
3.	Mortlach	c. 1005	13.	Glenlivet	3 October 1594
4.	Torfness	c. 1040	14.	The Trot of Turriff	13 May 1639
5.	Lumphanan	15 August 1057	15.	Megray Hill	15 June 1639
6.	Slioch	December 1307	16.	Brig o' Dee	18 June 1639
7.	Barra	23 May 1308	17.	Justice Mills	13 September 1644
8.	Culblean	30 November 1335	18.	Fyvie	28 October 1644
9.	Harlaw	24 July 1411	19.	Alford	2 July 1645
10.	Corrichie	28 October 1562	20.	Inverurie	23 December 1745

Map 1.

course of events. Much changed as most of them are, they are still rewarding places to visit.

I have called this book Grampian Battlefields. In so doing, I am guilty of perpetuating that famous slip of the pen made by Francisco dal Pozzo in the late fifteenth century when *ad montem Grampium* was substituted for the original *ad montem Graupium*. For all its dubious origin as a word however, the adoption of two-tier local government has given 'Grampian' a new lease of life as the adopted name of Scotland's north-eastern regional council. And by fortunate chance, Grampian Region continues to represent the cultural and historic North East with its ancient sheriffdoms of Elgin, Banff, Aberdeen and Kincardine. This is the area which forms the subject of this book.

Our knowledge of the whereabouts of the Grampian battlefields has been acquired surprisingly recently. Early maps of Aberdeen and Banff show few battle sites and even these are not ones well-attested by history. The crossed swords symbol of battle at Mortlach brae, the 'Bloody Butts' at Lendrum, the 'Bloody Pitts Camp' at Gardenstown, and an obscure engagement on the Sinclair Hills near Fraserburgh are no longer marked on modern maps, and only the 'sair field of Harlaw' seems to have been remembered from early times. Some Grampian battles, such as Justice Mills, whose site has long been covered by houses, or Mons Graupius, about whose site there is much controversy and little agreement, still remain unmarked on any of the Ordnance Survey's maps.

I have attempted to reconstruct the course of the principal Grampian battles using, wherever possible, the chronicles, narrative histories and letters written at the time or soon afterwards. Sometimes the available information may be contradictory or insufficient to form a clear picture; and old battles can and have been refought in different ways. I have benefited from the researches and published work of Scottish historians, although I have not necessarily adopted their conclusions. I should mention in particular the broad canon of published work by the late W. Douglas Simpson, but I am also indebted to Professor Ranald Nicholson on Culblean, Professor G.W.S. Barrow on the Wars of Independence, Professor J.K. St Joseph on Mons Graupius and Graeme Cruickshank and the late Dr F.W. Wainwright on Nechtansmere. I have tried to place the battles in their contemporary social and political context, and to bring out their historical significance, without unduly detracting from the blood and thunder of the field. On some of the more rose-tinted episodes of ballad tradition, I have shown due scepticism. North-eastern contemporaries regarded civil warfare and battle with fear and revulsion, although an element of unseemly gloating sometimes enters the record. Not for the North Easterners the fox-hunting spirit of merrier wars in sunnier climes. The Grampian battles were mostly short, embittered and desperate. Fortunately they were of rare occurence.

I hope that readers who might not otherwise have done so will be encouraged to walk over our battlefields and form their own conclusions on the positions of the warring forces and what took place there. Most are on private land and permission should then be sought before leaving the footpaths and tracks, but this is normally readily given. Visitors to Nechtansmere, Bennachie and Culblean enjoy magnificent elevated vistas over the surrounding land, and even the less accessible sites like Corrichie or (for different reasons) Justice Mills ultimately reward the perseverance needed to discover their secrets. Most Grampian battlefields remain quiet areas of open north-eastern countryside. Cattle placidly graze the Bruce Field at Barra; a chessboard of square dyked fields crowns the hilltop at Harlaw and coniferous forest, grouse muir and steep rounded bens form the backcloth to the battlefield of Glen Livet. Nothing but the sound of distant roads and the occasional passing war-plane need stand between the traveller and his contemplation of the past.

PART I

Ancient and early medieval battlefields

The reconstruction of ancient battles presents considerable, indeed sometimes insurmountable, difficulties. Our sources are always inadequate, often obscure in meaning and seldom consist of more than a scrawled line or two, usually by writers with little or no knowledge of military matters. We know little more about the people who fought them or about the circumstances which led to the conflict. And in most cases the site of the battlefield itself is unknown. The site of Nechtansmere was not located beyond reasonable doubt until 1948 and antiquarians have been searching for the site of Mons Graupius for the past two hundred and fifty years. The obscurity of these conflicts often belies the resounding fame of the leading personages involved, such as Macbeth, Thorfinn and Agricola. An examination of the known circumstances and traditions surrounding the battles, together with a cautious leavening of reasoned conjecture, can sometimes add flesh to the very bare historical bones of this period, providing that the investigator does not insist on certainties. The first four chapters of this book, spanning a thousand years of early Scottish history, offer attempts at such reconstructions. They cannot always be described in the same narrative style as later and better documented battles, for the evidence will not admit such an approach. But in the fashion of a detective one can, by sifting through the evidence (and trying to resist the temptation to squeeze it too hard), suggest what might have happened and why.

What kind of people were they who fought these half-forgotten battles in the long dawn of Scottish history? The earliest known inhabitants of the North East were a mixture of Celtic tribes who are best known by the collective name, 'Caledonians'. A confederation of these Iron Age peoples stubbornly resisted the Roman invasion of 83–84 AD, which culminated in the terrible battle at Mons Graupius. We know very little about them. According to the Roman historian, Tacitus, they had red hair, fought with large blunt-ended swords and small round shields, and used war-chariots.[1] We must, for lack of any evidence to the contrary, assume that they were the ancestors of the Picts, who burst into history two hundred years later, during the declining years of the Roman Empire.

Picti (painted people) was a nickname bestowed by a third century Roman historian to the barbarian raiders living north of the Antonine wall and referred either to some woad-like war-paint or to a form of tattooing which they may have indulged. Their warrior aristocracy formed a number of petty kingdoms in the North and East of Scotland, whose wealth was counted in cattle. The war-like nature of the Picts is portrayed on some of the 'symbol stones' of the age, particularly those in northern Angus. They show parties of soldiers, some mounted on ponies, others on foot, bearing spears, broad-bladed swords and small round shields reminiscent of the Highlander's targe. Some wear helmets with prominent nasal guards and knee-length tunics. Some of the riders wear a plaid or cloak. Many of the hill-forts or duns and coastal promontory forts, which are such conspicuous landmarks in Aberdeenshire and Angus, are Dark Age Pictish sites. They are variable in size, reflecting the relative power and wealth of their owners, but the largest, such as the great promontory fortress at Burghead, are elaborate edifices with massive ramparts and sunken wells, and they must have required considerable social organisation to build. This was probably made possible by a system of provincial government under sub-kings or *mormaers* (literally, 'great stewards'). According to the *Book of Deer*, the provinces of Moray, Buchan, Mar and Angus were each the responsibility of a *mormaer*, who was owed dues and military service from his property holders or chiefs. In times of war, a chief and his kindred *clann* would gather under the banner of his respective *mormaer*.

The hill-fort at Dunnichen, near modern Forfar, was the scene of the most resounding victory the Picts ever won. This was the battle of Nechtansmere (658 AD), recorded by contemporary English and Irish annalists, in which an invasion force of Northumbrian Angles, under their king, Egfrith, was annihilated. The kingdom of the Angles at that time included the whole of Lothian and extended across the central Lowlands and Fife as far north as the Tay. The technology and social organisation of the Angles was far more advanced than that of the Picts, but the Northumbrian soldier probably shared much the same weaponry, shields and headgear, if contemporary carvings are anything to go by.[2] Some of the Northumbrians possessed tunics reinforced with iron rings or possibly chain mail, while for King Egfrith and his principal war chiefs, we might expect rich and elaborate harness, a barbaric version of a fifth century Roman general.

The end of the independent Pictish kingdom came, as every schoolboy knows, when Kenneth MacAlpin became king of both the Picts and the Scots in about 843 AD. How the Scots King Kenneth achieved this merger is not entirely clear, since his fame rests on no more than three short lines of a contemporary annal. Possibly the two peoples submerged their differences in the face of a common enemy who was slaughtering Pict and Scot alike at this time—the Vikings. The North East scarcely figures in the recorded history of the Viking Age and archaeology has so far yielded little to fill the vacuum. Were it not for the strength of tradition and the Viking's own testimony, of which the most illuminating is the *Orkneyinga Saga*, it would be easy to assume that the Vikings never came at all. In the Saga, the Norsemen beat the Scots with monotonous regularity. Their successes were probably due to a combination of heavier armour, more advanced weapons and superior military skill. The Viking sword, in particular, was a work of craftsmanship. A well-preserved example was uncovered during the construction of a railway line near Gorton in Moray, in the nineteenth century. The well-balanced, tapering blade measures thirty-five inches and is damascened along the centre, whilst the pommel and guard are inlaid with silver. Such a sword would have been a precious possession, handed on from generation to generation. There is evidence, too, that Viking warriors habitually wore a protective shirt or byrnie of chain mail, while the Scots wore a knee-length leather coat which was presumably less effective against sword slashes.[3] The Scots successes against the Vikings in the early eleventh century, as recorded by native tradition, may have been due to the adoption of Viking hardware and phalanx formation in battle. The Scots king, 'Karl Hundason', for instance, is said to have worn a 'mail coat, famous for its strength and brightness'.[4] Other weapons and projectiles mentioned by the sagas include short bows, javelins, 'darts' and spears. With their exuberant, bloodthirsty poetry, the sagas tell us much about the love of adventure and military glory of the Viking, together with his cruelty and barbarity. The following extract evokes a naval battle fought off Deerness in the Orkneys:

> All their swords and boards were swimming
> In the life-blood of the Scotsmen;
> Hearts were sinking—bowstrings screaming,
> Darts were flying—spear-shafts bending;
> Swords were biting, blood flowed freely,
> And the Prince's heart was merry.[5]

It is a pity we know so little about the Vikings in the North East. No permanent settlements are known, although there is some evidence of Viking colonies on the Buchan and Moray coasts. Tradition records a number of battles, but some of these encounters may be imaginary. The early Scots historians who record them freely invented history in order to fill out the meagre early chronicles, whilst local tradition, as enshrined in the Statistical Accounts, tends to assume, fallaciously, that groups of cairns and other prehistoric features are evidence of great battles in days gone by. Those Viking battles with the best claims to historical fact are examined in chapter three.

The last of the ancient battles to be described is perhaps the most obscure of all: the mystery of Macbeth's death at Lumphanan. In retrospect this event can be seen as one of the turning points in Scottish history, for, with his death, Celtic society began to be transformed by an infusion of Anglo-Norman ideas under Macbeth's supplanter, Malcolm Canmore, and his successors. The rift between Highland and Lowland culture and society, which was to be a dominant feature of future wars in the North East, had its origin in a violent clash of arms in the dark woods of remote Lumphanan.

CHAPTER 1

MONS GRAUPIUS

> Battles against Rome have been lost and won before, but hope was never abandoned, since we were always here in reserve. We, the most distant dwellers on earth, the last of the free, have been shielded until today...

Words attributed to Calgacus in *The Agricola*

The stirring words, given to Calgacus by the Roman historian Tacitus, have echoed down the centuries. Calgacus' great speech in defiance of Rome preceded perhaps the biggest and bloodiest battle ever fought in northern Scotland and marked the climax of the Roman Conquest of Britain. After Mons Graupius, there was little left of Britain for the Romans to conquer: they had reached the northernmost limits of the classical world. One might therefore have expected this battle to be one of the best known in our history, and the battlefield a popular attraction along the lines of Bannockburn or Culloden. For its relative neglect, Tacitus himself is, paradoxically, largely to blame. His *Agricola* was first and foremost a biography, written as a eulogy of his famous father-in-law. The detailed geography of north Britain and the customs of her native inhabitants were largely irrelevant to his purpose and in the whole of *The Agricola* Tacitus provides a bare dozen place-names. He fails, in consequence, to provide sufficient detail to enable a curious posterity to locate the site of the famous battle.

The findings of archaeology and, more recently, aerial photography have filled some of the gaps in our knowledge, notably the discovery of a line of temporary 'marching camps' stretching across the North East from Stonehaven to the Moray Firth. Three of these camps have been favoured by different historians as the most plausible sites for the elusive battlefield and since all three lie in the North East they firmly establish Mons Graupius as a Grampian Battle. In order to keep the main narrative of the battle free from digression, I have placed the thorny problem of the site of the battlefield in a separate section at the end of the chapter. The reconstruction of the battle which follows remains non-committal about its exact position.

4

Agricola and the invasion of the far north

Britain was invaded by the legions of Emperor Claudius in 43 AD. The lowlands of the south and east were quickly over-run and settled, but the conquest of the remainder of Britain was a stop-go affair, the pace of which was governed by the political situation in Rome and the Empire. By 78 AD, the Roman conquest had penetrated, in a leisurely fashion, as far north as present day Yorkshire. Since the rebellion of Boadicea in 60 AD, the Romans had been content to consolidate territories gained rather than to advance further. The appointment of Gnaeus Julius Agricola as governor of Britain in 78 signalled the beginning of a new aggressive drive northwards.

We know more about Agricola than any other Roman governor of Britain, thanks to the pen of Tacitus. He was of aristocratic background, the son of a praetor. His career was conventional for someone of his upbringing and promise, alternating military positions in the provinces with government service in Rome. Agricola had served as military tribune under an earlier governor of Britain, Suetonius Paulinus, and was present during the bloody rebellion of Boadicea in the 60s. He backed the successful candidate for emperor during the Roman civil war of 69 AD, and was rewarded by high office and ultimately the governorship of Britain in 77 or 78 AD. Tacitus presents him as an archetypal imperial general, austere, self-controlled and hard-working, a disciplinarian who did his duty. He was, Tacitus says, 'in love with military glory'. A modern historian, who can afford to be more dispassionate than Tacitus, discerns no evidence of truly outstanding ability along the lines of a Pompey or a Trajan: Agricola was 'a good general with a great biographer'.[1] Nevertheless, no other Roman governor of Britain seems to have achieved so much in terms of military conquest, road construction and the Romanisation of 'wild' Britain.

Agricola's period of high office began with a dramatic exploit. With the campaigning season already drawing to a close, he despatched a picked body of men to invade the Druid stronghold of Anglesey by swimming across the Menai Straits with their horses. The astonished Druids gave in at once, and Agricola's military reputation was henceforth assured. For the next six years he embarked on a series of offensives aimed at subjugating the north. By 81 AD he reached the Forth-Clyde line without great difficulty, and consolidated his advance with a series of timber forts and garrisons. In that year a new emperor, Domitian, wishing to bolster his own prestige with military successes, gave Agricola permission to move on and subdue the last remaining portion of Britain.

North of the Tay lay a 'huge and shapeless tract of country'[2] of chartless forests, bogs and hills. Its climate Tacitus described, simply and accurately, as 'wretched'. This forbidding land was occupied by various tribes of Celtic origin. Ptolemy's map of Scotland, which was made in the second century but derived mostly from information gathered in Agricola's day, provides Romanised names for the principal tribes of northern Scotland. We know sadly little about any of them. The lowlands and glens of Fife and Angus were occupied by the *Venicones*. North of the Mounth, in what is now

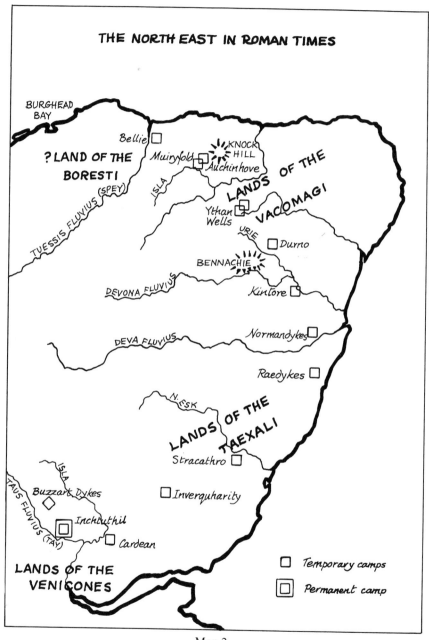

Map 2.

Aberdeenshire, were the *Taexali*, whose 'capital', Devana, has been identified by some with Aberdeen and by others with the remains of a prehistoric settlement near Loch Davan in mid-Deeside. On the lowlands of the Moray Firth were the *Vacomagi* and, finally, in the remote highlands about the Great Glen were the best known of them all, the *Caledoni*. Tacitus, who was not particularly concerned by the niceties of tribal geography, seems to have lumped them all together as 'the inhabitants of Caledonia'.

The Caledonians were comely people with reddish hair and large limbs, which led Tacitus to speculate that they were of Germanic origin. By the first century they had discovered the use of iron, which they used to tip their spears and arrows, whilst the less valuable metal bronze was relegated for use in making pots and bangles. They were probably a warrior society, whose wealth was counted in cattle, and whose lives were spent in perpetual raiding for more cattle and slaves. The Romans successfully exploited traditional rivalries between the various tribes and factions, in the same way as the American whites did in the Wild West and the British in India, seventeen hundred years later.

During the campaigning season of 83 AD, Agricola marched cautiously northwards through central Scotland, camping by navigable rivers where he could be supplied daily by his fleet. His aim seems to have been to build a chain of defensive forts guarding the entrances to glens north of Strathmore leading into the wild Grampians, with their line resting on the Firth of Tay. The Roman army was customarily divided into three columns with scouts or *exploratores* reconnoitering in advance of the army. After the day's march, Agricola's surveyors and engineers would supervise the building of a fortified temporary camp. A well-drained site with an adequate water supply would be sought, preferably one commanding an adequate view over the surrounding countryside. Within the single-line rampart and ditch, the men would dig latrines and pitch their tents in orderly, regimented rows, whilst some form of turf and timber structures would form command posts and places of religious observation.

During that year, the native tribes of the north appear to have agreed to settle their differences in order to join forces to resist the invader. Of the truces, pacts and urgent mobilisation of resources which must have taken place, we know nothing. But their reasons for resistance are clear enough. Tacitus says that the Caledonians feared they would be enslaved or left to face starvation as the Romans looted their granaries and roasted their cattle. They had heard about the conscription into foreign armies, the forced labour on the roads and in the mines and the heavy taxation which characterised the Romanisation of their neighbours in the south. In 83 AD the Caledonians very nearly succeeded in halting Agricola's remorseless advance. Avoiding pitched battle ('a pack of spiritless cowards', complained Agricola), and making use of the protection afforded by the 'woods and marshes', they launched a series of raids, culminating in a night attack on the isolated Ninth Legion. The Roman sentries were killed and the Caledonians managed to cross over the ramparts and break into the camp. Confusion reigned and only when Agricola, hurrying to the scene with three fresh divisions, joined the fray were they beaten back and a disaster averted. Attacks such as this strained the nerves of Agricola's men, particularly his auxiliary troops. One group of Germans mutinied, murdering their centurions and sailing off in two of the precious ships. It must have been with relief that the Romans reached the Tay and established winter quarters inside the more secure walls of a permanent fort at Inchtuthil.

As spring ushered in the campaigning season of 84 AD, Agricola suffered a personal tragedy. His infant son, born in camp the year before, sickened and died. The governor went on with his military preparations. His intention was to break the resistance and complete the conquest of Britain by bringing the troublesome Caledonians to battle and defeating them. He would therefore advance with deliberation through the heart of their country and force them into the open. His ability to defeat any combination of native tribes in open battle was not in doubt. The Roman field army of the 84 AD campaign may have numbered between 17,000 and 20,000 men, for it included contingents from all four legions stationed in Britain, auxiliary troops from the European provinces, a force of native Britons, and over 3,000 mounted troops. The core of the army was the Roman legions and their morale was high: 'they declared that nothing could stop men like them, that they ought to drive deeper into Caledonia and fight battle after battle until they reached the furthest limit of Britain'.[3]

We know very little about Agricola's actions in the spring and early summer of 84 AD. From the apparently remote location of the ensuing battle, we must suppose that he marched far into the north, and Tacitus' silence might be taken to mean that the march itself was relatively uneventful. The Romans settled into their routine of daily marches and nightly camps. They crossed unknown rivers, trackless forests and bleak, monotonous hills. And eventually, late that summer, says Tacitus with maddening brevity, Agricola 'reached Mons Graupius which he found occupied by the enemy'. Agricola had at last achieved his purpose of bringing the Caledonians to battle.

The battle

In massing together to defend a prominent hill position, the Caledonians were repeating what was evidently a traditional way of war, already adopted in previous decades by British leaders, such as Caractacus. The Romans were therefore familiar with this form of defence and had formed their own solutions to it. In the case of Mons Graupius, the Caledonians had made a supreme effort to meet the Roman menace. Embassies had gone out to the scattered settlements and tribes, women, children and cattle were withdrawn to the safety of the hills, sacrifices to the Gods were performed and the warriors, warned of the proximity of the Romans, assembled to fight them at the rendezvous of Mons Graupius. The tribes poured in from the surrounding countryside. Tacitus estimates their numbers at 30,000. This figure is intended to magnify Agricola's subsequent victory and need not be taken literally; half that number would have been remarkable. Only one of the leaders of this confederation is named. This is Calgacus, a man 'of outstanding valour and nobility', who is given a rousing speech by Tacitus, reminiscent of that of Henry V before Agincourt. This speech is, alas, not historical, but a literary device used often and with great effect by Tacitus and other classical writers. Indeed, Calgacus himself is probably a literary invention: the name means simply 'swordsman' and if he ever existed we might expect to know more about him and of his fate after the battle. In *The Agricola*, he walks on stage, delivers a speech, and promptly vanishes like smoke. Historical or not, however, his speech is deservedly famous:

> You have mustered here to a man, and all of you are free. The clash of battle—the hero's glory—has become the safest refuge for a coward. Battles against Rome have been lost and won before, but hope was never abandoned, since we were always here in reserve. We, the most distant dwellers on earth, the last of the free, have been shielded until today ... Now, the furthest bounds of Britain lie open to our enemies; and what men know nothing about they always assume to be a valuable prize. But there are no more nations beyond us; nothing is there but waves and rocks ... Pillagers of the world, the Romans have exhausted the land ... A rich enemy excites their cupidity; a poor one, their lust for power ... To robbery, butchery and rapine, they give the lying name of 'government'; they create a desolation and call it peace.[4]

As befits his austere character, Agricola delivered a much more matter-of-fact report, a typical army commander's 'Sitrep'. He proposed to fight the battle with his auxiliary troops, leaving his precious—and less expendable—legions in reserve. Tacitus calls this decision 'glorious', an odd choice of word. The troops were marshalled by their centurions in battle order. The four legions were stationed in the rear, by the camp rampart, together with the mounted reserve of four cavalry squadrons. A force of 8,000 auxiliaries, consisting of four cohorts of *Batavi* and two of *Tungri*, both originating from lower Germany and Belgium, plus an unknown number of native Britons, formed the front line. Like the legionnaires, they were clad in bronze or iron helmets and corslets, and bore flat oval shields. Most were armed with spears and the short, sharp, leaf-shaped Roman sword which was designed for use in close-quarter fighting, stabbing rather than slashing. Probably among them were half-naked irregular troops, armed with clubs or slings. Agricola guarded each flank with a total of 3,000 mounted troopers. Armed with swords and spears like the infantry, these sat on tough little ponies of less than fourteen hands. They acted as skirmishers and mounted infantrymen; massed cavalry charges were not much in fashion in the warfare at this period, and the Romans are said to have lacked the benefit of the stirrup. Some, indeed, rode bare-back into battle, without saddle or body armour.

The Romans faced an awesome spectacle. The front-line ranks of the Caledonians stretched out over a mile or more on the plain, and behind were yet more lines which 'seemed to mount up the sloping hillside in close-packed tiers'. In the no man's land between the armies, individual groups of Caledonians ran forward, shouting their defiance. Native charioteers man-oeuvred noisily about in front, throwing up clouds of dust as they showed off their skill. Agricola was probably unimpressed: chariot warfare was already regarded as obsolete by most of the tribes of the western world, and he knew how to deal with them from his experiences in the rebellion of Boadicea. Seeing that the enemy were nonetheless in greater numbers than he had expected, and that more were still arriving, he opened out his ranks to cover a wider front. Agricola sent his own horse to the rear—perhaps in a conscious imitation of Julius Caesar—and took up his position on foot in front of the standards. Then he gave the order to advance.

Once the Romans were within range, the Caledonians rained a shower of stones, spears and other missiles at their front ranks. The auxiliaries replied with javelins but, Tacitus states, 'the Britons showed great steadiness and skill in parrying our spears with their huge swords, or catching them on their little shields'. Agricola ordered his veteran Batavian and Tungrian cohorts forward, and the two great armies crashed together with the deafening noise of sword against shield, splintering wood and the screams of the wounded. In the roaring, confused, hand-to-hand fighting, the auxiliaries had the upper hand, whilst the Caledonians found no room in the crush to swing their unwieldy and blunt-pointed swords. Soon the Batavians were 'raining blow after blow, striking them with the bosses of their shields, and stabbing them in the face'. As the Caledonians began to give ground, the remaining infantry cohorts joined in, cutting, stabbing and clubbing their way into the crowded ranks. In a short time, the Caledonian front line had been driven back, creating confusion in the rear ranks. The battle at this point must have been a seething, heaving mass, the Roman auxiliaries hacking their way forward, the Caledonians increasingly giving ground.

In the meantime, the Roman cavalry had made short work of the native war-chariots. They now wheeled to attack the enemy in the flank. Their manoeuvre failed however, to break the Caledonian ranks. The rough ground at the base of the hill made concerted cavalry attacks difficult and the impetus of their advance slowed to a standstill. The main danger to both sides came from runaway chariots and riderless horses 'careering about wildly in their terror ... plunging into the ranks from the side or in head-on collision'. A Roman prefect of a cohort, Aulus Atticus, was killed after his horse went out of control and carried him deep into the enemy ranks.

The first phase of the battle on the plain had brought speedy victory to the Romans, but the Caledonian 'tiers' on the hillside were still intact and in a strong posture for defence. Unfortunately they were not content to stand and wait. Caledonians had already started to descend the hill from opposite sides, hoping to envelop the rear of the Roman army while the main engagement was being decided. Anticipating this, Agricola ordered his four reserve squadrons of cavalry forward to scatter them. The little horses pursued groups of fleeing Caledonians, sticking them with lances and cutting them down. Some were taken prisoner, only to be slaughtered in cold blood as a third and final native force descended the hill.

The battle now dissolved into a rout. The Roman horse regrouped and attacked the remaining Caledonian force from the rear. Isolated groups of natives were now fleeing into the hills, while others made last despairing, suicidal charges, flinging themselves against the Roman spears. Some escaped into the shelter of the surrounding forest and, rallying, managed to ambush and turn the tables on their pursuers. The Romans were obliged to form a cordon around centres of resistance in the forest, and squads of provincial troops were sent in to flush them out. Meanwhile the cavalry moved through the thinner parts of the forest, killing any fugitives they could find. The mopping up and pursuit of the wretched natives carried on until dusk, by which time the soldiers' limbs ached with killing. Then they set about looting the battlefield.

The Romans lost 360 men at Mons Graupius, most of them auxiliaries. There is no evidence that the legions were involved at all and only one senior officer, Aulus Atticus, was killed. Tacitus says of the Caledonians that 'some 10,000 fell', in which case two-thirds of their number had managed to escape. Again, we need to be mindful of the importance to Agricola and Tacitus of a propaganda victory, to justify the immense resources used up in this campaign. Still, it is probable that the native casualties were heavy.

The next day dawned to an eerie sight. On the plain and by the edge of the forest, 'equipment, bodies and mangled limbs lay all around on the bloodstained earth... An awful silence reigned on every hand; the hills were deserted, houses smoking in the distance, and our scouts did not meet a soul'. After scouting the neighbourhood to ascertain that no new enemy force was massing in the hills, Agricola marched on. Within a short time, as the brief northern summer drew to a close, he reached 'the territory of the Boresti', probably the lowlands of the Moray Firth, where he re-established contact with his supply fleet. A detachment of troops were placed on board and the admiral was ordered to sail north to explore the coast to the furthest point of land. Their landing parties met no resistance for 'the terror of Rome had gone before'. In the meantime Agricola took hostages from the Boresti and began the long withdrawal to winter-quarters at Inchtuthil, 'marching slowly, in order to overawe the recently conquered tribes by the very deliberateness of his movements'.

Agricola's cherished hopes for completing the conquest of the far north were soon dashed. Having now completed two full terms as governor, he was recalled to Rome by Emperor Domitian. He was rewarded with an *ornamenta triumphalia*, the highest honour that a non-member of the imperial family could hope to attain, but, according to Tacitus, the emperor feared his prestige and refused to consider him for the further high appointments his success had earned. Whatever the truth of this, Agricola was not employed again. Perhaps Agricola's Mons Graupius campaign was not regarded as the decisive triumph which Tacitus claims, for no territorial annexation resulted and the northern tribes—'the last of the free'—remained free. Moreover, only two years later, the fort at Inchtuthil was dismantled and the legions withdrawn south of the Forth-Clyde line. Tacitus saw this as a great betrayal: north Britain had been 'completely conquered' and then immediately let go. From the emperor's point of view, it was a perfectly sensible decision. The Roman imperial frontier was already over-extended and the far north of Britain held nothing worth the enormous cost of maintaining a garrison there. Perhaps even Agricola had recognised the impossibility of holding the vast hinterland of Highland Scotland. The natural line of defence was the neck of land between the Forth and the Clyde. Much more serious military threats existed elsewhere on the imperial frontiers.

Agricola's invasion of the north of Scotland was not the last time Romans set foot there, but we know little about subsequent expeditions. In 208 AD, a tribal rebellion proved sufficiently threatening for Emperor Septimius Severus to conduct a Scottish military campaign in person, at the head of a powerful army. He seems to have spent most of his time in operations between the Forth and the Mounth, but at least part of his army is said to have marched north as far as the Moray Firth, possibly in the footsteps of Agricola. Here in 209 AD the emperor received the surrender of the Caledonian tribes but the campaign had no durable result, for no attempt was made to refortify the territory north of Hadrian's Wall. A third offensive to 'the remote parts of Scotland' by Constantius Chlorus and his son, Constantine in 306 AD proved equally inconclusive, despite victories against northern tribes who were now being called Picts. After Constantius' death at York later that year, north-eastern history sleeps for another three hundred years.

The Roman victory at Mons Graupius is in some ways reminiscent of the battles against the Zulus and other tribesmen in the heyday of the later empire of Queen Victoria. From the standpoint of our own post-imperial age, it seems less glorious than it did to the Roman public at the time. The Caledonians were ill-prepared to meet professional, well-equipped soldiers in pitched battle, and the result was almost inevitable. Had they continued to employ the more sensible tactics of guerilla warfare, which came close to success in 83 AD, they might well have forced Agricola to withdraw without his propaganda victory. The German tribes of the Rhine had annihilated three Roman legions and won a war by such means. By committing themselves to a single decisive battle the Caledonians threw away most of the advantages of fighting on their own ground in the way they were best accustomed. But it was a mistake that they did not repeat and, unlike the other parts of Britain, Caledonia was never under permanent occupation.

Attempts to locate the battlefield

Tacitus did not regard the exact geographical location of the battle of Mons Graupius as a matter of any importance. He assumed, perhaps rightly, that his Roman audience would not be very interested in exact geographical information about a cold, remote land which none of them wanted to visit. 'The task of extracting history from The Agricola,' wrote one despairing modern historian, 'has a certain rather irritating attraction, akin to crossword problems'.[5]

Antiquarians, historians and archaeologists have been playing the Find the Battlefield game for nearly three hundred years. Sir Robert Sibbald, in his commentary on The Agricola (1707), suggested Ardoch, for no very good reason. Alexander Gordon (1726) was confident that Dalginross in Perthshire was the site, while another Perthshire site, Fortingall, was favoured by the Reverend John Horsely (1732). General Roy (*c.* 1750) suggested a site near Stonehaven[6] and William Maitland (1757) pointed to the nearby, newly discovered Roman camp at Raedykes as the likely place.[7] The Reverend James Playfair (1797) took an independent line, claiming that the battle had been fought at Buzzart Dikes near Blairgowrie and citing the remains of Caledonian and Roman camps in the vicinity as evidence.[8] His 'Caledonian camp' is in fact a medieval deer enclosure.

We need not linger long over most of these suggestions. They tend to be based on the supposed resemblance of a landscape to the imperfect description of Tacitus or on remains which were then thought to be contemporary with the battle. Most historians now believe that the suggested sites in Strathearn and Tayside are too far to the south to be tenable and only Raedykes survived the rigorous pen of O.G.S. Crawford.[9] The real clues to the site of the battlefield are the finds of modern archaeologists.

Let us review what Tacitus actually tells us about the battlefield. The Roman approach march is described thus: Agricola 'sent his fleet ahead to plunder at various points and thus spread uncertainty and terror; then, with an army marching light... he reached Mons Graupius, which he found occupied by the enemy'. The Caledonian front line was situated on a plain, but behind them, 'other ranks seemed to mount up the sloping hillside in close-packed tiers'. Tacitus also tells us that the Romans had built a defensive camp near the battlefield. He further implies that the Romans had already marched a long way north from their winter quarters at Inchtuthil by the Tay. And that is about all. To find the battlefield, therefore, we must look for signs of a large Roman camp situated not far from a prominent hill and separated from it by a level plain. We can supplement this information with what the late Colonel A.H. Burne described as 'inherent military probability'.[10] Since the Caledonians themselves decided to rendezvous and fight at Mons Graupius, they presumably chose not only a prominent landmark but one which must have been of some strategic importance and which they expected the Romans to pass. We might expect to find the remains of native settlements and fortifications in close proximity.

Valuable evidence was provided when the Roman legionary fortress at Inchtuthil, by the Tay between Perth and Dunkeld, was excavated in the 1950s. There is no doubt that this large timber fortress, which contained baths and a hospital, was founded by Agricola in 83 AD, for coins of emperor Domitian have been discovered on site. Inchtuthil would have been the advanced base and winter quarters for the Mons Graupius campaign of 84 AD and the battle must therefore have been fought well to the north. Aerial photography over the past thirty years has gradually revealed a chain of marching camps stretching north eastwards from Inchtuthil. The last permanent fort is Stracathro in the Mearns. From here, there are a series of temporary camps, about a days march apart from each other: Raedykes, Normandykes, Kintore, Durno, Ythan Wells, Auchinhove and Muiryfold at Strathisla, near the north coast. Most of these are large camps of 90–140 acres in size, and capable of sheltering a full-sized Roman expeditionary force. It is tempting to assume that the camps provide Agricola's line of march through the North East, but unfortunately the evidence cannot sustain that assumption. No material has been excavated which can establish the date of their construction. The relatively small camps at Stracathro, Ythan Wells and Auchinhove possess common details in the outline of their gatehouses which archaeologists attribute to a single invasion force, supposed to be that of Agricola. They are less certain about the larger camps, although some assume that they were built by Emperor Septimius Severus in 208–11 AD.[11] Professor J.K. St Joseph pointed out, however, that the uniformity of size of the larger north-eastern camps suggests that they were built by the same force and that camps of this size would have been necessary to contain the whole of Agricola's field army.[12] So far, no compelling evidence has emerged to assign these camps to a particular date and it is perfectly possible that they too were built by Agricola, although subsequent invading forces may have refortified them. With these precepts in mind, let us look at some of the recent attempts to find the battlefield:

1. RAEDYKES. This unusually well-preserved Roman camp has been championed by many writers and historians over the past two hundred years as Agricola's camp at Mons Graupius. It overlooks an important strategic position where the hills form a natural barrier between the Mearns and the lowlands further north. Furthermore, it is unusually irregular in shape, suggesting that it was built in a hurry. It has been suggested that the battle was fought on the nearby hills of Meikle Carewe and Curlethney or, alternatively, on Kempstone Hill further to the east.[13] Further supposed evidence was provided when the remains of three wheels and an iron axle-ring were excavated from the northern rampart of Raedykes by Sir George MacDonald in 1914. O.G.S. Crawford (1949) connected this find with the native war-chariots used on the battlefield. Modern opinion is that the wheels belong to a Roman supply wagon—interesting in itself, since Tacitus states that Agricola had travelled unencumbered by heavy baggage. Raedykes was for many years the only known Roman camp which seemed to provide all the necessary features of the battlefield but, in the light of more recent discoveries elsewhere, its claims are less convincing. Raedykes is not among those camps which are thought to be Agricolan in date and the flattish hills about the camp scarcely match the description of Tacitus, especially his reference to the Caledonian ranks arrayed 'in close-packed tiers' on the hillside. In the light of our knowledge of further Roman camps extending far to the north, Raedykes seems an improbably southerly location for a battle which was apparently fought near the northward limit of Agricola's march.

2. DUNCRUB. This site, a hill near Dunning in Strathearn, was put forward by archaeologist Richard Feachem in 1970, largely on etymological grounds.[14] Duncrub is thought to be derived from the Celtic *dun Crup* ('hill of the hump'), perhaps the root of Tacitus' *Graupius*. Nearby is the rampart of a large Roman camp which is thought to be of Agricolan age. The site scarcely matches Tacitus' 'world's end' location, however, and lies in an area

which was probably secure in Roman hands by 84 AD. Moreover, Duncrub seems too small and insignificant a hill to contain the vast Caledonian force.

3. SILLYEARN HILL. This northerly site, at the Pass of Grange on the frontier of the lowlands of Moray, was first mooted by Glasgow historian A.R. Burn in 1953.[15] The site satisfied the details of Tacitus better than any so far put forward, and the broad ridge of Sillyearn Hill was close to the then most northerly known Roman camp at Auchinhove, which archaeologists believe was built by Agricola. On strategic grounds, the site is a strong contender, particularly if one accepts the identification of *the Boresti* of Tacitus with the inhabitants of lowland Moray. Nevertheless, objectors point out that Auchinhove is much too small to contain the whole of Agricola's army and the camp lies to the west of, and therefore *beyond*, the Caledonian position, whereas one would expect it to lie on the east side, blocking the Roman line of advance. A second and much larger Roman camp has subsequently been discovered at Muiryfold but its date is unknown and, like Auchinhove, it too lies to the west of Sillyearn Hill.

4. BENNACHIE. The last of our sites is also the most recently proposed. During the course of an aerial reconnaisance flight on 26 July 1975, Dr J.K. St Joseph discovered an unsuspected Roman camp at Durno on the north side of the Urie, between Pitcaple and Old Rayne. Subsequent aerial photographs and a preliminary excavation revealed that this camp was exceptionally large, measuring 900 yards across, and enclosing about 144 acres. The ditches originally measured eleven feet broad and four feet deep. This is the biggest known Roman marching camp north of the Antonine Wall. Two miles away, the bold outline of Bennachie dominates the skyline, and its northern slopes form a great natural ampitheatre facing the camp. In 1978, St Joseph suggested that this hill and no other is Mons Graupius.[16] The main points in its favour are as follows:

(i) Bennachie is the most distinct and widely visible *Mons* along Agricola's probable route. It would be a natural choice for an assembly point.

(ii) There are many prehistoric settlements and hill-forts in the area, including two on Bennachie itself.

(iii) The Durno camp is large enough to hold the entire field army of Britain, estimated as some 20,000 men.

(iv) The Durno camp interrupts the normal spacing of the marching camps. Furthermore, the two nearest camps, Kintore (110 acres) and Ythan Wells (33 acres), together equal the size of Durno (*c*. 144 acres). This is consistent with the supposition that a reconnaisance force had advanced ahead to Ythan Wells but was withdrawn to join the main Roman army after the enemy had been sighted.

(v) This site agrees more closely with the description of Tacitus than any other. The north-facing slopes of Bennachie are steep and concave in outline, which means that the Caledonian ranks would indeed have appeared to rise up in tiers as seen from the plain of the Urie. Fur-

1.   Bennachie from the north, showing the possible site of the battle of Mons
Graupius.

thermore, Tacitus' phrase *summa collium*, 'the top of several hills', is
a good description of the serrated profile of Bennachie.

St Joseph sums up his argument neatly:

> Readers will form their own judgement ... (the above) considerations, taken
> individually, might be judged of little account, but the chances are over-
> whelmingly against there being in some other locality the significant associ-
> ations which is so evident at Durno—Bennachie.

Many recent books about Roman Britain have accepted St Joseph's argu-
ments, but nevertheless some anomalies remain. The camp lies over two miles
from the hill and the river Urie passes between them. No finds came to light
during St Joseph's excavation and the identification of the Durno camp with
Agricola is uncertain. St Joseph's identification is based, of necessity, on
circumstantial evidence, and there may well be other large camps awaiting
discovery, perhaps even beyond the Moray Firth.[17]

The site of the battle of Mons Graupius must remain a matter of opinion
until more substantial evidence is produced by the spade of the archaeologist.

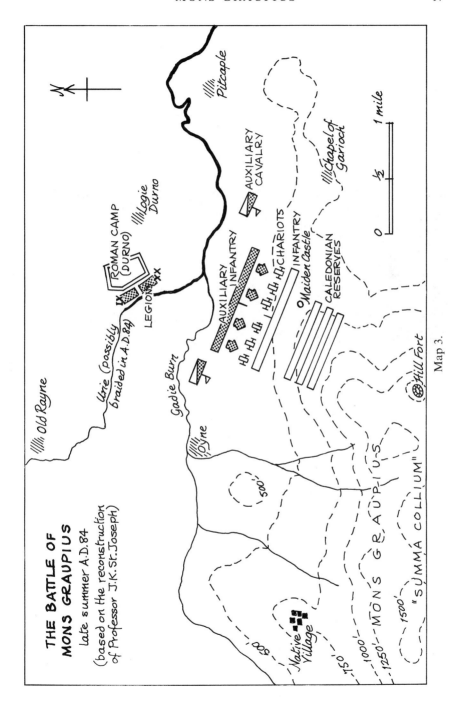

THE BATTLE OF
MONS GRAUPIUS

Late summer A.D. 84

(based on the reconstruction
of Professor J.K. St. Joseph)

Old Rayne

Urie (possibly
braided in A.D. 84)

ROMAN CAMP
(DURNO)

Logie
Durno

Pitcaple

IX

LEGION XX

AUXILIARY
CAVALRY

Gadie Burr

AUXILIARY
INFANTRY

CHARIOTS

INFANTRY

Maiden Castle

CALEDONIAN
RESERVES

Chapel of
Garioch

Oyne

500'

Native
Village

750'

1000'

1250'

1500'

"SUMMA COLLIUM"

MONS GRAUPIUS

Hill Fort

0   ½   1 mile

Map 3.

No wholly convincing site has been put forward, and, as one Roman scholar has written recently, with pardonable exaggeration, 'Mons Graupius could be almost any hill in Scotland'.[18] The rhetoric which Tacitus places in the mouth of Calgacus—'nor will it be inglorious to fall at the very limit of the created world'—has led one authority to locate the battle in Sutherland or Caithness,[19] although others believe that this phrase could apply to anywhere in the north of Scotland.[20]

I would add one personal remark. If one visits Durno with a copy of *The Agricola* in hand, as I did, and turns south to face Bennachie, it takes a strong determination not to feel that here one is indeed standing in Agricola's footsteps. Obscurities in Tacitus become clearer and the battle can be refought in one's imagination. As I stood there in the Roman camp on a blustery autumn day, with clouds scudding over the Mither Tap, I felt that here and nowhere else was fought the famous battle at the world's end.

Already, the ballad makers are at work:

> The fiery cross sped throu' the lan
> By Don an' Dee an' Deveron fair,
> An' seen wiz mustert on Bennachie
> Thretty thoosan' men or mair.[21]

Mons Graupius today

Bennachie dominates central Aberdeenshire like a great four-masted galleon riding on the choppy seas of Garioch and Donside. That well known lilt,

> O, gin I war whaur Gadie rins
> At the back o' Bennachie

describes the probable scene of the first recorded event in the North East's history. Today the 'back o' Bennachie' is traditional north-eastern farming country, blending into rough pasture and conifer plantations on the flank of the hill. The area is rich in historical associations and antiquities, and Bennachie itself is open to the public via the Forestry Commission's forest walks and the hill tracks which link the summit craigs.

In such an area we might reasonably hope to see some features associated with the time of the battle. But, as so often is the case with ancient battlefields, such evidence proves elusive. The farm of Westerton lies within the boundaries of the Roman marching camp of Durno, but its outline is visible only from the air as crop marks and, even then, only in certain seasons. In Professor St Joseph's reconstruction of the battle, the Roman front line lay between the Manse of Oyne and Mill of Carden, occupying a mile or so. A good overall impression of the battlefield as a Roman auxiliary might have seen it can be obtained from the Gowk Stone, a prehistoric stone standing on a low hill near the Manse.

A Caledonian's eye-view of the battlefield can be obtained by walking from the Forestry Commission's car park, along the 'Maiden Causeway' to the summit of Mither Tap. The vitrified fort at Mither Tap probably post-dates the battle, although it could well be the site of the Caledonian 'command headquarters' and might even be the place where Calgacus delivered his great speech. At the foot of the hill near the car park lies another antiquity, the 'Maiden Castle', apparently an Anglo-Norman motte. It is not easy to find, being crowned by beech trees and shrouded by plantings and regenerating scrub woodland. A third feature of the hill, which is more likely to be contemporary with the battle, is a prehistoric settlement situated in a forest clearing, just west of the Back o' Bennachie car park. This consists of an enclosure wall containing a number of smaller stone circles. Although we cannot prove that this settlement was inhabited at the time of the battle, it has the appearance of an Iron Age site and thus offers corroborative evidence for Tacitus' implication that Mons Graupius stood amid a well-populated district.

The antiquities of Bennachie add little to our knowledge of the battle but they lend interest and atmosphere to an exploration of the battlefield. The best way to bring this battle to life is to visit the area with a copy of *The Agricola* in your hand. The thunder of battle will ring from those dry, laconic pages.

CHAPTER 2

NECHTANSMERE

AD 685. In this year in Britain it rained blood, and milk and butter were turned into blood.

Anglo-Saxon Chronicle.[1]

Of all the battles in this book, Nechtansmere had the most far-reaching consequences. It is also among the least known battles, although it has been given a certain notoriety by a claim that the field is haunted by the ghosts of Dark Age warriors.[2] This is the only battlefield in this book which lies outside the confines of Grampian region. I have included it for two reasons: the battle involved the native Pictish people who inhabited the North East at that time and it influenced profoundly the course of history in the north and east of Scotland.

By 685 AD, the land which was, much later, to become Scotland was inhabited by a variety of kingdoms and tribal lands. In the far west dwelled the Scots of *Dalriata*, where St Columba's Christian foundation at Iona was already at work evangelising the north. In Strathclyde was the still important kingdom of North Britons. To the south and east lay the Anglo-Saxon realm of Northumbria which, after a period of expansion during the seventh century under a succession of aggressive and powerful kings, occupied much of Galloway and the eastern lowlands as far north as the Forth. And to the north of the Forth lay the Pictish kingdom of *Fortriu*, a name variously given to the heartland of Strathearn or to the whole of Pictish lands south of the Mounth. Further north still, Pictish peoples inhabited the lowlands of the North East, the Moray Firth and the far north of *Cait* or Caithness. What little we know about Pictish history has to be pieced together from annals and ecclesiastical writings of Irish and Northumbrian monks. The Picts have left us no writings of their own, apart from cryptic inscriptions on their symbol stones. By contrast, the cultural flowering of Northumbria under the early Christian church was at its height. This was the age of the Venerable

Bede and the great and influential founding fathers of the Roman church in Britain, Saints Cuthbert and Wilfred. Through the eyes of these men and those of their counterparts in Ireland, we can discern the general drift of events which led to the great battle at Nechtansmere in which Northumbria suffered her most grievous defeat.

The issue which was to be resolved at the battle of Nechtansmere was whether the eastern half of north Britain would be ruled by the English or the Picts. By 658, a powerful Northumbrian king, Oswy, ruled over the whole of Lothian as far north as the Forth, seemingly by a combination of military might and a family alliance with the Pictish king of Fortriu. For the first time the Anglo-Saxons and the Picts had a common boundary. According to Bede, Oswy 'subjected the greater part of the Pictish race to the dominion of the English'.[3] The extent and form of this 'dominion' is uncertain. Possibly it involved tribute and hostages. There is no evidence of permanent English settlement north of the Forth, but contemporaries agree that the Picts regarded themselves as 'oppressed' or even 'enslaved'. A frontier outpost, including a monastery, was established by Oswy at Abercorn on the Forth, and its new bishop, Trumwine, was there to ensure the consolidation of Northumbrian influence among the Pictish clergy and aristocracy.

King Egfrith and King Bridei

Egfrith, son of Oswy,[4] succeeded to the Northumbrian throne in 671. We are given a few personal glimpses of him by Bede and his contemporary, Eddius Stephanus, both of whom were acquainted with close associates of the new king. Egfrith had spent much of his youth in rather menacing circumstances as a hostage at the court of the rival Saxon kingdom of Mercia. His subsequent marriage, to a saintly woman who insisted on perpetual virginity, must have been an additional misfortune. He endowed the church with lands on a lavish scale, and at least for the first half of his reign, was on good terms with the leading churchmen of the time. Eddius refers to him in conventional terms as a 'most devout and Christian king' but also a ruthless warrior chief, 'tough and relentless' and 'a man of unwavering purpose'.[5] The power of the early English kings depended to a large extent on their ability to annex new land holdings with which to reward their followers. In order to win support, Egfrith was compelled not only to maintain but to extend his father's conquests. His reign was therefore spent in continual warfare, hopping from one beleaguered frontier to another. Eddius assures us that Egfrith was a gentle ruler of his own people and merciful to defeated enemies, but 'quick in battle, impatient of delay' and capable of dealing out ferocious retribution when defied.

The quick and impatient side of Egfrith's nature was demonstrated in his treatment of the Picts. In about 676 the Picts, taking advantage of Egfrith's preoccupations elsewhere, attempted to throw off the Northumbrian yoke and expelled a puppet king set up by Egfrith's father. Eddius describes, unsympathetically, how 'swarms of them gathered from every cranny of the north, like ants in summer sweeping up an earthwork to protect their home from ruin'. Egfrith responded to the Pictish rebellion by a ferocious military subjugation. Pictish armies are said to have fallen before him like corn to the reaper. Two rivers were choked with the slain, so that the Northumbrian host was able to cross over dry-shod in order to massacre the rest. Thus, according to Eddius, were the Picts reduced once more to slavery.

The Northumbrian church recorded the bloody suppression of the Pictish revolt with approval: their building projects were partly financed by the plunder, and king Egfrith could be seen as instrumental in bringing about the triumph of the Roman church in north Britain. A few years later, however, Egfrith quarrelled with the two most influential of his advisors, the austere saints Cuthbert and Wilfred, and from then on the monkish chronicles of the time are full of dire predictions of doom. Portents included a comet in 678— 'a tall column of bright flame ... which every morning shone like sunshine'[6]— and, in 685, the year of the Nechtansmere battle, the very heavens are said to have 'rained blood, and milk and butter were turned to blood'.

The action which incurred the Church's greatest disapproval was Egfrith's Irish campaign of 684. A Northumbrian sub-king, a roughneck called Bert or Beorht, was sent across the sea to Meath at the head of an expeditionary force. The brutal harrassment which followed, of 'an inoffensive people who had always been friendly to the English', was accompanied by the indiscriminate pillaging of Irish churches and monasteries. Clerical opinion in Northumbria was outraged and the events of the following year, which brought disaster to Egfrith and Northumbrian hegemony in the north, was thereafter seen as a judgement of God.

In the meantime, the Picts had a new ruler. In about 682, Bridei, son of Bili, succeeded to the Pictish kingdom of Fortriu. Here was a king with more than the usual resources to draw on. Bridei's father had been king of the Strathclyde Britons, based at Dumbarton, and had been succeeded there by Bridei's brother, Owen. Fortriu is described as 'the inheritance of Bridei's grandfather' on his mother's side. The accession of Bridei, therefore, may have represented an alliance with the still considerable kingdom of Strathclyde.[7] Suggestions of Bridei's unusual power appear fleetingly in the chronicles of the age. He besieged the fort of Dunnottar at the boundary between the northern and southern Pictish kingdoms.[8] He harried the Orkneys. In 685 his military campaigns culminated in a great battle which reversed the tide of Northumbrian expansion for ever.

The battle

The battle of Nechtansmere has been called 'the best documented event in Pictish history'[9] and was clearly regarded by contemporaries as an event of supreme importance. It is mentioned in a dozen early annals and saints' lives although few commit themselves to any detail more substantial than the date, place, and the names of the two kings. Nevertheless, the information which one can sift or reasonably surmise from the evidence is impressive for a battle fought in a remote place at this early date. Some contemporaries could undoubtedly have told us a great deal more about it, but chose not to. Bede, for example, was bent on demonstrating the triumph of Anglo-Saxon Roman Christianity over the Celtic church; he wished to stress an alleged Pictish desire to follow the Northumbrian lead in this great matter and would not have wished to over-emphasise an event like Nechtansmere, which resulted in the Roman church's discomfiture. Adomnán, St Columba's hagiographer, might have been able to tell us even more, for he visited both the Northumbrian court and the lands of the Picts shortly after the battle and is said to have been a close friend of King Bridei. But he had no particular interest in doing so; secular history had not yet been re-invented and our knowledge of political events in this distant age has to be glimpsed in the occasional gaps in the hagiographic mist.

An outline of the campaign and battle can be suggested from the evidence. Egfrith was determined to subdue the lands between the Forth and the Mounth, important both strategically and in terms of agricultural value, but either underestimated or failed to understand the particular difficulties facing him. There is no evidence that he maintained garrisoned forts and lines of communication, and he seems to have relied mainly on terror to assert his overlordship. How and why he was provoked into making a second punitive expedition into the land of the Picts is uncertain. There had, presumably, been some form of rebellion against Northumbria on a scale which required the king's personal intervention. Bridei may have taken advantage of Northumbrian preoccupations in Ireland and elsewhere to reject Egfrith's overlordship. What is certain is that Egfrith decided to rush northwards, like a bull at a gate, and that his action was regarded by some of his closest advisors as rash and unwise. They counselled caution, but the king brushed their doubts aside. 'This', says Bede, 'was Egfrith's punishment [for the rape of the Irish churches], that he now refused to listen to those who tried to save him from destruction'. Perhaps we should take Bede's remark with a pinch of salt: his account benefits from hindsight, and is coloured by his tendency to regard all historical occurrences as manifestations of divine will. So far as we know, there is no reason why Egfrith should not have supposed that his second expedition beyond the Forth would be as successful as his first.

Egfrith's plan of campaign is also uncertain. However, his father, Oswy, had lived in the lands of the Picts in his youth, and Egfrith had already visited the province at least once. He must have known something of the layout of the land with its river crossings, Roman roads and hill forts. He might well have intended to repeat the tactics that he had successfully used to trounce the Picts nine years before. On this occasion, Eddius informs us, his professional household troops had been mounted. He had laid waste the land to subdue the hostile tribes, and defeated the rebels in pitched battle at two river crossings, possibly the Avon and the Carron near present day Grangemouth. The Picts had been hampered by the lack of a resolute leader, and the ease in which Egfrith had suppressed the rebellion may have given him a low opinion of their fighting capabilities and an inflated one of his own.

Thus we can imagine the impatient king setting out with his war-band from Edinburgh or Abercorn as the return of spring beckoned in a new campaigning season. With many troops pinned down in Ireland, the North-umbrian force may have been smaller for the purpose than was wise, although we know nothing at all about its numbers or composition. Part of the force was probably mounted. If the Pictish settlements of the Tay were his main objective, Egfrith would have had to cross the Forth at Stirling, and follow the Roman military road. The king, we can be sure, was not in a merciful mood. He devastated Pictish lands and settlements, says Bede, 'with brutal and ferocious cruelty'. A cryptic note in the Ulster Annals suggests that it was Egfrith who burned a Pictish settlement called Tula-Amon, thought to lie between Glen Almond and the Tay.[10] As in the days of Agricola, the Tay was a natural frontier. Beyond it lay a little known country where Angles might fear to tread. Entering it was an act which, all Northumbrian chronicles agree, was 'extremely rash'.

Egfrith's advance into Strathmore was dominated by a desire, so far denied him, to bring the Picts to battle. The Picts adopted tactics used by guerilla forces many times before and since, by refusing to risk all in an unequal battle and making use of the natural protection afforded by the landscape. They may have raided the Northumbrian column, strung out along the woodland tracks, and picked off stragglers. They may have strained Northumbrian nerves with night attacks. Cursing the Picts, like Agricola before him, for a pack of miserable cowards, Egfrith's war-band stumbled on. They may have suffered from hunger, finding only burned out settlements in their path whose cattle had been wihdrawn into the neighbouring hills. There would have been little fodder available for the horses. And so, says Bede, 'the enemy pretended to retreat and lured the king into narrow mountain passes'. The neigh-bourhood of Forfar is, even today, a complex of ridges, sudden hills, lochs and swamps. In the Dark Ages, it must have been still more confusing, especially to unwary strangers. It is probable that Bridei, working to a prearranged strategy, deliberately lured Egfrith into an ambush. Perhaps, after so many weeks of frustration, with his army growing weaker and casualties mounting, Egfrith at last sighted a Pictish raiding party. The Northumbrians charged forward, anticipating easy victory. And then Bridei sprung the jaws of the trap at a site which, we have good reason to believe, is now called Dunnichen Hill.

The battle of Nechtansmere opened, Bede tells us, at three o'clock in the afternoon. The lie of the terrain suggests what may have happened. While one detachment of Picts engaged the Northumbrians from the east, another launched a downhill attack from the hill fort, raining down arrows, stones and other missiles. 'One can imagine', writes Professor Wainwright, 'the Northumbrians bursting through the cleft in Dunnichen Hill and realising, too late, that Nechtan's fortress and possible reinforcements for the enemy lay three or four hundred yards to their left'.[11] The Northumbrian army became trapped between the hill and the loch at it's base. With their backs to the water, Egfrith's men turned at bay to face the mass of painted warriors pouring down the hill. Floundering among the reeds, with no room to manoeuvre, they were surrounded and cut to pieces. Bede provides us with a last fleeting glimpse of the Northumbrian housecarls massed about their

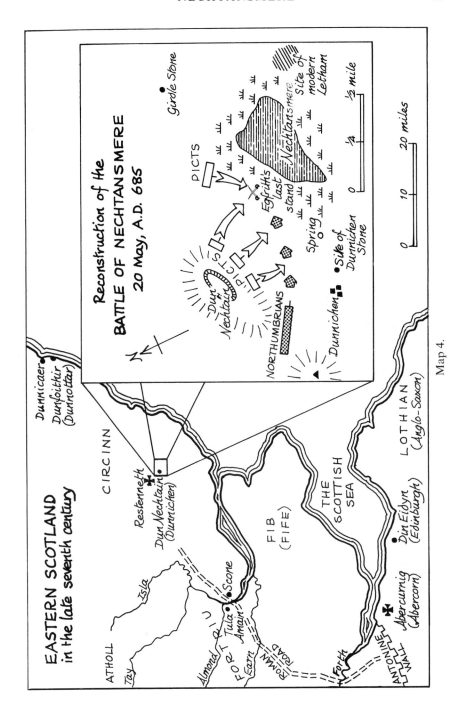

EASTERN SCOTLAND in the late seventh century

Reconstruction of the BATTLE OF NECHTANSMERE 20 May, A.D. 685

Map 4.

fallen king and fighting to the death with axe and sword before darkness fell.

Although the details of the Nechtansmere battle have not been passed down to us, comparisons can be found in frontier warfare elsewhere. One is inescapably reminded of General Custer and the battle of the Little Big Horn. Another parallel, closer to Nechtansmere in time and geography, is the disaster which befell three Roman legions in the forests of Germany in the year 9 AD. In both cases, the 'barbarians' defeated a technologically more advanced enemy by forcing him to fight on ground of their own choosing: the lure followed by the ambush. In both cases, the enemy was eventually surrounded and slaughtered like cattle. At Nechtansmere there were at least a few survivors who managed to make their way back to Northumbria.[12] But the flower of Northumbria fell in the battle, food for 'the horn-beaked raven and the hungry hawk'. Egfrith himself was slain with his bodyguard, hewn by 'black draughts'. His body, it seems, was treated honourably and was conveyed to his half-brother and successor, Aldfrith, at Iona, where it was buried among the kings and saints of the Scots.

Vivid reactions to the news of the battle have been preserved from both Anglo-Saxon and Pictish points of view. Bede's *Life of St Cuthbert* relates a story of how the great saint was given a premonition of the disaster. While visiting the ruins of a famous Roman fountain in Carlisle, Cuthbert was 'suddenly disturbed in spirit'. Leaning heavily on his staff, he murmured to a priestly companion: 'Perhaps at this moment the battle is being decided ... Do you not see how strongly disturbed the air is? Who can fathom the judgements of God?' In a sermon the following morning, he repeated his fears of impending catastrophe. In due course, a fugitive from the battle brought confirmation of what Cuthbert had feared. 'The same day, nay, the very same hour that Cuthbert received the message as he stood by the fountain, the king and all his bodyguards had been slaughtered by the enemy'.[13] It is noteworthy that Cuthbert was grieved by Egfrith's fate; he was, after all, the principal patron of Bede's monastery at Jarrow.

What looks like an authentic reaction to the battle is also preserved in a curious verse fragment from one of the Irish annals:

> This day the son of Oswy was killed in a battle with green swords ...
> This day the son of Oswy was killed, who had black draughts,
> Christ has heard our prayers, they saved Bridei the brave.[14]

This cryptic stuff is the voice of the Columban church of Iona, which Bridei had presumably adopted in favour of the Roman church of the Northumbrians. Like most later wars, both sides were confident that they held the monopoly of divine favour.

The news of Egfrith's defeat and death at the hands of the despised enemy probably took everyone by surprise. It meant a permanent end to Northumbrian pretensions of overlordship north of the Forth. Both Picts and a 'considerable part' of the Britons recovered their liberty, which they still held at the time when Bede was writing, nearly fifty years later. Many Northumbrians were killed, enslaved or forced to flee southwards, among them bishop Trumwine together with a cortege of monks and nuns. The fortunes of the Northumbrians, wrote Bede, quoting Virgil, 'began to ebb, recede and sink' while war-bands of Strathclyde Britons and Picts prowled the central Lowlands. The next king, Aldfrith, 'nobly restored the ruined state of the kingdom', says Bede, but 'within narrower bounds'. After Nechtansmere, Bridei fades once more into the impenetrable mists of Pictish history. He died in about 692 and wrapped up in 'a block of hollow withered oak', was buried, like Egfrith, on Iona by his friend Adomnán.

The site of the battle

Tracing the sites of early battlefields is usually a difficult, often an impossible, exercise since place names have changed over the centuries and the chronicles seldom provide many clues. In the case of Nechtansmere we are more fortunate. True, the Anglo-Saxon Chronicle simply refers to a battle 'by the northern sea', a reference to the Firth of Forth, which is vague enough, whilst Adomnán, the earliest source of all, refers only to 'Egfrith's battle'. However, the Irish Annals of Tigernach and Ulster mention *bellum duin Nechtain*, the

2. Site of the former Loch of Dunnichen, beside which the battle of Nechtansmere was fought.

battle of 'Nechtan's fort', indicating a hill-fort, and an early Welsh source, *Historia Brittonum*, refers to the *Gueith Lin Garan*, 'the fight of the pool of herons', indicating a loch. The name *Nechtansmere* is first recorded by the twelfth century chronicler, Simeon of Durham, but since Simeon is thought to have incorporated ancient Northumbrian annals, now lost, it is reasonable to suppose that this name was current much earlier.[15] Possibly it derives from the Pictish King Nechtan, mentioned by Bede, who founded a monastery in the area, although more than one king bore this name. The Northumbrians had evidently named the battle after the loch by whose shores their king had perished. The loch, presumably, took its name from the Pictish fort.

The correlation of ancient *Duin Nechtain* with the modern parish of Dunnichen was first made by George Chalmers in his monumental work, *Caledonia* (1824). Confirmation was provided by a twelfth century charter to Arbroath Abbey referring to the settlement of *Dun-Nechtan*. By Chalmers' time the ancient loch had already been drained, but its site was believed to be Dunnichen Moss, the area of level boggy ground below Dunnichen Hill. In unusually wet seasons, the loch can even briefly reappear, as Professor Wainwright discovered in the wet winter of 1946–7. The original Nechtansmere was probably a shallow pool, roughly triangular in shape, with broad, marshy surroundings. The latest editions of the Ordnance Survey maps place the crossed swords symbol of battle on the site of the loch itself, although the fighting probably took place slightly to the north in the vicinity of the present-day East Mains of Dunnichen.

Nechtansmere today

The country east of Forfar, with its lochs, moors and hills, is rich in antiquities of the Pictish age. Two miles south west of the town, the landscape is dominated by Dunnichen Hill, whose south-facing ramparts slope steeply downwards towards the leafy village of Dunnichen and a shallow, bowl-shaped depression in the nearby crop fields which marks the site of Nechtansmere.

This area has changed considerably since the time of the battle. In about 1760 most of the Loch of Dunnichen was drained,[16] but in the 1840s a remnant of it still existed,[17] surrounded by marshy ground liable to flooding in winter. Further drainage attempts were ultimately successful, and the only trace of the loch left today is a patch of marshy ground east of Dunnichen church.

The *Statistical Account* records the remains of a stone rampart on Dunnichen Hill but this was evidently dismantled shortly afterwards to provide material for dyking, and much of the remaining portion was obliterated by a quarry in 1833. Nevertheless, this flat topped hill retains a prominent shelf on its southern face, which probably formed part of the original fortifications. The destruction of Dun Nechtan is a sad loss to archaeology, but a magnificent panoramic view of the battlefield can be obtained on the walk to the summit of the hill. From here it is not difficult to recreate in the mind's eye the appalling situation of the Northumbrians, trapped between the steep hill and the loch with no hope of escape.

3. The battle monument at Nechtansmere, erected in 1985 on the 1300th anniversary of the battle.

There are two inscribed stones of Pictish age in the neighbourhood of the battlefield. At the junction of the eastward road from Dunnichen and the northward road from Letham is the Girdle Stone, a flat boulder bearing circular marks. It was placed here to mark the boundary of Letham parish, although its original site may have been Greystone, five miles to the south. The better known Dunnichen Stone is now in the Royal Scottish Museum in Edinburgh but a plaster replica stands on the triangle of grass in front of Dunnichen Church. The stone's original position is uncertain, for Dempster purloined it to adorn the grounds of Dunnichen House, from whence it was removed to Arbroath Abbey. The stone is well-preserved, displaying a group of enigmatic Pictish designs: a 'disc and Z-rod', a 'mirror and comb' and 'pot' symbols. Both stones are of the Class One type, in which the faces are undressed, and no recognisably Christian emblems are present. It is thought that this type of stone dates back to the Nechtansmere period, though we cannot know whether either the Dunnichen or the Girdle Stone had anything to do with that event. A good view of the battlefield can be obtained from the yard of the nearby church.

The Statistical Accounts for Angus record ancient burial sites in the Dunnichen area which contained human bones, stone coffins and decorated clay urns, although the bones quickly turned into dust when exposed to the air. Graves found on a gravelly knoll near the Den of Letham also contained bones and the rusted remains of iron weapons. Antiquarians of the last century liked to regard such sites as evidence of ancient battles, quite without justification. Modern archaeological techniques would undoubtedly yield more information about Pictish settlement in this area, but there have been no recent excavations.

Although there are therefore few visible reminders of the battle at Dunnichen, a graphic picture of the Picts in warlike mood is preserved on the Aberlemno Stone four miles to the north, which stands by the west porch of Aberlemno church. Graeme Cruickshank has recently made the interesting suggestion that the battle scene depicted on one side of the stone may even be that of Nechtansmere. Some of the figures bear distinctive helmets with nose-guards, and these may represent Northumbrian soldiers. A fallen warrior being pecked by a large bird may even be Egfrith himself.[18]

A third edifice not far from the battlefield reminds us that at least one fruit of the battle proved to be transitory. The Columban church, which had prayed for Brude's victory, was to be rejected by the Pictish King Nechtan only twenty-five years later, in favour of the Roman church of St Peter. According to Bede, King Nechtan asked for English stonemasons to construct a church, 'built in the Roman manner', in the heart of Pictland. The site of this church is traditionally identified with Restenneth Priory, built on the promontory of another vanished loch. It is possible that the lower part of the surviving priory tower may be part of this very church. Its square, primitive masonry is certainly pre-Norman and similar in many respects to the Anglo-Saxon monastery at Monkwearmouth, of which Nechtan's new church was to be a copy.

There remains one last aspect of the battlefield to recount: its ghosts! In

4. The Aberlemno Stone. This stands four miles from the battlefield of Nechtansmere, and it is possible that it depicts that battle.

January 1950, Miss E.F. Smith, a resident of Letham, was obliged to walk home in the dark along the Brechin road, after a car accident. Snow lay over the fields but the bitterly cold night air was clear. As she drew nigh to Letham Miss Smith began to see eerie lights moving from the direction of Dunnichen Hill, which gradually resolved into torches borne by dark figures in antique dress. The spectral figures were apparently searching the battlefield, looking for their own dead among the corpses. The psychiatrist, who interviewed Miss Smith and published the results thirty years later, believed she had experienced a genuine apparition while in an altered state of consciousness.

On the 1,300th anniversary of the battle of Nechtansmere, a monument commemorating the battle was raised at Dunnichen Church by Letham and District Community Council.

CHAPTER 3

VIKING RAIDS

A furore Normannorum libera nos, Domine.
'From the fury of the Northmen deliver us, O Lord', attributed to Church litany in the ninth and tenth centuries.

The history of the North East during the age of the Viking incursions, which could be said to have lasted from about 794 to about 1150, is very obscure. Few contemporary writings survive to record the impact of the Scandinavian raiders on north-eastern society. The best known stories and traditions of this time were already garbled by the time they were first written down in the fourteenth century, and the original core of historical fact had become embroidered into a web of romantic fantasy. When attempting to untangle it, the archaeological record is only of negative use. Scandinavian finds are rare in the North East and confined to a couple of graves on the Spey and a handful of objects at Culbin, Knockando and Dorback burn on the Findhorn.[1] The Vikings may well have refortified old promontory forts, such as Burghead and Portknockie, as local tradition and at least one saga suggest, but we have no direct evidence that they did. Again, the tenth century Norse hero, Tryggri Ulfkelsson, is said to have belonged to a family in 'Buchanside', but if he did live in Buchan, we don't know where. If the Vikings ever built settlements between the Spey and the North Esk, we have not yet found them.

Battles with the Vikings have long been part of the folk memory of the North East, however, and the traditional battlefields, which were often given romantic names like 'the Bloody Butts' and 'the Bloody Pits', appear on the earliest editions of the Ordnance Survey's maps. The historical sources for these battles—traditional ballads, religious homilies, forged charters and skaldic verses—scarcely inspire much confidence. Nevertheless, there were certainly Viking raids on the North East coast between the ninth and twelfth centuries, and the stories and ballads about them probably enshrine real events, embroidered by the imaginations of much later generations. They

show the Vikings in search of the movable wealth of churches and monasteries, sometimes striking inland leaving their boats beached in the bays and
estuaries of the coast. They show the peoples of the North East putting up a
very good account of themselves, sometimes outwitting their foes by the use
of 'a stratagem'. They build churches on the sites of battle and stick Viking
skulls into the masonry. The sagas and folk-tales are appropriately partisan:
in the local tales, the North East usually wins; in the sagas, the Vikings carry
all before them.

The nature of the Viking raids changed as time went on. Initially, the
raiders were mere freebooting pirates, anxious to seize the wealth of the
monasteries and be gone. In the years following the sack of Lindisfarne in
793, the dreaded longboats brought increasing devastation and terror 'to all
the islands of Britain'.[2] As the coast of Britain became more familiar to the
Scandinavian marauders, a different type of Viking began to emerge.
Although he may have been equally keen to pillage and rob, he was also a
coloniser, a farmer and a trader. Such groups founded the later Viking
earldoms in Orkney, the Western isles and the west coast, as well as the Viking
kingdom of Dublin. Political alliances were formed between the Vikings and
the native kingdoms, and the Scots were to become adept at exploiting them.
The growing wealth of the Scottish and Irish Vikings in turn attracted the
rulers of the Viking homelands, who demanded their slice of the trading
profits.

These developments still lay in the future in the mid-ninth century, when
much of Scotland was at the mercy of the invader. At this time, as elsewhere
in Europe, the Vikings began to winter in these islands and strike inland in
large well-disciplined armies. Their impact on the peoples of the north was
devastating, and their effect was to bring about the eclipse of the Pictish
kingdom. We see the events of this time only in the brief glimpses allowed us
in the Irish annals, but that is enough to convey the horror and hopelessness
of the situation. In 839, the Vikings invaded the Pictish heartland of Fortriu.
In a great battle, Picts and Scots 'almost without number' were slain. The
survivors were obliged to pay tribute. In 866 AD, Olaf, King of Dublin, in
alliance with the Scottish Vikings, invaded the lands of the Picts and again
defeated them at Fortrenn, after which 'they plundered all the territories of
the Picts and took hostages'.[3] Olaf was, apparently, still rampaging about the
central parts of Scotland in 870 when he besieged Dumbarton, the 'capital'
of the Britons of Strathclyde, and enslaved the inhabitants. Five years later,
the Picts were massacred by the Dane, Halfdan of Dublin. The twilight of
the Picts seems to have been a time of opportunity for the Scots. In the 840s,
Kenneth son of Alpin, a Gaelic Scot of allegedly 'marvellous astuteness', won
posthumous glory for himself by founding a dynasty of Scots kings who were
henceforth to rule over most of that part of the north which had not already
succumbed to the scourge of the Vikings. The old nationality and culture of
the Picts was replaced, by inscrutable means, by that of the Scots. Hence, by
the close of the ninth century, the Vikings had destroyed the old kingdoms
of the north. The new kingdom of the Scots, variously called 'Alban' or
'Scotia', was hemmed in by the equally new northern Viking earldoms of

Orkney, Caithness and the Western Isles and by the Vikings of York to the south.

It is not clear to what extent the Picts and Scots of north eastern Scotland shared in the disasters which befell their compatriots south of the Mounth. Their lands were certainly under pressure in the 860s by Thorstein the Red of Caithness and Sutherland and it is from this direction, and from Orkney, that the Viking raiders to the North East appear to have come. Nor is it clear whether the early MacAlpin Scots kings ruled over this area. From the fragmentary evidence available, it would appear not. The Irish annalists recognised the chieftains of Moray as kings in their own right until well into the eleventh century, and that province was a source of disaffection for at least two centuries after that. The kingdom of Moray may have been founded by Scots from Argyll migrating northwards up the Great Glen in the face of the Viking conquests. Their overlordship may have extended over all the old Pictish kingdoms north of the Mounth, and if so they probably inherited the ancient antipathy between the northern and southern kingdoms.

The first well-attested raid of the North East came not from Norseman or Dane but from Anglo-Saxon England, now ruled by its powerful king, Athelstan, styled King of all Britain. The object of the invasion was to punish the King of the Scots, Constantine II, for entering into an alliance with the Dublin Vikings. The invasion was on a scale unprecedented since Roman times. Athelstan's army was 'drawn from the whole of Britain' and supplied by a fleet which raided coastal townships as far north as Caithness. The land army advanced north during 934 AD, laying waste the countryside as they went. They had proceeded as far as 'Wertermorum' and 'Dunfoeder', before Constantine, the 'hoary-headed traitor' of the English chronicle, was induced to surrender.[5] Wherever Wertermorum might have been, Dunfoeder is almost certainly Dunnottar Castle. Its name is thought to derive from Dun-o-thir, meaning Fort of the Low Country, for this stark rock guarded the strategic pass between the rich farmlands of the Mearns and the wilder Highlands beyond and may have marked the northern limit of the realm of Scotia. Dunnottar had been a Pictish stronghold at the time of King Bridei and it was probably the scene of a battle between the Scots King Donald II and the Vikings in about 900, in which Donald was slain 'upon the brink of the waves in his broad gory bed'.[6] At any rate, Constantine duly offered Athelstan hostages and swore oaths for future good behaviour. Thus satisfied, the English departed.

Fleeting glimpses of the North East in the annals of the Viking age recorded the untimely demise of several more of these shadowy early Scots kings. The second half of the tenth century consisted of a bewildering succession of rival kings whose reigns appear to have been nasty, brutish and short. King Malcolm I (943–54) lost his life in the Mearns while fighting the men of Moray. The Pictish Chronicle states that he was slain at *Fodresart*, which an early tradition places in the vicinity of Stonehaven, probably at Fetteresso, although the Chronicle of St Andrews asserts that he fell at Fordoun. A wooded knoll near Kirkton of Fetteresso known as Malcolm's Mount is his traditional place of burial. The great cairn which once crowned the knoll has

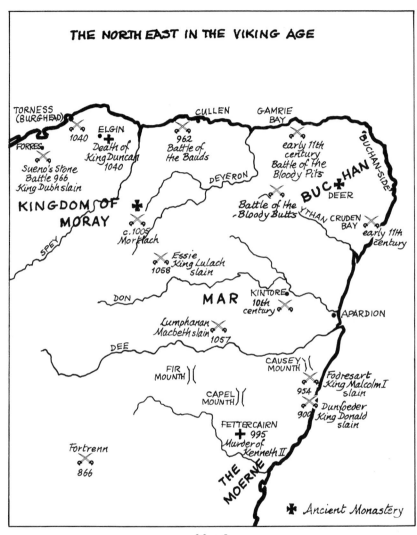

Map 5.

long since been quarried away for use as dyking stone, but a cist grave, originally discovered here in 1822, was excavated in 1975. Its structure reveals the grave in its true colours as a Bronze Age site and Malcolm's Mount must have acquired its name by mistaken association with the Scots king, whose death post-dated the earlier burial by about two thousand years.

Malcolm was not the last king to die in the course of a dispute with Moray. King Dubh (962–6) was killed at Forres 'by the treacherous nation of Moray'. His headless body was hidden for a time under the bridge of Kinloss and it is said that the sun refused to shine until it was found and transported to Iona, where it was buried with honour. The death of Dubh may be the scene depicted so graphically on Sueno's Stone (see below). These disputes with Moray foreshadow conflicts in the eleventh century, when the Scots rulers of Moray seem to have allied themselves with the Vikings against their fellow Scots south of the Mounth.

Dubh's predecessor, Indulph (954–62), fought a battle against the Vikings at *Invirculen*, which is thought to be at the mouth of the Cullen burn on the north Buchan coast.[7] Local tradition calls this conflict the 'Battle of the Bauds', after the place-name, Bauds of Cullen. Three prominent rocks on the shore of Cullen Bay are known as the Three Kings, fancifully named after three Viking leaders slain in the fighting, although more probably derived from the Gaelic *ceann*, meaning headland. The same folk-memory is preserved in a local saying, 'three kings there buried be, between Rannachie and the sea'. Tradition would seem to agree with the Pictish Chronicle that Indulph was successful in repelling the Viking fleet. A later record asserts that Indulph himself was slain in the fighting and was buried in the Kings Cairn at Cullen. This last is another fable. Indulph was buried on Iona like most early Scots kings, and the Cullen cairn is probably another Bronze Age site. An even more unlikely tradition names the leader of the Vikings as the infamous Eric Bloodaxe, blithely ignoring that fierce warrior's death in battle on the moors of northern England some eight years previously. The attribution of well-known names like Eric Bloodaxe, 'Sueno' and Canute to recorded incidents on north eastern shores was a habit of early antiquarians but there is rarely any contemporary warrant for these myths; they are the romantic fancies of Victorian ministers and schoolmasters.

King Kenneth II (971–95) was another king who died by violence in the North East, but in his case it was not in battle but by an elaborately plotted murder carried out at Fettercairn 'by his own subjects'. He is credited with a victory over the Viking raiders near Kintore after which he drove the survivors back to their longboats, beached at Donmouth. The battlefield is alleged to be a heath between Kinellar and Kintore, on which there were once 'a great number of tumuli which indicate it to have been the scene of a most sanguinary conflict'.[8] This battle is not mentioned in any early source and, as passed down to us, seems to be myth rather than history. The king is said to have used a cunning stratagem to defeat his enemies: he dressed up a herd of cattle with oak leaves which deluded the short-sighted Vikings into believing that the Scots army was larger than it rally was—an echo of the Macbeth legend.

The Moray raids and the battle of Mortlach

A dim ray of light filters through the murk of these distant conflicts when we turn to the affairs of Moray between 990 and 1040, for this is the time of the *Orkneyinga Saga*, the story of the Viking earls of Orkney who reached the apogee of their power under Earl Sigurd the Stout and his son, Thorfinn. According to the Saga, Sigurd's claim to the suzereignity of Caithness and Sutherland was disputed by Findlay, the ruler of Moray. The result was a pitched battle at Skidmore in 995 in which, after many hours in which the battle had swayed this way and that, Sigurd had the victory. In alliance with the Vikings of Dublin, Sigurd over-ran the disputed territory and harried the coast of Moray, raiding deep into the interior. He was resisted by Moray chiefs, one of whom has passed into legend as Maelbrighde the Tooth. The nominal characteristic of this chief was 'one huge buck tooth, sharp and black'. According to the legend, he challenged Sigurd to a trial by combat with forty horsemen on each side. Sigurd agreed but, with the craft and deceit of his race, brought along two men on each horse. Thus tricked, the forty men of Moray, including Maelbrighde, were all miserably slain. Retribution for the foul deed was not long in coming: Sigurd slung Maelbrighde's severed head to his saddle-bow as a trophy and, as he spurred his horse forward, the head twisted and sank its famous buck tooth deep into Sigurd's leg. The wound grew septic and soon Sigurd was dead, his blood poisoned by the dead chief's fatal bite.[9] This yarn probably recalls a real event involving a leader called Maelbrighde but the outcome must have been different, for the real Sigurd survived the encounter by nearly twenty years and fell in battle at Clontarf in 1014.

For aid in repelling Sigurd, Findlay of Moray appealed to the latest king of the Scots, Malcolm II. Malcolm was to prove a more successful king than any of his immediate predecessors and eventually managed to crown the achievements of a long reign by dying in his bed at the age of eighty. He seems to have been ruthless and opportunistic, like his ancient predecessor Kenneth MacAlpin, and perhaps saw Findlay's entreaty as a chance to assert his authority in the troublesome and hitherto independent province of Moray. Accordingly, he marched north. The first battle took place at Nairn and, after a stiff fight in which the king himself was wounded, the Vikings withdrew to their ships.

Next year the longships were back again, pillaging and burning their way along the north coast. Banff was put to the torch. Once more King Malcolm buckled on his sword and set out to repel them. The stage was set for the great battle of Mortlach, famous in north eastern tradition and entirely unsung in the Orkneyinga Saga—perhaps because the Vikings were defeated. Our only information about the battle is in narrative chronicles written long afterwards. Fordun, the author of the earliest of these dates, the battle to the year 1005, soon after Malcolm's accession. The story was taken up with gusto by Hector Boece, whose *History of Scotland* (1527) devotes considerable space to it. The jist of what he has to say is this:

The Vikings, warned of King Malcolm's approach, moved inland in order to deny him access to the coastal plain. The Vikings approached from Carron House on Speyside, four miles to the west, whilst Malcolm had come up from the east via Glen Fiddich, having camped the previous night at Auchindoun. The two armies collided near the monastery of Mortlach, in the secluded glen of the Dullan Water. Catching sight of the assembled Vikings, the Scots attacked with more haste than sense, and three of their leaders fell in the first onslaught. Losing heart, the Scots fell back in confusion but found their line of retreat impeded by the narrow confines of the vale, with its 'deep trenches full of water and mudde'. At this moment of crisis, King Malcolm, who had been borne along in the press, fell on his knees and, facing the chapel on its brae above the Dullan, prayed to God and St Moluag for victory. In return the king vowed to build a cathedral church on the site of the chapel to testify 'that by God's support our realm hath been defended'. Their courage thus renewed, the Scots rallied to the king's banner and fought on with resolution. The Viking captain, one Euecus, 'who was prancing up and down the field without any helmet on his head', was dragged from his horse by Malcolm, assisted by 'a bushment of stout warriors', and slain. Thereupon the Vikings retreated in their turn and were pursued with great slaughter by the victorious Scots. Thus writes Hector Boece.[10]

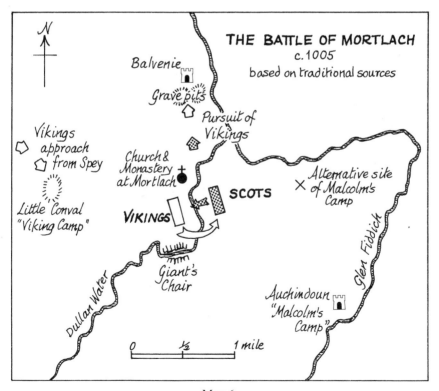

Map 6.

Boece's story can be supplemented by local tradition. The Vikings are said to have camped before the battle at the hillfort on Little Conval, overlooking Mortlach from the west. The grave of Euecus was marked with 'a bulky, cylindrical stone', later built into a dyke, while the common soldiers were buried in a great pit near Balvenie Castle. Within Malcolm's votive addition to the church, there were once three holes which are said to have held the impaled heads of three Viking chiefs. The last of these disappeared in about 1760, after having been 'tossed about by schoolboys' (*Old Statistical Account*). According to Lachlan Shaw's *History of the Province of Moray*, 'human bones, broken sabres and pieces of other ancient armour' have been discovered in the vicinity of the battlefield from time to time. A more fanciful local tradition asserts that King Malcolm won the battle by a stratagem. The Scots had dammed the Dullan Water above the narrow linn known as the Giant's Chair and were able to release a torrent of water down upon the hapless Vikings who had gathered further downstream![11]

How much real history is contained in the narrative of Hector Boece and these local yarns? Had Boece access to contemporary or near-contemporary accounts of the battle, which have since been lost? We do not know for certain, but it is unlikely. Boece's main source was Fordun's history, written a century before, but Fordun has little to say about the battle of Mortlach except that the Vikings were 'ramscuttered' by the victorious Scots and that, in gratitude, Malcolm extended the church by three spears lengths. When Boece's evidence is uncorroborated, he is a most untrustworthy source. He has been dubbed by later, more critical, generations as the 'Father of Lies' and his 'history', a colourful narrative modelled on the style of Livy, is full of invented melodramas and credulous 'marvels'. His account of the battle of Mortlach appears to be a gloss on the tradition that King Malcolm II founded the Mortlach See on the field of the battle. This was a subject that greatly interested Boece, for he was also the author of another largely fictitious history, that of the bishops of Mortlach. The charters which formed the basis of this tradition are now known to be forgeries, the earliest of which in any case attributes the foundation not to Malcolm II, but to his great grandson, Malcolm III.[12] The tradition that some sort of battle did take place at Mortlach in the early years of the eleventh century is, however, surely strong enough to be trustworthy. The treasures of an early Christian monastery would have proved a powerful attraction to the raiders and there is firm evidence that such a settlement existed at Mortlach in the Dark Ages. This settlement is said to have been founded by the Columban missionary, St Moluag or Moloch of Lismore, in about 570 AD. The most solid piece of evidence for its later existence is contained in a papal bull of 1157, which refers to 'the town and monastery of Mortlach with five churches and lands appertaining to them'.[13] This description implies that Mortlach was the seat of the northern bishops before its translation to Aberdeen in the twelfth century. Whether they were originally appointed by the kings of Scotland or the kings of Moray is uncertain, but the bishop could presumably call upon the king of the moment to aid him in the event of an attack on the monastery. If there is any solid evidence for the events of that fateful day in the early eleventh century, it probably lies buried beneath the walls of the present-day parish church.

Mortlach today

The ancient church of Mortlach stands on its brae above the pleasant, wooded vale of Dullan Water, amid the whisky houses of modern Dufftown. The interior of the church has been heavily restored but the oldest parts—three east facing lancet windows—date back to the fourteenth century. Sixty years ago two Pictish stones were found in the churchyard. The larger one is called the Battle Stone, in commemoration of the battle of Mortlach, although it is probably much earlier in date. A seven foot high pillar, it stands at a drunken angle in the centre of the kirkyard amid the modern head stones. One face shows a Celtic cross and early Christian symbols—paired fishes and a lamb. The opposing side is uncompromisingly pagan: a bull's head, a snake and a mounted hunter with his dog. This stone was probably associated with the early Christian foundation of St Moluag, as was the smaller 'Pictish' slab, housed in the porch of the church.

Hector Boece undoubtedly knew the church of Mortlach at first hand and his description of the battle fits in well with the local topography, which can be explored with ease by taking the public footpath from the church along the Dullan Water to the Giant's Chair. The traditional site of King Malcolm's prayer and the turning point in the battle lay (at least in Boece's imagination) on the haugh below the kirk-brae, which is now a walled cemetery. Despite the growth of modern Dufftown, this is a most pleasant area to explore on foot, heady with history and the malty tang of the Glen Livet distillery.

The battle of the bloody pits

The ballad-famed battle of the Bloody Pits also dates from the period of Earl Sigurd's raids on the North East coast, during the first decade of the eleventh century. The battle takes its sonorous name from a series of circular excavations by the shore at Gamrie Bay, in which the dead are said to have been buried. According to tradition, a party of Vikings were defeated here by a posse of local levies, mustered by the sheriff of Banff. Three Norse kings were slain in the fighting, and their severed heads were built into the masonry of a church, founded on the battlefield in thanksgiving for the victory. The skulls feature in an evocative piece of balladry by Sir William Geddes:

> Over brine, over faem,
>   Through flood, through flame,
> The ravenous hordes of the Norsemen came
>   To ravage our fatherland.
> The war I ween had a speedy close
> And the Bloody Pits to this day can tell

5. The Battle Stone, Mortlach Churchyard. Though traditionally held to commemorate the battle of Mortlach, in reality it probably dates from a much earlier period.

How the ravens were glutted with gore
And the Church was garnished with trophies fell.
  'Jesu, Maria, shield us well!'
Three grim skulls of three Norse kings,
  Grinning a grin of despair,
Each looking down from his stony cell—
  They stared with a stony stare.

There undoubtedly were human skulls on display both in this church and in others in the North East, but they were not necessarily Viking ones. Skulls in churches are likely to have held a sacred purpose as saintly relics; the skulls of enemies and traitors ended up on poles at the town gates, not in shrines. In fact there is no reason, apart from the weight of tradition, to suppose the Battle of the Bloody Pits ever happened, for no early annal mentions it. There is sound charter evidence for a medieval church at Gamrie Bay, although the present ruined church of St John (displaying the surprising date of 1004 on its gable) dates from no earlier than the sixteenth century. The three skulls were probably transferred from the earlier church, and a visitor in 1832 recalled seeing them 'grinning horrid and hollow in the wall where they had been fixed directly east of the pulpit'. Unfortunately they grin there no longer. A fragment of skull 'taken from the wall of the old church of Gamrie' was in the possession of Banff Museum by 1908,[14] and an unlabelled skull showing no signs of earth burial was found lying among a jumble of other artifacts recently, although whether or not it was one of the original heads is uncertain.[15]

The 'bloody pits' can still be seen as a series of grassy hollows, presently much overgrown by whins, near the coastal footpath at map reference NJ 786648. Archaeological spoil-sports assert that they are natural subsidence features, just as the 'Danish Camp', a pattern of variously angled features on the ground surface to the immediate north of the church could be a natural rock outcrop rather than the remains of a fortification. Only excavation can provide the answer.

Another 'traditional' battle, this time at Cruden Bay, is linked with this period of Viking raids. The fighting is said to have taken place on what are now the Links, and the enemy was eventually driven back to his ships moored in the bay. A church was established on the battlefield immediately west of the modern village (Grid reference NK 088363), in thanksgiving for the victory. Curiously enough, it was dedicated to St Olaf, himself a Viking, who had changed sides and fought against Sweyn Forkbeard and other marauders. After his death in c. 1000 Olaf became a cult figure and a number of churches throughout Britain were dedicated in his name. No trace of the original church survives but an excavation in 1857 found a rough font and a grave, said to be that of a 'Danish' chief, on its site. A notice in the present church states that the ancient kirk at Cruden was founded in 1012 by Malcolm II and is mentioned in a Papal Bull of Pope Adrian IV.

The battle of Torfnes

Reddened were the wolf's-bit's edges
At a place—men call it Torfnes—
It was by a youthful ruler
This was done, upon a Monday,
Pliant swords were loudly ringing
At this War-Thing, south of Ekkial,
When the prince had joined in battle
Bravely with the king of Scotland.

attributed to Arnor, Earl's Skald, *Orkneyinga Saga*[16]

The greatest of the Viking earls was Thorfinn, who, at the height of his power, ruled over no less than nine earldoms in the north and west, in addition to 'a great dominion' in Ireland. Most of what is known about Thorfinn is told in the *Orkneyinga Saga* which, although written down much later, enshrines oral tradition handed down from one generation to the next. The portrait it paints of Thorfinn is of a huge, ugly, warlike Viking:

> Of large stature and strong, but ungainly, he was uncomely, sharp-featured, dark-haired, and sallow and swarthy in his complexion. Yet he was a most martial-looking man, and of great energy; greedy of wealth and renown; bold and successful in war, and a great strategist.

The saga tells of the war between Thorfinn and a Scottish king named 'Karl Hundason' (literally Karl, son of dog!). The Scottish and Irish annals record no one of that ilk, perhaps a derisive Viking nickname, and opinions differ as to who he might be. The main possibilities are Duncan (1034–40),[17] Macbeth (1040–57) or an unrecorded king of Moray.[18] I have followed P.B. Ellis[19] and others in attributing this extraordinary name to Duncan and the events leading to the battle of Torfnes to the year 1040.

According to the saga, Thorfinn had received the title and revenues of the earldom of Caithness at the hands of a King Malcolm, perhaps Malcolm II but possibly a king of Moray, also called Malcolm. King Duncan attempted to revoke this endowment and exact tribute for Thorfinn's lands on the northern mainland. Thorfinn and the Vikings of Orkney did not take kindly to Duncan's demand. His reply is unrecorded but we can safely presume it was unsatisfactory for, as a result, Duncan named his nephew, Moddan, as earl of Caithness and sent him north with a force of Atholl men to bring the recalcitrant Vikings to heel. Thorfinn assembled his Orkney men for the showdown and, the saga insists, Moddan took one look at their bristling ranks, decided that discretion was the better part of valour, and withdrew. A second expedition was planned. Moddan would return north in greater force while Duncan would lead a fleet of eleven longboats to the Pentland Firth and cut off Thorfinn's army in Caithness in a pincer movement. Of course (since our only source is the Viking saga) the plan went wrong. Thorfinn fought and defeated Duncan in a naval engagement south of Sandwick in the Orkneys. Duncan got away but was chased as far south as the

Moray coast. In the meantime, Moddan's force, camped at Thurso, was attacked by night by Thorfinn's lieutenant, Thorkell Forester. Moddan himself lost his head to a Viking sword whilst leaping from a flaming window. The surviving Scots marched back to Moray.

Thorfinn now took the offensive. Joined by the victorious Thorkell, he fortified a coastal site, named Torfnes in the saga, and harried the coast with sword and flame. Duncan had sent far and wide for reinforcements including levies from Ireland and the west coast—but not, apparently, from Moray, which may be significant. The two armies met on the day before the Feast of Assumption, on 14 August 1040. According to the saga, Thorfinn stood among the foremost of his warriors, under the raven banner of the Norsemen with 'a gold-plated helmet on his head, a sword at his belt, and a spear in his hand'. The first Viking charge broke the ranks of the ill-armed Irish, who were 'immediately routed and never regained their position'. Duncan's main force then moved forward and for a while there was fierce fighting.

> High his helm the Lord of Hjaltland
> Bore amid the clang of weapons;
> In the battle ever foremost,
> Reddened he his gleaming spear-point
> In the wounds it gave the Irish.
> Thus my lord his mighty prowess
> Showed beneath his British buckler—
> Taking many warriors captive;
> Hlodver's kinsman burnt the country.

Thus sang Arnor, Jarl's skald. Despite their numerical superiority, the Scots were beaten, and the battle ended with the flight of King Duncan. The Saga writer was uncertain of Duncan's fate although he adds, with a perceptible shrug, 'some say he was slain'.

Where did this historical struggle take place? The saga mentions three placenames: 'Torfnes, on the south side of Baefiord' and 'south of Ekkial'. 'Ekkial' is the river Oykell, in which case 'Baefiord' might be the Dornoch Firth and 'Torfnes' the present-day cape of Tarbatness. If so, the battle would have been fought on the march land between Viking Sutherland and Caithness and the kingdom of Scotland.

Circumstantial evidence points to an alternative site at modern Burghead, which the Vikings called 'Torness'. This siting involves straining 'south of Ekkial' to mean 'south of the border' in the Scots kingdom of Moray and not on Viking lands, but there is a strong local tradition of a battle near this site, possibly in the vicinity of Standingstone.[20] Burghead is the site of an unusually large and important Pictish fortification which was burned in the ninth century, probably by the Vikings. It may have been refortified by Sigurd and Thorfinn as an operational base, severed from the mainland by the saltings and tidal inlets of the Loch of Spynie. The local inhabitants of Rose Isle are said to have been forced to cut and convey timber to the nearby shipbuilding yards of the Vikings. Advocates of the Burghead site suggest a dramatic battle, with the Scots struggling across the saltings of Spynie to

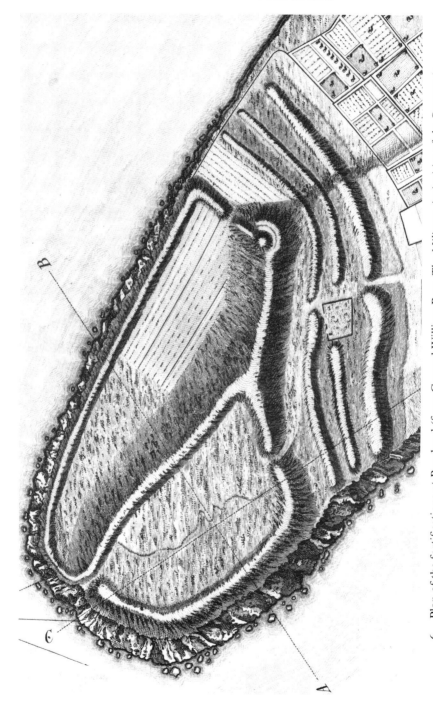

6. Plan of the fortifications at Burghead (from General William Roy, *The Military Antiquities of the Romans in Britain*, London, 1793). These Pictish fortifications were burnt in the ninth century, possibly by Viking raiders.

attack the Vikings, massed in readiness on the ridge of dry ground to the north. It is only fair to remind the reader, however, that this scene may be imaginary.

Sagas are hazardous sources of historical information when uncorroborated by contemporary evidence or by the findings of archaeology. In the case of the battle of Torfnes we have a few grains of information from Irish chronicles written not long afterwards, but they are concerned less with the battle than with its aftermath—the fate of King Duncan. The *Chronicle of Tigernach* states that the king 'was slain by his own subjects at an immature age'. The *Chronicle of Marianus Scotus* adds that his death took place 'on the day before the feast of Assumption [14 August 1039 or 1040] by his general, Macbeth, son of Findlay'.[21] This single sentence has damned Macbeth in the eyes of distant posterity as a regicidal villain. Contemporaries, apparently, were glad to be rid of Duncan—whose fate was no different to that of the majority of his predecessors. A very old tradition, cited in Fordun's *Scotichronicon*, states that Duncan was mortally wounded in a blacksmith's shop ('Bothgowan', now Pitgaveny) and taken to Elgin where he died. In this belief King Alexander II founded a chapel in the cathedral church in 1235 where masses were sung for Duncan's soul. That Macbeth is named as Duncan's slayer is not surprising since the two had long been at feud. Macbeth had inherited the kingdom of Moray from his father Findlay but he also represented a cadet line of the house of MacAlpin and had a viable claim to the throne of both kingdoms. In this context it is more surprising to see him named as Duncan's general. At any rate, the outcome seems to have been that Macbeth was acclaimed as the first ruler of both Moray and 'Scotia' and he may have owed his subsequent long and prosperous reign to this circumstance.

After the battle of Torfnes, Thorfinn is said to have devastated the north as far as Fife with fire and sword:

> the earl's men went over hamlets and farms and burnt everything, so that scarcely a hut was left standing. Those of the men whom they found they killed, but the women and old people dragged themselves into woods and deserted places, with wailings and lamentations.
>
> Fast the flames devoured the homesteads;
> Lives that day were in great peril;
> Fire the Scottish kingdom ravaged—
> All reduced to smoking ashes.

Perhaps the saga exaggerates the extent of Thorfinn's conquests. Some believe that relations between the great Viking and King Macbeth were peaceful and productive, and it has even been suggested that they were one and the same person![22] Such speculation is possible because we actually know very little. Even the date of Thorfinn's death is uncertain, although he may have lived until about 1065.

Burghead today

An eleventh century Scot would find this area changed out of recognition. The ancient Loch of Spynie has all but disappeared and rich farmland covers the reedbeds and flats of Viking times. The landward ramparts of the great promontory fort at Burghead were destroyed during the building of the modern town between 1805 and 1809, although their original dimensions are preserved in a plan included in General Roy's *Military Antiquities* (1793). The walls were originally at least eighteen feet high and technically well-constructed out of stone, laced with wooden planks and beams. Roy reputedly discovered coins, spearheads and other antiquities on the site, but these finds, which might have told us so much about the archaeology of the site, have all been lost. Recent excavations have established that the fort is of Pictish age, not Roman as was originally thought, and was probably built between 400 and 600 AD. Although a number of interesting finds have been discovered in the vicinity, including incised carvings of bulls and a rare early Christian 'slab-shrine', no Viking objects have come to light, and the question of whether or not Sigurd and Thorfinn re-fortified the site remains an open one.

The fort of Burghead now consists of the remains of an upper and lower enclosure at the seaward end of the promontory. The ramparts on the north eastern side are still well-preserved, but those on the western side have been eroded by the tides and are steadily crumbling into the sea. The most interesting feature on the site is a unique rock-cut well, the original freshwater supply for the fort, which consists of a square vaulted chamber and rock-cut basin, reached by a flight of steps. The well, a scheduled ancient monument, is signposted from the main street and can be visited by obtaining the key from the neighbouring house.[23]

The Sueno's Stone battle

The dramatic sandstone pillar at Forres known as Sueno's Stone is a kind of Bayeaux Tapestry in stone of a long-forgotten northern battle. Carved in dense ranks on one face of the stone are armies of helmeted warriors, some mounted, most on foot with raised swords and spears. A figure in a quilted kilt, evidently the leader, stands facing us. Two warriors engage in combat with massed ranks of swordsmen standing behind. Near the base of the pillar are grisly scenes of piled heads, prostrate bodies and an arched feature which is probably intended to be a bridge. The reverse side shows, by contrast, a Christian cross below which a badly eroded scene appears to portray a burial.

Sueno's Stone is one of the finest carved stones in all Britain and it surely commemorates an event of great importance. Local tradition, enshrined in the stone's name, insists that the Danish King Sueno (Sweyn) defeated King Malcolm of the Scots at or near this place. The carving, however, is similar in style to native Pictish stones and is clearly not a product of the very different Viking art. Indeed, an earlier name for the stone was *Rune Pictorum*,

7. Sueno's Stone, Forres. The stone might commemorate either an eighth century battle between the Picts and the Scots, or a tenth century conflict between a king of the Scots and Picts (by now united) and the men of Moray, during which the king was killed.

the stone of the Picts. In 1823 eight complete human skeletons were found after the land to the immediate west of the stone was ploughed.

In a recent article[24] local archaeologist Ian Keillar suggests that the stone is more ancient than is generally believed. Among the Irish annals is a reference to a battle fought at 'Forboros' in about 740 AD, between the indigenous Picts of Moray and the Scots of Dal Raita, in which the Picts were victorious. Keillar believes that 'Forboros' is synonymous with modern Forres. It may derive from the Gaelic *foir*, an edge or border, and the Pictish *ais*, a place, suggesting that this was the boundary of Pictish and Scottish lands at that time. Perhaps the Picts put up the stone as a warning to future Scots trespassers!

There is evidence for another battle at Forres, however, in the tenth century, much closer in time to the Viking incursions. The annalists record that King Dubh of the Picts and Scots was slain in battle by the 'treacherous men of Moray' in about 966 AD. The battle is said to have taken place at the bridge of Kinloss, which is depicted on the stone. The stone's kilted figure may be Dubh himself, and a frame around one of the severed heads hints at his fate.[25] If the scene on the obverse side is indeed a burial, it could illustrate the funeral of King Dubh who was buried hereabouts. Although we know next to nothing about him, Dubh must have been highly regarded in his time since the MacDuff stewards and earls of Fife claimed kinship and descent from him.

The Aberdeen raid

King Eystein's raid on Aberdeen, probably in 1151, is the last and best-known of the Viking raids in the North East and is of special interest as one of the first appearances of Aberdeen in Scottish history. The primary reason for this Norse king's excursion into Scottish waters was not, however, to raid towns but to force the independent-minded Earl Harald of Orkney to swear fealty to him. He duly captured Earl Harald's ship 'of thirty banks of oars and nearly eighty men in her' and took the rebellious earl into custody until he had paid a ransom of three gold marks. *Heimskringla*, the Saga of the Kings of Norway, tells us that Eystein then turned southward along the east coast of Scotland with three small longboats, and 'attacked in Scotland the market town that is Apardion, and slew there many men and plundered the town'. The skald Einar Skulisson then breaks into verse:

> I have heard that
> Apardion's people fell;
> The King broke the peace;
> Swords were broken.[26]

Was the object of this raid to punish the men of Aberdeen for their support for the errant Earl Harald? It is difficult to be sure, but it is tempting to tie the consequences of the raid to a royal visit three years later by King Malcolm IV. Although Aberdeen was probably already a royal burgh, it was neither regularly nor frequently visited by the Scottish kings of the time.[27] According to the *Orkneyinga Saga*, Sweyn Asleifson who, with the exception of Thorfinn, was reckoned to be the greatest of all the Vikings of Orkney, visited Aberdeen as a guest of the young Scots king. The relevant passage runs as follows:

> Then Sweyn went over to Ness (Caithness) and through Scotland. He found Malcolm, King of Scots, who was then nine winters old, in Apardion. Sweyn spent a month there and was well entertained. The King of Scots insisted upon his enjoying all those emoluments of Caithness which he had before he became Earl Harald's enemy ... the King of Scots and he parted very good friends.[28]

This cosy friendliness between Viking adventurer and young king was due to Malcolm's support for Sweyn's client, Erland, a rival claimant to the earldom of Orkney. The complicated diplomatic manoeuvring between Norway, Orkney and Scotland is best read in the pages of the Saga. What is of relevance here is that Aberdeen seems to have played a significant role in the high politics of the north even in that early period. Perhaps we should see Eystein's raid in that perspective and not as a simple raid for booty and slaves.

CHAPTER 4

MACBETH AND LUMPHANAN

Before my body
I throw my warlike shield. Lay on, Macduff;
And damned be him that first cries, 'Hold, enough'!
Exeunt fighting.

The last words of Macbeth according to Shakespeare.

There can be few historical figures, except perhaps King Arthur, who are as well known as Macbeth and about whom so little is known for certain. What is evident is that Macbeth reigned in Scotland from 1040 to 1057, that he was finally killed by a rival at Lumphanan, and that most of the notorious crimes attributed to him are later inventions. To make anything at all out of his reign, one has to disregard the legends, nourish every tiny scrap of information grudgingly passed on to posterity by his contemporaries and fill in the gaps with reasoned conjecture.

The reign of Macbeth appears to have represented a popular Gaelic re-action against the spreading English influences of his two predecessors. After the battle of Torfness, Macbeth killed the previous king, Duncan, and was crowned in his place on the ancient stone of destiny at Scone. Later gen-erations asserted that Macbeth 'usurped' the throne, but this is an anach-ronism. The Gaelic custom of tanistry governed the succession of the early Scots kings, whereby any senior heir of the royal line whose father, grand-father or great-grandfather had been king was eligible for the throne; only minors were debarred. In the previous century, the crown had been passed to and fro like a shuttlecock from one branch of the royal house to another. In 1040 Macbeth was the senior surviving tanist. The other potential claimants, Duncan's two sons and Macbeth's own step-son, Lulach, were minors and therefore not yet eligible. Thus Macbeth's accession appears to have been in accord with the customs of the time, even if he obtained the crown by violent means.

The first fourteen years of Macbeth's reign appear to have been relatively prosperous; as an early chronicler put it, 'there were productive seasons'.[1] The king was evidently generous to the church within his limited means, which ensured him a good press from the only literate section of early Scottish society, the bishops and their clerics. St Berchan, an Irish chronicler, described Macbeth's appearance as yellow-haired and red-faced, which sounds rather like England's William Rufus, except that Macbeth was also supposed to have been tall and handsome. We do not really have any evidence to say whether he was a 'good' king or a 'bad' king, but, in order to keep his throne for fourteen years, he must have been a reasonably capable one. In 1054, however, storm clouds were gathering on the southern horizon.

The late King Duncan's two sons had been brought up in the court of the king of England, Edward the Confessor. Macbeth had no reason to fear them whilst they were still boys but, by 1054, the elder of the two, Malcolm, was in his twenties and eager to back his claim to the throne with force. It was in the political interests of Saxon England to lend Malcolm military support and during the summer of that year a powerful Anglo-Danish army raised in Northumbria crossed the border.

We know a little about this campaign. The commander of the invading army was not Malcolm but Siward, the fierce Danish earl of Northumbria. We can find a hint of the tactics of the Scots in the contemporary English chronicle, *Vita Edwardi Regis*.[2] The anonymous chronicler dubs the Scots 'an uncertain race of men and fickle; and one which trusts rather in woods than in the plain, also more in flight than in manly courage in battle'. In other words, Macbeth avoided committing his own inferior forces to open battle and used the guerilla tactics of Bridei the Pict and William Wallace in like circumstances. The English reached Scone without resistance and moved on to the tiny Taymouth settlement of Dundee, where Siward's supply fleet had docked with reinforcements. Shortly afterwards a great battle was fought. Tradition places it at Dunsinane Hill, and this does seem a likely position for Macbeth's army, threatening Siward's communications between Scone and Dundee and cutting him off from his land-base. There is a large hill-fort with triple ramparts on one of the summits of Dunsinane, but Macbeth evidently chose to fight in the open, perhaps on the advice of the Norman mercenaries who aided him. The battle, fought on the Festival of the Seven Sleepers on 24 July, was long and bloody.[3] There were 1,500 English killed, including Siward's son, Osbern, and his sister's son, Dolfinn. But in the end the larger army had the victory and Macbeth took flight, leaving the greater part of his army—numbering 3,000 it is said—dead in the field. According to a tradition nurtured by the Menzies, their kinsmen joined the English against Macbeth, bearing branches of rowan trees plucked from Birnam Wood near Dunkeld for good luck. And thus Birnam Wood came to Dunsinane.

Despite appearances, the English success—and Malcolm's—was only partial. Siward had to hurry home with his surviving housecarls to quell a rebellion in his own province, which he duly did 'with swords and other kinds of tortures' only to die immediately afterwards. Malcolm was installed as king of Cumbria by the English and may have controlled southern Scotland, but Macbeth managed to cling to his throne in the north for three more years.

These three years, which separate the battle at Dunsinane from the fatal field of Lumphanan, are passed over in silence by the early chroniclers. We must assume that there was no major battle in the intervening period. Then, quite suddenly, Macbeth makes his last appearance in the chronicles as a fugitive, hunted down and killed in an obscure skirmish at the back of beyond, at Lumphanan. What had happened? The Chronicles of the Kings of Scotland state without elaboration that Macbeth 'was killed in Lumphanan by Malcolm, Duncan's son, and was buried on Iona'. The Chronicle of Melrose says much the same: 'Duncan's son, named Malcolm, cut him off by a cruel death in Lufnaut [Lumphanan]'. The earliest source of all, the Irish monk Marianus Scotticus, gives us the date of Macbeth's death: 15 August, the Day of the Assumption, in 1057.

This is meagre fare indeed. To make anything at all of the events of 1057, one is forced to fall back on chronicles and historical narratives written long after Macbeth's time, and also on local tradition in the hope that it contains scraps of history. The first additional details are given by John of Fordun in his *Scotichronicon*, compiled in the late fourteenth century. This is what he says:

> Macbeth, seeing his own forces daily diminishing and those of his adversaries increasing, suddenly left the southern parts of his kingdom and fled to the north, in whose narrow passes, and in the depth of whose forests, he hoped to find safety. Malcolm, however, quickly followed him across the mountains to Lunfanan, where he slew him in a skirmish, with his few followers, on 5th December 1056.[5]

Despite his getting the date wrong, Fordun provides a plausible motive for Macbeth's precipitate departure to the north, which may be based on earlier annals, now lost. Andrew de Wyntoun, writing a few decades later, puts the story into verse:

> Thus Makbeth slew thai thun
> In-to the Wode of Lunfanan
> And his Hewyd thai stak off thare
> And that wyth thame fra thine thai bare
> Til Kynkardyne.[6]

This is probably a gloss on Fordun's chronicle, although Wyntoun adds several colourful details of his own, including a leading role for the character of Macduff, who was torn from his mother's womb and could thus fulfil the prophesy of the 'thre werd systrys' by slaying Macbeth in single combat. Wyntoun was capable of making up such stories as he went along but he is more likely to be repeating surviving oral traditions about the battle.

In local traditions Macbeth crossed over the Fir Mounth into the North East, was surprised by an attack from Malcolm's men on Queen's Hill near Aboyne, drank from a nearby well during the pursuit and turned at bay at the Peel of Lumphanan, 'under whose fosse, Macbeth received his death wound'.[7] Some say that he was slain while leading a charge of his bodyguard. His severed head was brought to the triumphant Malcolm: on a pole according to some, on a golden platter according to others.

Out of all this romantic embroidery a few strands seem clear. Lumphanan was not a battle royal on the scale of Dunsinane, but a local skirmish notable only in that it encompassed the death of a king. Macbeth was evidently overtaken by his enemies on his way north, and perished in the ensuing fight. Reliable evidence is very thin, but it is possible to attempt a reconstruction of the events of late summer 1057, which may not be far from the historical truth.

By summer 1057, Macbeth's hold on the throne had been seriously weakened. There had been no pitched battle since 1054, but many of the leading thanes and churchmen in the south of the country had switched their allegiance to Malcolm. England lent political and, probably, material support. Thus encouraged, Malcolm decided that the time had come for an all-out attempt to topple Macbeth from the throne. It has been suggested that Macbeth's palace at Scone was attacked by night and the king wounded, a supposition based on a verse from the contemporary 'prophesy' of St Berchan:

> On the floor of Scone he will vomit blood
> The evening of a night in much contention.[8]

Macbeth fled northwards with a small following. He probably intended to raise a force in his former mormaerdom of Moray where the people were still loyal. Malcolm's obvious course was to prevent Macbeth from raising reinforcements. The straightforward way to deal with the problem—and Malcolm was probably a straightforward man—was to intercept and murder the fugitive king before he could reach his homelands.

If we accept local tradition, Macbeth's party passed over the Grampians via the Fir Mount drove road, perhaps wishing to avoid the lowlands, and crossed the Dee at a ford near Craig Farrar. Turning east, he intended to pass over the low, rolling hills of Cromar towards Donside and Strathbogie. Malcolm, it seems, was there before him, and was based at Kincardine O'Neil, several miles to the east with a much larger force. Perhaps he had taken a more direct route to Mar over the Cairn o' Mount pass. Malcolm's men were apprised of Macbeth's whereabouts and attacked his small force on the slopes of Queen's Hill near the Tarland or 'Bloody' Burn. A subsequent running engagement ensued, which drove Macbeth in the direction of the tiny woodland kirktoun of Lumphanan.

Dense marshes and a wide shallow loch have lain at the western approaches to Lumphanan until comparatively recent times. This remote settlement lay athwart the ancient mounth road from Donside to the Cairn o' Mount, where St Finnan had preached the gospel to the heathen Picts several centuries before. Lumphanan's best-known feature is the Peel, a medieval motte surrounded by a swampy moat. The Peel is linked with Macbeth in popular memory, although a recent archaeological excavation found no evidence of

8. The Peel of Lumphanan. Though traditionally associated with Macbeth, the fortifications that survive are of much later (thirteenth century) date.

occupation before the thirteenth century.[9] Possibly some form of fortification existed here in Macbeth's day although we know nothing at all about it. Two other Lumphanan sites are also associated with his death. The first of these is the Macbeth Stone, a natural boulder two hundred yards south of the Peel, which is said to mark the place where the king fell. Another tradition places the final skirmish on Parkhill, to the north of the village. At one or other of these places, Macbeth chose to make a stand. At the head of his household, he charged into the midst of Malcolm's troops. A flurry of blows from heavy iron swords, the thrust of a fence of spears, and the last of the old Gaelic kings was dead. His head was brought to a gloating Malcolm, but his body was rescued and given honourable burial amongst his ancestors on the island of Iona.[10]

There remains a postscript to the battle. Once Macbeth's death became known, his supporters in the north acclaimed his step-son, Lulach, as King. This unfortunate monarch was no match for the brutality and low cunning of Malcolm. In March 1058 Lulach, posthumously known as 'the Simpleton', was slain at Essie, now the parish of Rhynie, at the strategic pass between Moray and Strathdon. This encounter is sometimes called the 'Battle of

Essie', but it is far from certain that any battle took place. The earliest source, the Ulster annals, states simply that Lulach was killed. The Chronicle of Melrose adds that Lulach 'fell by the arms of Malcolm ... thus alas! through lack of caution, the hapless king perished'. The Irish annalist Tigernach adds that Lulach was 'slain by treachery'. Perhaps Malcolm lured the simpleton king into his camp on pretence of a parley, and then murdered him. Or perhaps his warriors ambushed those of Lulach near the pass below the Tap o' Noth, where the *Statistical Account* conveniently records an ancient conflict. With Lulach out of the way, Malcolm's hold on the kingdom was at last secure. He returned over the Mounth and was crowned king at Scone on 25 April 1058. A new Anglo-Norman phase in Scottish history was soon to begin. Lumphanan was, in some ways, Scotland's equivalent of the Battle of Hastings.

A legend is born

Shakespeare's Macbeth parts company with history in almost every detail, but the Bard's immortal play is not based on invention. His Macbeth may

9. Macbeth's Cairn, Lumphanan. Traditionally claimed as the site of Macbeth's burial, his body later being moved to Iona. In reality, the cairn is prehistoric in date.

even have some characteristics in common with the historic king. Macbeth was probably a superstitious regicide in fact as well as fiction, but he seems to have ruled with the approval of his contemporaries. Between the true king and Shakespeare's villain lies a series of historical twists.

As the ultimate loser in a power struggle, Macbeth's posthumous reputation was probably vilified from the start. When he first resurfaces in the late fourteenth century chronicles of Fordun and Wyntoun, the legend is already shaped. Wyntoun, in particular, was anxious to 'prove' that the royal line of Scotland stretched back to the dawn of history; Macbeth had attempted to supplant this manifest destiny and therefore he had to be classed as a villainous usurper. Fordun introduces the probably fictional character of Macduff, and Wyntoun makes him the instrument of Macbeth's death. We have to wait for Macduff's motive for opposing Macbeth until the sixteenth century, when Hector Boece duly provides one; Macbeth murdered Macduff's wife and children. Boece also brings Banquo and Lady Macbeth into prominence for the first time. Macbeth's real queen was named Gruoch, and was herself of royal lineage, but there is no evidence that she in any way resembled the evil harpie that Boece creates. Banquo was invented to provide a convenient ancestor to the Stewart kings. Boece's version of the legend was adapted by Holinshed who was, in turn, the source for Shakespeare's play.

It is unlikely that Shakespeare regarded the Macbeth story as historical fact, and in any case he used considerable artistic licence when adapting it for dramatic purposes. Lumphanan was telescoped with the battle of Dunsinane. The role of Banquo as the ancestor of the Stewarts was expanded to please Shakespeare's patron King James VI and I, who had recently inherited the throne of England. Shakespeare further flattered the King by pandering to his interest in witchcraft. His three witches are the descendants of the 'thre werd systrys' in Wyntoun, but it took Shakespeare's dramatic art to shape and polish them into his memorable trio of prophetic hags. By a strange coincidence, a coven of alleged witches living near Lumphanan had been publicly burned only a few years before Shakespeare wrote his masterpiece.

Macbeth's transformation from popular monarch to hated ogre has an ironic counterpart in his contemporary ruler, Edward the Confessor, King of England.[11] Edward, in reality a weak and mediocre king, became the patron saint of the realm after his death, a model of justice and piety which lesser kings should emulate. History's verdict is sometimes capricious.

Lumphanan today[12]

As befits his prominent place in literature and folklore, Macbeth has become associated with a number of features in and around the place of his death. He has a stone, a cairn and a well, in addition to the Peel of Lumphanan itself. Latterly he has even been commemorated by a hotel, the Macbeth Arms (formerly the Lumphanan Hotel)—although Macbeth inconveniently died over a century before the art of heraldry was first conceived. Even the very dim King Lulach has a pair of standing stones to his credit.

Whether any of these is a genuine battlefield relic is another matter. Macbeth's Cairn on Perk Hill, marked by a copse of beech and pine trees, is certainly prehistoric. When opened in 1855, this large circular heap of stones was found to contain a 'short cist' burial chamber, together with bones and ashes. They are not the bones of Macbeth, who lies in Iona, but those of an anonymous chieftain buried about three thousand years before. The higher slopes of Perk Hill are liberally sprinkled with smaller cairns, and sword blades, stone battle-axes and other 'memorials of warfare' are reported from this area in the pages of the *New Statistical Account*, which concludes in consequence that 'very likely this is the spot' where the battle took place. It is as likely as any other, but the artifacts could be, and probably are, relics of earlier times. Associations of small cairns like those on Perk Hill are nearly always found, on examination, to be field clearance heaps, not burial sites.

Macbeth's Stone stands on an island of grass in a field by the now disused railway track. It is a natural boulder projecting some two feet out of the ground and is said to mark the place where the king was slain. There is no inscription and the stone is remarkable mainly because it is so ordinary. Similar stones must once have been common in this neighbourhood, but they were broken up and cleared when the land was improved for cultivation. That this particular stone was left alone suggests that the tradition is a long-standing one, although its prominent position facing directly onto the Peel of Lumphanan may be the reason for its association with Macbeth. It is said that a team of oxen ran away at the first attempt to till its site, and the stone has always been carefully preserved by the proprietors of the nearby farm of Cairnbeathie.

Macbeth's Well is inset into the base of a steep roadside bank near the railway bridge, about one hundred yards from St Finan's church. Its waters are cold and clear, and a chain hangs from one of the stone lintels which would once have held a drinking cup. It may have been the original village water supply and it is even conceivable that Macbeth drank from it, as he is said to have done. He seems to have been a particularly thirsty king, drinking from a variety of natural springs and wells between Aboyne and Lumphanan (although he probably did not drink at the Macbeth Arms hotel). An alternative tradition has it that the king's severed head was washed here after the battle.

The Peel of Lumphanan offers what seems, at first sight, a more substantial link with the battle. However, a four-year excavation of the Peel mound by Dr Eric Talbot of the Department of Archaeology, University of Glasgow, indicates that the fortification dates back only to the first half of the thirteenth century. It is, in fact, a fairly typical (and rather late) Anglo-Norman motte. If there were earlier defence works on the Peel mound no signs of them have been found, and it is probable that the steepening and shaping of the hillock to form the motte would in any case have destroyed all traces of them. In fact we do not even know what a fortification of Macbeth's time looked like. The Peel of Lumphanan was originally a small, detached hillock or 'tump' surrounded by marshes, and if there ever was a Dark Age fort at Lumphanan this would have been a natural choice of site. That is about all one can say.

Tradition places the site of the battle of Essie on the north-western side of Tap o' Noth, where there is a group of ancient cairns. Once thought to be burial cairns, these are now known to be clearance piles, part of an ancient field system. The precise field of battle, if battle there was, is unknown.

King Lulach's pair of stones stand on hillsides about a dozen miles apart. 'Lulach's Stone', a handsome pillar of schist among whin scrub at Bridgend of Mossat in Donside, is about six miles from the king's death place and probably owes its name to that circumstance. The other, named 'Luath's Stone', crowns a ridge of Green Hill in the parish of Tough. There is some doubt whether 'Luath' is King Lulach or, alternatively, whether the hound of the Gaelic demi-god, Cuchullin, is meant. The size and prominence of these stones argues that they served a commemorative purpose and were not mere boundary stones. They must be considerably older than the eleventh century, however, and it is unlikely that they were originally associated with Lulach. W. Douglas Simpson has commented that the names of these stones argue a sympathetic folk-memory of the simpleton king in the North East.[13]

None of the foregoing monuments therefore have sound credentials as contemporary relics of the battlefield. What they do emphasise is that folk-myths and traditions can linger in peoples memories, even when contemporary chronicles are silent. This may go some way to explain why Lumphanan is both the least-known and one of the best-known battles in this book.

PART II

Battlefields of the Middle Ages

The age-old Celtic customs of the North East were gradually transformed during the twelfth and thirteenth centuries by the introduction of feudalism. Successive Scottish kings had strengthened their authority by granting lands to subjects in return for military service. In principle this entailed a mutual acceptance of lordship and homage between two free persons, the lord and his vassal, and it could be applied at all levels of landed society. It strengthened the bonds of loyalty to the crown whilst the vassal benefited from the comparative security of tenure it gave his lands as well as his right to enjoy his lord's patronage and protection. The outward manifestations of feudalism were military: the knight and the castle. The first recorded knight's fees in the North East were created by King William the Lion (1165–1214) when landed estates in the Mearns and Deeside were granted out to the Bissets and other leading barons. The same king granted a royal charter to the burgh of Aberdeen, giving the town trading monopolies, freedom from tolls and other privileges. By this time Aberdeen and Banff possessed royal castles whose sheriffs were nominees of the king and presided over regular courts to which the tenants of a barony could attend as of right. By such means, the power of the Scottish kings extended even to remote parts of the realm which they rarely visited in person. On the other hand, feudalism did not always keep the peace between the king's chief vassals. The thirteenth century North East is riven with conflict between Durward and Bisset, Strathbogie and Comyn, Comyn and Bruce. The war of 1307–8 was, in the North East at least, essentially a private Bruce-Comyn dispute, whilst the battle of Culblean in 1335 settled a land dispute between the Strathbogie earls of Atholl and the Gordons as tenants of the earls of Mar. The battle of Harlaw (1411) was first and foremost the consequence of a feudal dispute, exacerbated by the enforced absence of the king.

The early castles of the North East were little more than fortified timber houses, usually standing on top of a steep hillock or motte. The larger castles contained a pele tower, with stables, storehouses and smaller dwellings of timber and thatch, sometimes with an adjacent fortified enclosure or bailey. Some were protected by a deep, encircling moat. By the latter half of the thirteenth century, the wealthier castles, such as Kildrummy, Coull and Banff, were built of stone which afforded much more effective protection than their smaller, wooden counterparts. Secure in his castle, the knight or baron was safe from all but the most determined and well organised attack. His stronghold would yield only to a prolonged siege or by the wasting of the surrounding lands in order to starve the defendants into surrender. Castles therefore dominated warfare in the Middle Ages and in the late thirteenth and fourteenth centuries were garrisoned in Scotland by English kings as a means of subjugating a hostile community.

The second factor which changed the nature of war was the rising professionalism of the knightly classes. As a consequence of feudalism, the knight's duties and equipment became increasingly elaborate and expensive. Depending on his rank, he would be expected to furnish mounted men-at-arms and foot soldiers in the service of his lord, the number depending on his wealth and social standing. By the time of the Wars of Independence, a knight's personal arms included a suit of mail, a helmet or *basinet*, a wooden shield, a sword, a spear and perhaps a battle axe, in addition to a strong warhorse with harness and caparison. Such equipment became still more expensive later on with the adoption of plate armour, which demanded powerful horses or *destriers*, usually imported from Flanders. The horses were themselves protected with coats of leather, hardened by steeping in warm oil or wax, and called *cuir bouillé*.

The horseless classes, who made up the greater part of the feudal 'Scottish service' were obliged to provide arms in accordance with their means. An enactment of Bruce's Parliament in 1318 obliged freeholders owning £10 worth of goods to provide a sword, a spear and gloves of plate plus either an *aketon* (a quilted coat) and *basinet* (a light, conical helmet) or a *habergeon* (a mail coat) and an iron hat. Husbandmen owning goods equivalent to the value of a cow were to provide a spear or a bow, but no armour. These were minimum demands. In practice the 'Scottish service' went into battle bearing a rag-bag assortment of weapons, spears predominating, but also longhandled Danish axes, bill-hooks and even farm implements.[1] It is unlikely that many owned a sword, since this was still an expensive and highly prized possession.

These men were summoned by the sheriff's levy and served under the banner of their laird. Their military training was probably minimal, although most men who worked on the land must have been reasonably fit and hardy. They were rarely called out for more than a few days at a time and their performance in that rare event, a pitched battle, depended on circumstance. When well led and with a stake in the outcome, as in the great patriotic battles of Stirling Bridge, Falkirk and Bannockburn, they could fight with great courage and endurance. On the other hand they were liable to desertion, particularly at harvest time and, being inexperienced in the arts of war, they lacked discipline. Most of the time was spent on the march and in making camp—the Scots were adept at makeshift shelters—and actual hand-to-hand fighting usually lasted minutes rather than hours. The Scots fought in massed formations of spearmen known as schiltroms, designed, like the later infantry 'squares', to deflect the enemy horse. The schiltrom was vulnerable to arrows and other missiles. Bruce won at Bannockburn because he could choose the ground on which to fight and because he was able to drive away the dangerous English archers with his light cavalry.

In general, the Scots avoided open battle against their better equipped and numerically superior English foes in favour of guerilla raids. Under masterful and talented leaders like Wallace, Randolph, 'the Black Douglas' and Andrew Moray, the amateur 'Scottish Service' was replaced by smaller but more effective mobile bands of professional soldiers. These *hobelars*, lightly armed and mounted on tough little horses, were well-paid—about six pence per day. They were experts in inflicting the maximum amount of damage to the lands of their enemies, whether English or fellow Scots, at the minimum cost to themselves. As a contemporary wrote, their main occupation was wasting, burning and 'taking beasts'.

A compelling contemporary portrait of the hobelars is given by Froissart:[2]

> These Scottish men are right hardy and sore travailing in harness and in wars ... they are all a horse-back, unless it be the followers and laggards of the host, who follow afoot. The knights and squires are well-horsed, and the common people and others on little hackneys and geldings; and they carry with them no carts nor chariots because of the diversities of the mountains they must pass through ... They take with them no provision of bread nor wine, for their usage and soberness is such in time of war that they will pass in the journey a great long time with flesh half cooked, without bread, and drink of the river water without wine, and they neither care for pots nor pans, for they seethe beasts in their own skins ... but on their horse between the saddle and the panel they truss a broad flat stone, and behind the saddle they will have a little sack of oatmeal; and when the stone is hot, they cast some of the thin paste thereon, and so make a little cake in manner of a cracknel or a biscuit, and that they eat to comfort withal their stomachs. Wherefore it is no great marvel though they make greater journeys than other people do.

This was all a far cry from the colourful banners and shining armour of the medieval knight. But these men won the Wars of Independence.

CHAPTER 5

ROBERT BRUCE'S CAMPAIGNS IN THE NORTH EAST

And certis tha suld wele haf pris
That in thar tym war wicht and wis,
And led thar lif in gret travale,
And oft in hard stour of battale
Wan gret pris of chivelry
And war voidit of cowardy
As was King Robert of Scotland.

Barbour, *The Brus*, c.1375.

The Bruces and the Comyns

When Robert the Bruce crossed swords with his sworn enemy, Comyn of Buchan, in the fall of 1307, Scotland had already suffered twelve years of intermittent war. The line of undisputed Scottish kings had ended with the sudden death of Alexander III one stormy night in 1286. His sole heir, 'the Maid of Norway', died soon afterwards in 1290. No less than thirteen candidates put themselves forward for the vacant throne, and in order to settle the ensuing dispute, known as Scotland's Great Cause, the appointed guardians of the realm invited Edward I of England to arbitrate between the claimants. King Edward eventually found in favour of John Balliol against his main competitor Robert Bruce, grandfather of the future king. Edward probably saved Scotland from civil war, but he took advantage of the crisis to secure recognition of himself as lord superior of the king of Scots and obtained the surrender of the Scottish royal castles. Thereafter, he chose to treat his nominee as a vassal. King John Balliol's humiliations deepened in 1295, when Edward demanded his services for an impending expedition against France. This was too much for the Scots to stomach and they forced

64

their king into open defiance. Scotland entered into an alliance with Edward's French enemies and, the following year, the Scots attacked Carlisle. King Edward returned from France, with smoke and brimstone in his nostrils. In quick succession he invaded Scotland, sacked the town of Berwick, defeated the Scots army and recovered the royal castles. John Balliol was obliged to confess his errors in an abject public ceremony and surrender his kingdom to Edward. He returned with the English as a prisoner. The latest Scottish crisis seemed to be settled. Scotland fell under English occupation while Edward returned south to other pressing matters with the remark that it does a man good to rid himself of a turd. The ancient stone of Scone, on which Scottish kings had been installed for centuries, travelled southwards among the baggage.

The Scots nobility were cowed by Edwards's blitzkrieg but others were ripe for revolt. In May 1297, a little known Clydesdale knight's son called William Wallace slew the sheriff of Lanark. At about the same time a revolt in Moray took fire throughout the north and North East, and the English sheriff of Aberdeen threw in his lot with the rebels. In September, the combined rebel forces defeated the English army in the field at Stirling Bridge. Wallace was knighted and appointed sole guardian of the realm. King Edward's Scottish policy stood in ruins, while Scots raiding parties caused havoc in the borders. Edward gathered his forces and rode north once more. Wallace chose to stand and fight at Falkirk and on 22 July 1298 the Scottish schiltroms of massed spears were decimated by cavalry charges and Welsh longbows. Wallace escaped to renew his earlier life as an outlaw leaving others to head the remains of the patriotic cause.

The guardianship of the realm was now invested jointly in Robert Bruce, earl of Carrick, and John, the 'Red Comyn', lord of Badenoch (and nephew of John Balliol), who represented their respective families' rival claims to the Scottish throne. The Bruces were of Norman descent and traditional friends of successive English kings, who had granted them lands in England. Bruce's father and grandfather had remained steadfastly loyal to King Edward despite his earlier judgement in favour of Balliol. On the other hand, Bruce and Comyn hated one another and their joint guardianship was beset with dissension. Bruce eventually resigned as guardian and retired to Galloway, where, in 1304, he succeeded to both his father's estates and his dormant claim to the throne. Fearing the restoration of John Balliol, Bruce submitted to King Edward and became his confidant in Scottish constitutional matters. He took no further part in the continuing patriotic struggle in which the Red Comyn was finally induced to surrender on lenient terms. But he did take part, perhaps not very enthusiastically, in the ensuing manhunt for Wallace, which resulted in the latter's capture and execution.

In February 1306 the constitutional position of Scotland was much as it had been in 1296. The nation was in practice a conquered province of Edward I, despite the continuing legal niceties over representation and succession. Suddenly the relative calm was torn asunder by a bolt from the blue: that famous meeting in the Grey Friars kirk in Dumfries in which Bruce and his followers stabbed the Red Comyn to death. Legend has it that Comyn had pretended to support Bruce's claim to the throne in exchange for gifts of land, but had then tipped off the English king as to Bruce's treasonable intentions. More probably, Comyn refused his support and Bruce killed him in an unpremeditated fit of temper. Bruce had managed to commit an act of simultaneous murder, treason and sacrilege. The alternatives before him were the throne or the gallows. With breathtaking audacity, he wrote to Edward demanding recognition for himself as king of Scots and shortly afterwards had himself crowned at Scone by a band of his close supporters.

By murdering his rival, Bruce had incurred the eternal enmity of the Comyn faction, who included the Red Comyn's powerful cousins, John Comyn, earl of Buchan, and John MacDougal of Lorne. Many Scots, as well as King Edward of England, now regarded Bruce and all who followed him as traitors. The Scottish clergy, on the other hand supported Bruce as the leader of a national crusade and took no notice of the Pope's demand for his excommunication. The English military machine rolled into action. Bruce and his small army were routed by the earl of Pembroke's cavalry as they attended to their cooking pots in Methven Wood near Perth. King Hob, as the English called him, took to his heels and fled westwards. His sisters, wife and daughter were escorted to Bruce's castle at Kildrummy in Donside by his brother, Neil, and John de Strathbogie, earl of Atholl. Despite its stout walls, Kildrummy did not hold out long against an English siege by the forces of the Prince of Wales and earl of Pembroke. According to legend, the castle garrison was betrayed by a blacksmith, who started a fire in the wooden and thatch buildings within. Neil Bruce and Atholl were conveyed southwards in chains and hanged. The royal women managed to escape northwards but were captured at Tain and taken into captivity in England. The confinement of Bruce's sister, Mary, and the countess of Buchan, wife of the Comyn earl, who had taken a leading part in the coronation and, it is said, offered other favours, was particularly severe. They were placed in 'cages', probably stone lock-ups, on the battlements of two of Edward's castles. The impulsive act of sacrilege in the kirk of Dumfries had reaped a terrible retribution upon Bruce's family and friends.

Robert Bruce himself managed to escape his enemies and spent a chilly winter on the isle of Rathlin and the Irish coast. There, aided perhaps by a lesson of patience and fortitude from a spider, he negotiated support and planned his return. In February 1307 his brothers Thomas and Alexander landed at Galloway. Their expedition was another disaster. The small force was quickly rounded up and the brothers were taken to Carlisle where they, like their brother Neil, were hanged. Bruce's prospects of regaining the throne appeared very bleak when he himself landed on the mainland in March. And yet from this moment the tide began to turn in his favour. Bruce abandoned all pretensions to the knightly code of chivalry and, like Wallace before him, began to conduct a successful guerilla campaign of hit-and-run raids, ambushes and night attacks, and assaults on enemy outposts and supply trains. Bruce probably had had some previous experience of this type of warfare in Galloway and was able to utilise his intimate knowledge of the hilly terrain to great effect. He was also lucky in his earliest supporters, men like James Douglas, Thomas Randolph, Gilbert Hay, Robert Boyd and Neil Campbell who were soon to become famous guerila fighters. His greatest stroke of fortune—though doubtless he had noted it and acted accordingly— was that King Edward was now old, sick and soon to die; bereft of his iron will, the English offensive against Bruce soon collapsed.

Bruce's ultimate success in the war of 1307–8 owed much to his personal qualities of leadership, resourcefulness and courage. He was regarded as the finest knight in Christendom at the time of his death, an attribute which owed at least as much to his gallantry and showmanship as to his successful career as a soldier; Barbour sums him up as 'debonair'. Such high praise comes from the pens of his admirers. Perhaps they overdo it: Bruce emerges from Barbour's pages as an adventure hero of myth, largely lacking the individual infirmities that all flesh is heir to, except, perhaps, for his hot and impulsive temper. We cannot claim a close acquaintance with the man inside the myth. Bruce's years of glory lay in the future; in 1307 he was widely regarded as a traitor and ruthless terrorist, whose record was spotted with descreditable acts and whose brief preposterous reign had ended in ignominy.

Bruce scored his first important success at Glen Trool in April. His tiny force ambushed an English column by rolling boulders down upon them. In May he defeated a detachment of English at Loudon Hill by carefully choosing his ground and digging trenches to counter the dreaded cavalry charges. On 7 July King Edward I died while gamely struggling north to quell this latest Scots rising. His son and successor, Edward II, had no enthusiasm for hunting Bruce in the cold hills of Scotland and soon turned back, taking his father's bones with him. Thereafter the English offensive in Scotland lacked resolute direction and changed to mere defensive resistance. The garrisons stayed cooped up in their castles while the rising tide of Scottish patriotism lapped at their battlements. Henceforth, Bruce's immediate foes were not so much the English as his Scottish rivals, the Comyns.

The battle of Slioch

On hearing of the death of King Edward, Bruce's 'false preachers' or propagandists as we would now call them, reminded their listeners of the prophesy of Merlin which held that the death of the tyrant would be followed by the union of Celtic peoples, who would henceforward live at peace with one another. This idyllic prospect was not at first apparent. By breaking out from the hills of Galloway and Ayr into the lands of his foes, Bruce began a short but bitterly fought civil war against the supporters of John Balliol. His available force was still very small—fewer than a thousand men—and he was incapable of taking war into the Lowlands, since they were still firmly in English hands. On the other hand, he could operate successfully in the hills, even on enemy territory, and enlist friendly support as he moved on. John MacDougall of Lorne and John Comyn, earl of Buchan were implacable opponents, and Bruce had to defeat them in order to control the north.[1] This was a task of no mean difficulty, particularly since William, earl of Ross, was also opposed to him. He could hope to gain adherents from his own estates in Garioch and Strathdon, and from the fiercely independent province of Moray, but in the meantime the military experience of his companions, and, perhaps, a personal sense of destiny, were his greatest assets.

While the heather purpled in the late summer sun, Bruce harried the lands of the MacDougalls and MacCans in the mountains of Argyll, pillaging, burning and filling his food bags and coffers as he went. John MacDougall of Lorne eventually accepted a truce, allowing Bruce unhindered passage across the Great Glen to the Moray Firth. The North East was, by this time, clustered with castles garrisoned by companies of Englishmen or by Scots loyal to their pro-English feudal lords. Most of these castles were wooden constructions but a few possessed stone towers. A very few, and these the most important like Kildrummy, also possessed stone curtain walls. Bruce had no siege equipment and he does not in any case appear to have spent time on long sieges. Wooden castles could be set on fire, walls could be scaled and, by harrying the surrounding countryside and cutting off supplies, he could always starve out his enemies, except for those in coastal castles which could be supplied by sea.

Moray was a potential source of recruitment for Bruce's small force. The area had been a centre of rebellion in 1297 and one of his captains, Sir Thomas Randolph, owned extensive lands there. According to a letter from the earl of Ross the king's army now numbered 3,000 men, most of them recruited locally in Moray. This was a much larger force than the king's enemies could quickly raise and with it Bruce managed to capture and destroy the royal castle of Inverness and burn the royal town and castle of Nairn.[2] At Elgin and Banff, he encountered stout resistance. On hearing of the approach of a force led by the earl of Buchan to relieve the sheriff of Banff, Bruce moved south to his own lands in Garioch and the moated motte and bailey castle at Inverurie, built many years before by his ancestor, David, earl of Huntingdon. Perhaps he intended to collect his rents and gain his force a brief respite from the rough living and constant marches which they had endured for many months past. Instead everything went wrong. Winter came early that year and snow began to fall. Bruce's health began to break down and soon the king had to be carried in a pallet or litter. He may have been suffering from pneumonia or pleurisy, a benumbing, Barbour says, brought on by his lying for so many nights in the cold. By the time the little force reached Inverurie the king was prostrate:

> Thar him tuk sic ane seknes
> That put him to full hard distress;
> He forbar bath drink and met.[3]

His only surviving brother, Sir Edward Bruce, took charge. The king was carried in his litter across the exposed lowland plain in bitter winter weather. The force halted at a refuge in the hills of Strathbogie which Barbour calls 'slevach'. It has been identified with a farm in the parish of Drumblade, now anglicised as Slioch. It evidently once consisted of a farm steading, a chapel,

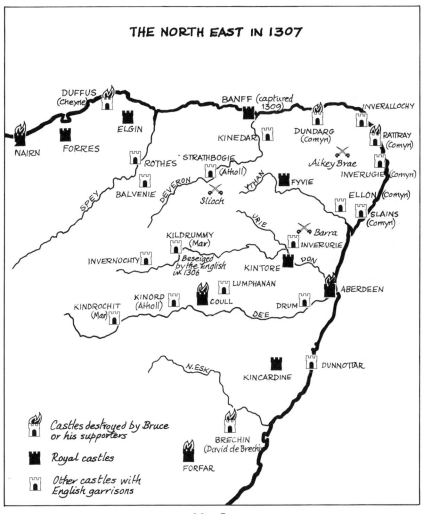

Map 7.

and a small motte known as Torra Duncan, which faced a still smaller mound
known as Meet Hillock or 'the justice seat'. Since Barbour describes Slioch as
a 'strength', there was presumably a timber pele tower and palisade crowning
the flat top of the motte, where the sick king was housed. The motte covers
only about two hundred square yards however and most of the king's men
probably camped in the boggy wood nearby.

By this time, Bruce's force numbered only 700.[4] John Comyn, earl of
Buchan, had been kept informed of Bruce's progress and state of health and
now saw the opportunity to kill or capture the king. He mustered a joint
force of Scots and English from the garrisons of the earldom which is said to
have outnumbered Bruce by two to one. Among their company were 'many
nobles', including Buchan's nephew, Sir David de Brechin, renowned in his
day as 'the flower of chivalry', and Sir John Moubray, a wealthy Scottish
knight who, like Bruce, had co-operated with Edward I. Buchan's force
reached the refuge at Slioch on Christmas Day. When he found Bruce's men
massed at the edge of the wood and ready for the fray, he seems to have
hesitated. His archers fired a volley of arrows to break them up, but Bruce
had bowmen of his own and the two sides sniped at each other for a while.
Buchan's archers eventually gave up or were driven off and, for some reason,
the earl decided against a direct assault. Fordun claims he was overwhelmed
by shame and confusion and asked for a truce, which the king 'kindly'
granted.[5] Barbour states, with greater plausibility, that the two forces skir-
mished inconclusively for three days with Buchan's men getting the worst
of the encounter. Buchan seems to have decided that reinforcements were
necessary and withdrew until their arrival on 31 December.[6] This second
assault was also a failure but by this time the king's men were hard pressed
for lack of food and medicine. Dispassionate military logic would suggest
that they were at Buchan's mercy.

This makes the outcome of the series of skirmishes forming the battle of
Slioch all the more surprising. For the king's men, massed around the litter
of the king, seem to have simply marched out of camp in full view of the
enemy. Buchan made no move to stop them making their way to the greater
safety of the Peel of Strathbogie for, explains Barbour, his courage had failed.
Buchan's inaction at this point is one mystery of the Slioch encounter. The
other is why Bruce allowed himself to become cornered in this unhealthy
boggy wood in the first place, instead of marching directly to Strathbogie a
bare three miles away. Possibly, as Dr Edward Meldrum suggests, Bruce's
objective was indeed Strathbogie, but Buchan had intercepted him and occupied the intervening hill.[7]

The battle of Barra

Uncertainty also surrounds the next stage in the story. According to Barbour,
Bruce sojourned at Strathbogie until he had recovered his strength, and then
advanced directly on Inverurie again. This second attempt resulted in the
battle of Barra, which took place, says Barbour, on Christmas Eve. Barbour

seems to have been guilty of telescoping two separate events for epic effect. Documentary evidence, in the form of letters to the English king, show that the decisive battle of Barra did not take place until well into the spring of 1308, which is the date assigned to the battle by the chroniclers Fordun and Bower. Bower's chronicle states explicitly that the battle was fought on Ascension Day, which in 1308 occurred on 23 May, and, in the light of other evidence, this seems to be the most probable date.[8]

This casts an interesting light on Bruce's strategy, for it is now clear that on regaining some of his strength at Strathbogie, he disappeared back to the west, leaving the earldom of Buchan still unsubdued in his rear. We hear of his force attacking the Comyn castle of Balvenie in Speyside, of the destruction of Tarradale Castle in the Black Isle and of Duffus Castle on the shores of the Loch of Spynie, near Elgin. Finally, on Palm Sunday (7 April) 1308, Bruce renewed his assault on Elgin Castle itself, and was again repulsed.[9] This is all remarkable work for a sick man operating in winter, although the king may not have been present in person at all of these events. It is clear, however, that between New Year's Day and Easter, there had been no decisive encounter. Comyn of Buchan was still in the field and his follower, Sir John Moubray, was able to relieve Elgin at the end of April, and report confidently to the English king that Bruce was in retreat.

It appears that after his repulse at Elgin Bruce struck southwards to his own lands once more. Whether he was following any coherent strategy is uncertain. His objective was to crush, once and for all, the military might of the earl of Buchan but the means may not have been obvious. Before the Comyn province could be subdued, the earl had first to be defeated in the field. By moving to Inverurie for a second time, Bruce may have hoped to provoke his rival into attacking him. If so, his judgement was sound enough, for subsequent events played into his hands.

Word reached Comyn of Buchan that Bruce was back. Buchan had disbanded his earlier force but, with the aid of Moubray and Brechin, he mustered a new joint English and Scots force of a thousand fighting men. According to Barbour, this was quite an impressive looking army, 'well-arrayed' with streaming banners and all the panoply of war. Whether it was an effective fighting force was another matter. Comyn and his knights found billets in the farmtoun of Meldrum[10] about five miles north-east of Bruce's camp at Inverurie, and prepared themselves for battle on the following day.

At dawn David de Brechin led a detachment of cavalry in a surprise raid on Inverurie. The horses galloped across the wooden bridge over the Urie at Balhalgardy and into the street of the little town. They cut down some of Bruce's outposts and sent the rest fleeing towards the safety of the moated castle. But Brechin did not have the strength to assault the king in his lair. Bruce was stung into immediate retaliatory action. The royal temper spilled over as the king rose unsteadily from his pallet and buckled on his harness, roaring that Buchan's attack had cured him better than any medicine could. The camp bustled with urgency as his followers, impressed by their master's sudden recovery and 'cheerful countenance', 'joyfully' prepared themselves for the fray.

10.   The Bass of Inverurie. This imposing motte and bailey castle must have become well known to Robert Bruce during his campaigns in the North East.

Comyn of Buchan, we are told, was quite unready for a swift counter-attack (Barbour represents him throughout as extremely dim). The alarm was raised by a scout who spied the king's banners descending the hill between Inverurie and Meldrum parish. Buchan hastily drew up his force athwart the Inverurie road, on the level ground between Barra Hill and the marshes of the Lochter Burn. Unsure of the reliability of his ill-armed feudal levies— 'the rabble' and 'small folk' as Barbour calls them—he sent them to the back and stiffened his front line with his knights and men-at-arms. They waited tensely as Bruce's force approached, for the king's reputation had preceded him, and he was regarded with awe and fear by his enemies.

Indeed, it seems to have been the king's reputation that won the battle of Barra. As the spears levelled and the ranks began to close, Buchan's men spied Bruce himself among his knights, his sick body propped up in the saddle by a man on either side. Terror overcame the 'small folk': they had been told that Bruce was sick and incapable of rising from his bed. The sight of the king, terrible and vengeful, was too much for them. A trickle of deserters turned into a flood and soon the greater part of Buchan's force were showing their heels, flinging away their billhooks and spears and leaving the field with all convenient haste. Buchan and his knights made desperate but futile attempts to rally their wavering line. Finding themselves forsaken in the face of the wrath of Bruce, they in their turn mounted their steeds and fled. And so:

> ... Quhen the kingis cumpany
> Saw that tha fled sa foulely,
> Tha chasit tham with all thar mane,
> And sum tha tuk, and sum has slane,
> The remanand war fleand ay   (remainder fled away)
> Quha had gud hors gat best away.

As it happened, Buchan's cavalry had quit the field just as quickly at the battle of Falkirk, nine years earlier.

Such was the ignominious rout of Barra. Those who were unfortunate enough not to own a good horse are said to have been slaughtered at the 'Bruce Field' by the boggy hollow of the Lochter burn. Edward Bruce's cavalry chased Buchan's men as far afield as the English-held Fyvie Castle, where some of them found temporary refuge.[11] Buchan and Moubray fled to England where the former died shortly afterwards. Whether he died from wounds, disease or shame is unrecorded, but his flight ended the century-long rule of the Comyns in the north.

How do we account for this extraordinary collapse, which the chronicler Fordun saw as the turning point in Bruce's career? There are a number of clues in Buchan's earlier behaviour. He had sat tight in his earldom during most of the campaign, and had done little to relieve his sheriffs and knights whose castles Bruce was busy knocking down more or less without hindrance. He had permitted Bruce to escape from Slioch just when he seemed to be at his mercy. Bruce himself showed his contempt for Buchan by turning his back on the earldom of Buchan after the Slioch episode, and by moving about the Comyn provinces almost at will. The probability is that Buchan could no longer rely on his tenants, and the new English king was unable or too incompetent to aid the failing earl. It is said that Buchan was obliged to punish some of his freeholders shortly before the battle, for voicing support for Bruce.[12] The cause of ex-king Balliol, represented by the Comyns, had become a dead issue: nobody wanted Balliol back. The patriotic cause was now the cause of Robert the Bruce.

The harrying of Buchan

If the account of the battle of Barra as passed down to us reads like comic opera, and one must allow for the fact that Barbour was more interested in praising Bruce than in disinterested history, its consequences were tragic. Bruce advertised the fall of the Comyns by reducing the earldom of Buchan to a desert. The 'harrying of Buchan' seems to have been a vindictive act of terror against a defenceless enemy, carried out with remorseless efficiency by Bruce's brother Edward. According to Barbour, the king

> gert his men brin all Bouchane
> Fra end till end, and sparit nane,
> And heryit tham on sic maner
> That eftir that wele fifty yher
> Men menit (remembered) the herschip of Bouchane.

The harrying of Buchan was the climax to the Bruce-Comyn feud, in which no quarter was asked or given. The events of the recent past had made any accommodation between them impossible, although the king treated most of his other erstwhile opponents with more clemency. During that flame-girt early summer of 1308, the crops and livestock of the Buchan farmers and freeholders were destroyed and a remnant of Comyn's army is said to have been routed with great slaughter at Aikey Brae, near Old Deer.[13] Fordun adds that the king killed whom he would and to those whom he would have live he granted life and peace. The castles which ringed the earldom were dismantled. Some, like Dundarg and Rattray, were levelled to the ground and their wells filled in with rubble. Others, like Slains, were later refortified and given to Bruce's loyal followers, in this case Sir Gilbert Hay.

   The Buchan war spilled over into Mar, where Bruce and his late supporter, the earl of Atholl, owned extensive lands. Local patriotic hands seem to have taken to attacking castles on Bruce's behalf with notable success. The record hints at what may have been happening. In 1304, when Bruce and Atholl were co-operating with the English, Atholl's stone castle of Coull, near Aboyne, was a lonely outpost among lands which were 'savage and full of evil-doers'. The earl 'had no other fortress where the country or his servants may be in safety, to keep the peace'.[14] By 1308, the royal castle of Coull was manned by a small garrison of archers, crossbowmen and mounted esquires

11. Dundarg Castle, built by the Comyn earls of Buchan in the thirteenth century inside the remains of a prehistoric fort, and demolished by Robert Bruce in 1308. The gatehouse, the only remaining standing structure, dates from the sixteenth century.

under a sergeant of the sheriff of Aberdeen in order to protect Mar from the forces of Robert the Bruce.[15] The garrison were owed at least a year's wages and we might surmise that they felt themselves forsaken in their moment of peril. Perhaps they surrendered, perhaps they made a fight of it, but at any rate the castle fell in 1308 and was reduced to the ruins we see there today.

The taking of the castle of Aberdeen is more mysterious. The famous story of how, on the watchword 'Bon Accord', the patriotic citizens of the town rose against their oppressors and put them to the sword has no contemporary warrant and first surfaces in the mainly fictional narrative of Hector Boece, over two hundred years afterwards. Only three things can be deduced with certainty; that like Coull, the garrison of Aberdeen castle had not been paid recently, that Bruce had some cause to feel grateful toward the burgesses of Aberdeen and that the castle's fortifications were afterwards razed and never rebuilt. None of these facts are at variance with the legend, and Barbour's omission of the episode may mean simply that his hero king was elsewhere at the time and had no direct hand in it. The castle seems to have fallen in

August 1308, for surviving accounts books show that the garrison ceased to occupy the castle during that month.[16] Whatever truth may lie behind the Bon Accord legend, the burgesses of the town later received a signal mark of royal favour when King Robert granted them the lands of Stocket Forest: the Freedom Lands.

The year 1308 was Robert the Bruce's *annus mirabilis* and the snowballing effect of his victories turned the tide firmly in his favour. By the end of the year, all castles north of the Tay except Banff were in his hands. The first evidence of settled government under King Robert's reign dates from towards the end of that year and in March 1309 the king convened the first parliament of the reign at St Andrews, attended by an impressive gathering of clergy and nobility. The civil war had become the patriotic war of liberation. The king was out of the heather at last and firmly on his throne.

The battlefields today

Bruce is an elusive quarry to track down in the North East: there are not many places where one can stand and say that, beyond doubt, 'Bruce was here'. The farmstead of Slioch, near Huntly, has long been identified with Barbour's 'Slevach' and Fordun's 'Slenach'. Both words are probably derived from the Gaelic, *sliabhach*, meaning hilly country or moorland. Slains Castle on the Buchan coast has been suggested as an alternative site of battle, apparently because of the similarity in names, but otherwise it has nothing to recommend it: Barbour makes it clear that Bruce's depleted force had left the coastal plain for 'that strinth' in the hills. The neighbourhood of Slioch is, in the words of the parish minister writing for the *New Statistical Account*, 'embosomed in hills'. A mile north-west of Slioch is a small motte named 'Torra Duncan', which may have sheltered the stricken king during those anxious days of Christmas 1307. A low ridge rising to the west, which separates the level farmland around Slioch from Strathbogie Castle and the modern town of Huntly, is known as Battle Hill. Tradition attributes this place name to an otherwise unknown (and anachronistic) conflict between the Comyns and the Gordons, but it is more plausible to suppose that the battle of Slioch is meant. To the south-east lies another low rise named Robin's Height which the *New Statistical Account* identifies with the site of 'Bruce's Camp'.

The Ordnance Survey place the site of battle midway between Torra Duncan and Slioch farm—a good compromise, since the precise site is unknown. The battlefield today is disappointing. A lush carpet of barley covers the area in summer, submerging all original detail. The Meet Hillock and another ancient mound have vanished, and even Torra Duncan has felt the plough and is not easy to pick out when the crops are ripe. A small rectangle of wet ground near the motte has been planted with conifers and evokes a distant remembrance of the long-vanished boggy wood.

The battle of Aikey Brae is recorded only in local tradition, although that is not necessarily to deny its historicity. According to the *New Statistical*

Account Edward Bruce camped on 'Bruce Hill', a mile west of New Deer. A cluster of 'tumuli' nearby were thought to mark the places where the dead had been buried, and the famous market of Aikey fair was established on the battlefield 'in memory of this victory'. One would have thought that the people of Buchan had scant cause to celebrate the event.

The battle of Barra took place on what are now the enclosed, cattle-grazed fields of the Mains of Barra, just south-west of Oldmeldrum, and known today as 'the King's Field'. A prehistoric fort on the Hill of Barra is traditionally associated with 'Comyn's Camp', but this is just another example of nearby antiquities becoming associated with a battle. A number of small elliptical trenches were found on the site, in one of which was found an English billhook.[17] The imposing tower house of Barra Castle, which stands to the south of the battlefield, is of early seventeenth century origin.

The Bass of Inverurie is a beautifully preserved example of a motte and bailey castle, despite the encroachment of the adjacent cemetery. This was almost certainly the site of Bruce's camp before the battle, although tradition places it at a prehistoric fort on a hill above the town, perhaps to counterbalance Buchan's camp on the hill of Barra. Needless to say, there is also a small cave near Inverurie which is said to be the one in which Bruce had that famous confrontation with a spider.

Of the north-eastern castles laid low by Robert Bruce or his brother, some have sunk without trace like that of Aberdeen; others, such as Ellon, are submerged by later building. Perhaps the most spectacular remaining ruins are the Buchan promontory forts of Dundarg and Slains; both are now shattered ruins, but one can still sense their ghosts. Dundarg is particularly dramatic, a sentinel of angry red sandstone riding above the pounding waves. It was one of the earl of Buchan's personal castles; if he really spent much time living in such an uncomfortable place, he must have been a tougher proposition than Barbour would have us believe.

CHAPTER 6

CULBLEAN

After Bannockburn (1314), the English were unable to seriously threaten King Robert's throne or realm. Indeed, the boot was on the other foot, and the Scots cheerfully devastated the borders as far south as Yorkshire in a series of mounted raids by guerilla bands. In 1328 the new English king, Edward III, conceded Bruce's right to the independent crown of Scotland at the Treaty of Northampton. The 'true, final and perpetual peace' was sealed by the marriage between Bruce's five-year old son David and Edward's sister Joan. Unfortunately King Robert was by now a very sick man. On his death in the following year, Scotland was again placed under the guardianship of leading nobles in the name of the community of the realm and the boy king, David II.

The War of Liberation had resulted in the disinheritance and exile of many Scottish barons and knights who now lived on their estates in England. Many had since died, but they left restless, ambitious sons, eager to recover their lands and impatient to take advantage of the new situation in Scotland.

The Disinherited, as they called themselves, encouraged Edward Balliol to resurrect his dead father's claim to the crown. An expeditionary force was raised, with the tacit but as yet undeclared support of Edward III, embarked on boats at the Humber and landed at Kinghorn in Fife. To their great surprise the Disinherited quickly won a string of victories, defeating the Scots army in the field at Dupplin Moor and capturing Perth and Edinburgh. Edward Balliol was crowned at Scone in September 1332 and issued letters patent to Edward III recognising him as lord superior. This was the only practicable step since Balliol enjoyed limited support among the Scots and could hold onto his gains only with English help. This was soon forthcoming when Edward III took advantage of renewed Scots raids and the summary expulsion of Balliol by the supporters of David II to revoke the Treaty of Northampton and lay siege to Berwick. A new Scots army was cut to pieces by English archers at the battle of Halidon Hill in 1333. Scotland's erstwhile leaders were now mostly dead. David II was spirited away to France and the Disinherited seized the fruits of victory.

As before, Scotland proved harder to hold than to take. The Disinherited were soon falling out among themselves, and those who had remained loyal to David II were able to organise resistance and push the English—and Balliol—out again. A major effort by the English king was now necessary in order to keep Edward Balliol on the throne. In July 1335, therefore, the two Edwards launched a massive two-pronged invasion of Scotland. The armies reached Perth without serious resistance and there Edward III received the submissions of many of David II's supporters. The Peace of Perth, signed that August, was virtually a capitulation.[1]

All this sound and fury in the south apparently had little impact on the North East. This was to change however in 1335, when David of Strathbogie arrived on the scene. Strathbogie was the son and heir of the earl of Atholl whose earldom included extensive holdings in the North East. Atholl had been disinherited by Robert Bruce after treacherously attacking the Scottish supply depot on the eve of Bannockburn, and had died in exile in England. Strathbogie had accompanied Balliol in 1332 as claimant to the earldom of Atholl, and after the latter's coronation was recognised as earl and as steward of Scotland. In 1334 Strathbogie was forced to switch his fealty to David II, but at the Peace of Perth he reassumed his old colours as a Balliol man. Despite these changes of allegiance Balliol still trusted or needed Strathbogie enough to name him king's lieutenant in the north and promise him the office of constable of Scotland. Strathbogie set off north, with a strong force including siege engines, to regain the North East for Balliol and dispossess those who retained their allegiance to David II.

Since the heroic days of 1306–8, the North East had been a bastion of loyalty to Robert Bruce and his son. Bruce had rewarded his followers—Hay, Leslie, Irvine and Seton among others—with the lands of the disinherited Comyns and Strathbogies. David of Strathbogie began an attempt to turn the clock back to 1306 by dispossessing the new landlords in favour of the heirs of the old. He and his Comyn kinfolk are said to have intended to root out every freeholder in the North East. They arrived with seige engines at harvest time, when the mind of every knight, husbandman and cottar was on bringing in the sheaves. The trail of devastated lands, burning ricks and slaughtered cattle, of evil memory, began anew. Strathbogie's vindictiveness and intemperance ensured him a very bad press from the patriotic Scots chroniclers. According to Andrew de Wyntoun, writing seventy years later,

> His hart fra Scottis all turnyd was;
> And Inglis man became agayne
> And gert his folk wyth mekill mayne
> Ryot halyly the cwntre   (ravage wholly the country)
> And lete, that all hys awyne suld be.[2]

Holinshed adds that he was 'greedie of government' and that he 'did most grevously oppress the giltless and poor people, and wickedlie ordered all things after his own fansie, without reason'. Others expressed themselves unable to find any words harrowing enough to describe him.

To establish his hold on the North East, Strathbogie had to capture the castles. The strongest of them, Kildrummy Castle, still held out and was garrisoned by 300 men loyal to David II under Sir John of the Craig, an erstwhile tenant of Strathbogie's. The king's aunt, Christian, was also sheltering within its stout walls. John of the Craig had been captured by Strathbogie some time before and released on the promise of a ransom, due on 30 November. Under the rules of war at that time, the castle would be surrendered on that date unless relief were brought.[3] In the meantime, Strathbogie met 'stout and manly resistance'. Wyntoun tells us that the defendants 'offtare scathyd thame wyth-out than thai dyd thame wyth-in'. With the surrender date approaching, however, Christian Bruce, doubtless remembering the unpleasant fate of her family in 1306, dispatched a messenger appealing to her husband, Sir Andrew Moray, lord of Garioch, for aid.

Moray was the effective leader of the Scottish resistance and the newly appointed guardian of the realm. While Strathbogie threatened Kildrummy, he was involved in peace talks with Balliol's commissioners at Bathgate in Lothian. When the news arrived, he was rather surprisingly given licence to assemble a force to raise the siege. Perhaps his opponents regarded the rescue of a wife as a chivalric imperative. Perhaps they also hoped that Moray might get himself killed in the process. Moray mustered a small but hardy and experienced band of 800 men, among them Sir William Douglas, the knight of Liddesdale, Patrick, earl of Dunbar and Sir Alexander de Seton, who had recently been obliged to surrender his north-eastern estates to Strathbogie.[4]

Moray rode north with all the speed of a husband in distress. By 28 November he had crossed over the Fir Mounth into Glen Tanar and was now poised to strike north, through the Howe of Cromar, to Kildrummy. Strathbogie, having received news of his advance, abandoned the siege and moved southward to Culblean, where he took up position across the main approach road, 'at the est end, rycht in the way'. He seems to have been inviting battle, confident in the strong hilltop position, not attempting to escape. He was followed, at a cautious distance, by John of the Craig with the 300 'wycht and hardy' men of Kildrummy at his back.

The rival armies sighted each other across the dark waters of Loch Davan, just as dusk fell on 29 November. Moray had forded the Dee at the Mill of Dinnet and occupied the 'Hall of Logy-Rothwayne', a moated house on the eastern shore of Loch Davan.[5] There he was joined by John of the Craig, and we may well believe, with Wyntoun, that 'he was glade of thare cummyng'. For Sir John had not only brought reinforcements, he had brought with him a detailed knowledge of the lie of the land.

Moray decided to approach Strathbogie's camp at night, in readiness for a surprise assault at dawn. He further decided to divide his force before the attack with one division under his own command and the other under Douglas. Such tactics were ambitious but not novel, for the Scots had gained experience of them in raids on Weardale and elsewhere in northern England.[6] A further reason for aiming at surprise was Moray's deficiency in numbers, for even with the addition of the men of Kildrummy he had little more than 1,000 men.

Two main tracks passed through the wood of Culblean with its lochs and marshes. One of these, which Wyntoun calls the 'Umast (uppermost) Way', was probably the drove road to Tullich on which Strathbogie had pitched his camp. The second, the 'Tothir (small) Way', may be the original Deeside road[7] but is more probably a minor track passing through the wood at a lower elevation than the Umast Way. Moray's plan was to pass around the south side of Loch Kinord then strike north towards the Umast Way, a distance which would take his mounted force most of the night to cover.

Moray probably left his cook fires burning as his mounted column filed out of camp. Perhaps he left behind a small body of camp followers to stoke the fires and make as much noise as possible to confuse the enemy: the waters of Loch Davan have excellent sound transmission qualities.[8] The column passed silently south towards the Dee, and then northwards along the west side of Kinord via the Tothir Way. As they drew nigh to Strathbogie's camp, with dawn now glimmering above the black hills of Culblean and Morven, Moray's force dismounted and left their horses coralled in the wood. The command of the main force he gave to Sir William Douglas. Moray would himself lead a second group around the enemy camp and attack downhill, from the heights of Culblean hill.

Strathbogie's position on the hillock gave him a panoramic view over the landscape below. He was well poised to strike at any force moving north up the Umast Way towards Kildrummy, which is probably the direction which he assumed that Moray would take. That a force would attempt to encircle his camp and attack from behind had evidently not occurred to him: possibly, with his English upbringing, he would have thought such a manoeuvre to be contrary to the knightly code. Suddenly there were warning cries, and a scout came running into camp with the news that a force was moving towards them from the south. The whinny of a pony or the chink of chain mail must have aroused a sleepy sentry. Strathbogie acted swiftly. Horns blared, the sleeping soldiery were roused and kicked out of their plaids and marshalled across the 'lytill path', facing south towards the steep valley of a small stream—the Burn o' Vat. Strathbogie is said to have tried to stiffen the resolve of his men by personal example. 'Be Goddis face', said he, indicating a large granite boulder nearby, 'we twa the flycht on us sall samyn ta': this great stone will flee the field as soon as I will. Sir Walter Scott borrowed this famous incident in *The Lady of the Lake*, when his hero, Fitz-James found himself in similar circumstances:[9]

> His back against a rock he bore,
> And firmly placed his foot before:
> 'Come one, come all! this rock shall fly
> From its firm base as soon as I'.

By the time Douglas reached the burn he found Strathbogie's men in a strong position along the slopes of the heathery ridge which runs parallel

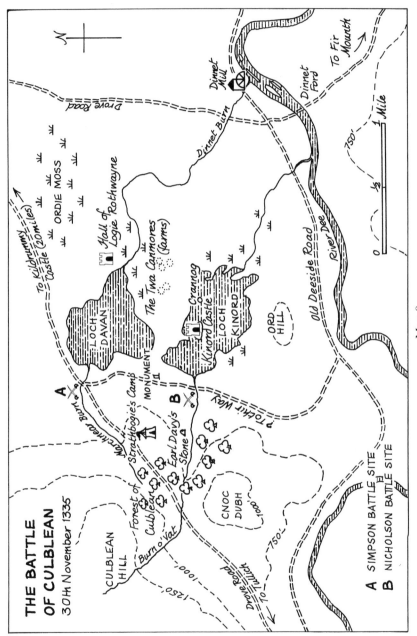

Map 8.

with the stream. The slopes of the burn were (and still are) rugged and strewn with bushes and boulders. The surrounding hillside was probably rather open woodland of birch, pine and oak, with plentiful juniper bushes. It would be impossible to maintain a close battle-line or schiltrom of spears in such broken country, and Douglas evidently realised this before his opponent did. Wyntoun relates how he restrained his more headstrong followers from charging down over the burn by holding his spear horizontally in both hands and crying: 'Stay, my Lords, a moment'. Strathbogie took this for hesitation and, seeing that their numbers were fewer than he had feared, cried 'Hey! apone thame tyte, for thai ar welle nere dyscumfyte'! His men rushed down towards the burn and in their haste, as Douglas had foreseen, broke ranks. Such headlong dashes were a feature of the undisciplined feudal armies of Scotland. Much the same behaviour lost the battle of Dunbar in 1296.

As Strathbogie's Athollmen poured across the ford of the Burn O' Vat, shouting in excitement and blowing horns, Douglas cried 'Now we!' and sounded the advance. His men straightened their spears and moved forward. The clash seems to have taken place in and around the ford. One of Strathbogie's knights, Sir Robert Brady, was slain and measured his length across the burn which, local tradition insists, ran red with blood.

Strathbogie was already doomed. During the hullaballoo around the ford, Moray had by-passed the enemy camp un-noticed and had lain hidden in the 'herberry', waiting until the greater part of the enemy force was engaged. Then, at a given signal, they rushed downhill on to the flank and rear of Strathbogie's army:

> With that Sir Androw of Murray
> Come in on side sa sturdely
> With all thaim of his cumpany
> That in his cummyng, as thai say
> He baire doune buskis (bushes) in his way.[10]

Strathbogie's army promptly collapsed. Small groups of fighting men remained on the field, but most of the terrified rank and file made a run for it, fleeing into the dense forest and swamps around Loch Kinord. Moray let them go; he was only interested in the leaders. Consequently the casualties were light:

> There war bot fewe slayne in that fycht
> For the wode held theme owt off sycht
> And thai fled als so hastyly
> That away gat the mast party.

Strathbogie saw that all was lost, and, placing his back to an oak tree, he fought on until overcome and slain: 'There by an aik deyd Erle Davy and sundry of his company'. Gordon tradition has it that he was killed in single combat with Sir Alexander de Seton who, as the recipient of Strathbogie's north-eastern estates, had good reason for wanting him dead. With him fell his son-in-law, Sir William Comyn, and another kinsman, Sir Thomas Comyn was, according to Holinshed, captured and beheaded the next day. Sir Thomas Brown was taken prisoner and knocked about by his captors.

One of Strathbogie's supporters, Sir Robert Menzies, managed to escape to his nearby pele tower on the island in Loch Kinord. There are two accounts of his fate: according to Wyntoun, the most probable, he surrendered to Moray the next day on promise of a safe conduct. Gordon legend, however, claims that Sir Alexander de Seton constructed a flotilla of timber rafts to convey his men to the island, stormed the castle and put its garrison to the sword.

Culblean was a battle which was seen as decisive in retrospect by later Scottish chroniclers. After Culblean, wrote Fordun, the fortunes of war favoured the Scots. At the time it may have seemed only a minor episode in the war. David of Strathbogie was eliminated but the war went on. Seven months after Culblean, King Edward III led a chivalrous dash to Lochindorb to rescue the late Davy of Strathbogie's wife, who was besieged by Moray— a kind of tit-for-tat for Moray's wife at Kildrummy. The North East suffered much in 1336. An English force entered Aberdeen, repulsed its defenders drawn up on The Green and, on the pretext that an English knight had been slain by the towns folk, put the entire town to the torch. It is said that Aberdeen burned for six days and nights.

But, like his grandfather Edward I, Edward III could not conquer Scotland, although he could seize its castles, ravage its lands and burn its towns. His successive invasions produced no lasting political settlement and the devastation that accompanied them seems to have united the nation to resist in a manner recalling the days of Wallace and Robert Bruce. Edward III lacked his grandfather's iron determination to enforce his 'rights'. He was more easy-going, an opportunist in love with military glory and quick profits, neither of which Scotland had provided. France, in 1337, looked much more promising. The English nobility, too, found their feudal duties in Scotland increasingly onerous and the Commons were increasingly reluctant to vote for taxation for Scottish garrisons. And so Balliol and the Disinherited were, by degrees, abandoned. The war fizzled out and in 1341 David II, now a young man capable of ruling, returned to his inheritance. Much of the credit was due to Sir Andrew Moray.

The site of the battle

There have been a number of different reconstructions of the battle of Culblean, which is not surprising when one considers the complexities of the landscape over which it was fought and the obscurities of Wyntoun's chronicle. In the nineteenth century the site of battle was thought to lie on the eastern side of Loch Davan, beneath the slopes of Mulloch Hill, but this left many details in Wyntoun unexplained. The first real breakthrough came in 1925, when G.M. Fraser identified the low, moated mound on the eastern edge of Loch Davan as the site of Wyntoun's Hall of Logy-Rothwayne.

Nearby place names such as the Mains and Mill of Logie and Nether and Upper Ruthven strengthened this conjecture. This identification was accepted by W. Douglas Simpson who in 1930 produced what has become the 'classic' reconstruction of the battle.[11]

Using the Hall as a starting point, Simpson set out to identify Wyntoun's 'Umast' and 'Tothir' Ways, which he rightly believed were the key to the battle. The one 'upper' track which almost certainly existed in 1335 was the Tullich drove road, and he placed Strathbogie's camp by this track at the west side of Loch Davan. This provided a basis for a reconstruction which was in apparent agreement with Wyntoun. Simpson suggested that Douglas marched around the north shore of Loch Davan on the line of the present A97 and that the battle took place over the Marchnear burn which passes in front of Strathbogie's position. There remained Moray's flank march. Simpson sent Moray and John of the Craig off into the forest to the north of Loch Davan and suggested a route for the 'Tothir Way' which would take them around Strathbogie's flank to attack him from the north-west.

Although there are some attractive features in this reconstruction, there are also flaws, both in terms of geography and military probability. The Marchnear burn is a mere trickle and the point where it crosses the Tullich drove road is an intricate little area, most of which would probably have been swamp and reedbed in 1335. Visiting it today, it is difficult to visualise the battle unless the numbers involved were very small indeed, but Simpson crams several thousand men into this locality. He also refutes certain details in Wyntoun that do not square with his theory. Although Wyntoun explicitly states that Moray moved from the Hall of Logy-Rothwayne down to the Dee, Simpson dismisses such a long detour as impossible—on the assumption that the army marched on foot. But his own version of the 'Tothir Way' is a straggling minor path which does not seem to lead anywhere, itself inherently improbable.

The military improbabilities of the Simpson version are self evident. In an age long before synchronised watches it would have been very rash indeed for Moray to have divided his force from the outset, as Simpson suggests. With anything less than perfect timing at the dawn attack, he would have left Strathbogie with a clear escape route to the south. From what we know of Moray, we can be sure that he had a better plan than this.

A variation of the Simpson theory was put forward by Fenton Wyness.[12] Without citing evidence, Wyness dismisses the supposed hall site as a 'prehistoric earthwork' and sites Moray's camp at an old farming settlement, a mile to the east. This is a step backwards: archaeologists have little doubt that G.M. Fraser's site *is* a medieval motte, and it bears no resemblance to the plentiful prehistoric sites in the Cromar area.[13] Like Simpson, Wyness divides Moray's force from the outset, but makes Douglas strike along the ridge of dry land between Lochs Davan and Kinord, whilst Moray's flank attack rounds the north side of Loch Davan. This theory carries the same military criticisms as that of Simpson with the added demerit that Douglas' attack is now on a dangerously narrow front with the only available burn some way *behind* Strathbogie's position.

There is, fortunately a third extant theory. In *Edward III and the Scots* (1956), Professor Ranald Nicholson provided a study in depth of the military and political struggles of the 1330s. The premise for his reconstruction of the battle of Culblean is based on several points which had hitherto been neglected or misunderstood. Firstly, Moray's strategy was based on mobility: his entire force was mounted and could therefore cover large distances comparatively quickly. They dismounted only immediately before the battle. Simpson encumbers Moray's 800 horse with 2,000 foot soldiers (for which there is no warrant in Wyntoun), on the assumption that 800 was a ludicrously small force. On the contrary, remarks Professor Nicholson, 'such a force was, in the circumstances, quite sizeable'. Once Wyntoun's night march to the Dee becomes possible, then local geography, the chronicle account and military probability at last begin to converge. Moray was not interested in merely turning the enemy's flank. He intended to cut off his line of retreat completely, attack him in the rear and finish him off with a flank attack which would drive the fugitives into the swamps. Wyntoun's Umast and Tothir Ways therefore take their place as the two probable medieval roads—the Tullich drove road and the Deeside road. Wyntoun's stream and ford becomes the substantial Burn o' Vat, not the tiny Marchnear Burn, with Strathbogie's camp situated on the hillock above—an excellent choice of site. We can ascend this hill today and, looking down over the battlefield, can readily appreciate Moray's mastery of guerilla warfare—mobility, surprise, annihilation.

Culblean today

A visit to the Culblean battlefield can form part of an enjoyable historical and archaeological walking tour, for this area is rich in antiquities including a beautiful Pictish stone and one of the finest concentrations of Iron Age settlements in Scotland.[13] The erstwhile heather grouse muir on the slopes of Culblean is now reverting back to the wooded conditions prevailing at the time of the battle, which were probably mixed forest of oak, birch and pine. The bushes which are mentioned in Wyntoun were very likely junipers. Because of the past management of burning and grazing there are only a few natural oaks or junipers remaining there today.

It has been generally assumed that the lochs and swamps would have been more extensive in 1335, and hence even more formidable obstacles. This is not necessarily so. The climate then was rather warmer than now, and much of the present swampland is encroachment over what was formerly open water. Loch Davan would probably have been somewhat larger in 1335, but the surrounding area might have been less, rather than more, marshy.

Both the Simpson site, the Marchnear Burn, and the Nicholson site, the Burn o' Vat, should be on the itinerary for an inspection of the battlefield and the visitor should make his own mind up about their respective merits. The former is now a tangle of planted and natural trees, three crofts and a pond, through which the burn passes almost un-noticed. The Burn o' Vat is

12. The monument at Culblean, commemorating the battle of 1335, erected by the Deeside Field Club. It stands about four hundred yards north of the probable battlefield.

less cluttered, although the battle was probably centred in the area now given over to car parks and the tea-rooms. Strathbogie's camp on the hillside above the tea-rooms provides a panoramic view of the ground below. A large prominent 'erratic' granite boulder perched on this slope is sometimes called Earl Davy's Stone, although it lies to the west of the earl's probable position.

A monument to the battle stands by the A97, roughly halfway between the Burn o' Vat and the Marchnear Burn. A rugged pillar of Craigenlow granite, it is thirteen feet high and weighs over seven tons. It was originally suggested and designed by Fenton Wyness and erected by the Deeside Field Club at the site where he thought the battle took place. It forms one of a trio of similar 'Clach na Cuimhne' stones on Deeside, the other pair commemorating the battle of Corrichie and the raising of the Standard at Braemar in 1715. On the face of the Culblean monument is a brass plaque which briefly describes the battle.

Of the two fortified sites mentioned in Wyntoun, the Hall of Logy-Rothwayne has vanished, but the low moated eminence on which it stood is still visible at the east end of Loch Davan. It has been planted over with pines and the moat has partially filled in, although it is still marshy in wet weather. Kinord Castle stood on the larger of the two islands on Loch Kinord (the smaller is a man-made island or crannog), and was linked to the north shore by a wooden causeway. In 1335 it would probably have been a wooden structure, although it was later rebuilt from stone. The castle was finally 'slighted' in 1648, after it had served as a Royalist garrison under the marquis of Huntly, and so thoroughly that even the rubble has vanished. The causeway survived until 1783, when it was used in the making of the first Ballater bridge.

Two final, apocryphal traditions are associated with the battle of Culblean. One is that a group of fugitives from the battlefield took refuge in the Deeside Mill at Dinnet. They were surrounded and all were killed except two, who were saved by the intervention of the miller. The other tradition is connected with the Tarland burn, to the north of Aboyne Castle; this, 'the bleedy burn', was said to be so choked with the slain that for twenty-four hours the waters ran red with blood. That the real battlefield lay six miles to the west did not deter the growth of this legend. As with many another battlefield, such glory fables live on long after the real events are forgotten.

CHAPTER 7

REID HARLAW

Gret pitie was to hear and see
The noys and dulesum hermonie
That evie that dreary day did daw;
Cryand the corynoch on hie,
Alas! Alas! for the Harlaw.

From the Battel of Hayrlaw, first published 1548.

The 'Sair Field o' Harlaw' has become one of the most enduring folk memories of the North East, the day of deliverance when the caterans of the lord of the Isles were turned back at the gates of Aberdeen at a terrible cost in lives. Yet although it is one of the best known of the north eastern battles, it is also one of the least understood. There is a thick layer of legend woven about the battle of Harlaw, and it seems to have been acquired unusually early. John Major, writing in the early sixteenth century, remarked that 'Harlaw' was a popular children's game during his schooldays at Haddington Grammar School in Aberdeen, rather like latterday Cowboys and Indians or Cops and Robbers.[1] And we still annually raise our glasses to 'the heroes of Harlaw' although few of us remember precisely why the battle was ever fought.

The difficulty of getting behind the legend to the bare truth about the battle is illustrated by our two earliest sources, both of which are lyrical rather than strictly historical. The first of these is the Gaelic battle song, composed for the MacDonalds by Lachlan Mor MacMhuirich, which, as one might expect, is a panegyric to the bravery of the clans.[2] According to this bard, the Lowlanders were 'quite defeated' and chased all the way to Aberdeen. The Lowland version of events, as recounted in the anonymous poem *Battel of Hayrlaw*, is at first sight very different. Here the bold earl of Mar and his band of knights surprise the Highlanders, who are represented throughout as an ill-disciplined mob, and, despite initial setbacks, fight the greatly superior

Highland force to a standstill. The Highlanders withdraw during the hours of darkness and Mar is justified in regarding the battle as a victory, having delivered the civilised Lowlands from an awful fate at the barbarous hands of the cateran. Both of these sources are obviously heavily biased and phrased in emotional language which is at once heroic and vague.

There are, unfortunately, no better near-contemporary sources to draw on, since this battle took place during one of those disconcerting gaps in Scottish history when the chronicles suddenly dry up. Fordun and Barbour were dead and Wyntoun chose, for inscrutable reasons of his own, to end his chronicle a few years before 1411. Bower, the abbot of Inchcolm, wrote a continuation to Fordun's history in the 1440s, within a generation of the battle, but despite his assertion, 'by Christ, he is not a Scot to whom this work is unpleasing,' he plainly had no eye-witness account to draw on.[3] In consequence he manages only to paint a rather stereotyped picture of Highlanders flinging themselves with mad courage upon thickets of spears. The only early historian who attempted to balance the conflicting versions of the battle was John Major who, in 1527, was writing at a time when oral tradition was perhaps still current:

> Though it be more generally said among the common people that the wild Scots were defeated, I find the very opposite of this in the chroniclers; only, the earl of the Isles was forced to retreat; and he counted amongst his men more of the slain than did the civilised Scots. Yet those men did not put (him) to open rout, though they fiercely strove, and not without success, to put a check upon the audaciousness of the man.

The ballads have built up a picture of racial hostility between the Gaelic 'wild Scots' of the Highlands and the 'civilised' Scots of the Lowlands which is partly anachronistic, and reflects the times of the ballad makers rather than the time of Harlaw. As historians have long since pointed out, the division between Highlanders and Lowlanders was, and is, cultural rather than racial, and Gaelic speakers would have been found on both sides at Harlaw. The principal antagonists, Donald of the Isles and Alexander of Mar, were related by marriage. Donald was, by all accounts, an intelligent, even a cultured man, whilst Alexander's early career included acts of barbarity which rivalled the bloodthirstiest deeds of the 'caterans'. It is doubtful whether the Lowlander of 1411 could claim much of an advance of civilisation over his fellows in the hills. This was a time of anarchy and lawlessness and some Lowland lairds lived the lives of brigands whilst the tenants and cottars who farmed the land were probably not much wealthier than the average Highlander. All the same, the cultural divide between Highlander and Lowlander was broadening and the increasing degree of hostility between them probably influenced the events which led to 'Reid Harlaw'.

The battle of Harlaw had its origins in a feudal dispute which could be resolved only by force of arms, since the king of Scotland, James I, who might have been able to adjudicate, was a prisoner in England. This was the period in which the Stewarts, under Scotland's regent, the duke of Albany, gained power in the North East. In 1405, Albany granted the earldom of Buchan to his son and, a year or two later, his nephew Alexander seized the earldom of Mar by the coarse but effective expedient of throwing the rightful earl into the dungeons of his own castle and marrying his wife. That such actions could be condoned was a sign of the times. In the meantime, the earldom of Ross had fallen vacant. The heiress, Euphemia Leslie, a little crook-backed girl, was persuaded by Albany to resign the earldom when she came of age in favour of her uncle, the Stewart earl of Buchan. She was then packed off to a nunnery. This was ill news for Donald, second lord of the Isles, who feared the growing power of the Stewarts and had put forward a claim of his own to the earldom of Ross, that he was the rightful possessor through his wife Margaret, sister of the dead earl and next in line of succession after Euphemia. Donald argued that by becoming a nun, Euphemia would be dead to the world and hence had no right either to hold or dispose of the earldom, which would therefore revoke automatically to himself as the *de jure* earl.

Like his father before him, Donald regarded himself as an independent ruler who could enter diplomatic negotiations with foreign powers on his own behalf. He had no difficulty in winning English support for his claim to Ross and, probably, also that of the captive Scottish king who had watched from afar the antics of his Stewart relatives with growing anguish. Highland raids into Moray increased in the years leading up to Harlaw. By 1411, Donald was determined to seize the earldom of Ross by force 'or else be graithed in his graif'. He called out his kin in the Isles, who mustered at his castle of Ardtornish, on the Sound of Mull. Donald is said to have chosen 6,000 of the best men and sent the rest home.[4] The force marched through Ross to Dingwall, where they were opposed by the Mackays. Outnumbered, the Mackays were defeated and the victors marched on to the town of Inverness and set ablaze its great oak bridge and castle. As Inverness burned, other clans pledged Donald their active support, including the MacIntoshes, MacLeans, MacLeods, Camerons and Clan Chattan. The resultant army was one of almost unprecedented size and a tribute to the power and patronage of the lords of the Isles in their heyday. It might even have numbered 10,000 men, as the ballads insist.

What did early fifteenth century clan warriors look like? We have little contemporary evidence apart from that of the Aberdeen priest, Fordun, who describes them as 'wild and untamed, rough and unbending ... comely in form but unsightly in dress'.[5] John Major gives a more detailed description, which must be close to the actual appearance of the men at Harlaw:

> From the mid-leg to the foot they go uncovered; their dress is, for an over-garment, a loose plaid and a shirt saffron-dyed. They are armed with a bow and arrows, a broadsword, and a small halbert. They always carry in their belt a stout dagger, single-edged, but of the sharpest. In time of war they cover the whole body with a coat of mail, made of iron rings, and in it they fight. The common folk among the Wild Scots go out to battle with the whole body clad in a linen garment sewed together in patchwork, well daubed with wax or with pitch, and with an overcoat of deerskin.[6]

We are told, largely on the evidence of Lowland writers, that Donald's intention was to sack the town of Aberdeen and plunder the Lowlands as far as the Tay. Probably his real purpose was to sieze the lands pertaining to the earldom of Ross in the sheriffdoms of Banff, Aberdeen and Kincardine.[7] He may have intended to lay waste the lands of the Stewart earls; in any case, there was little he could do to prevent the pillaging and disorder which always attend the progress of a wild, undisciplined army. Booty was the Gaelic warrior's price for support. Leaving the embers of Inverness smouldering behind them, the clans marched behind their banners and pipes along the road which would take them to Harlaw.

The man responsible for the defence of Aberdeen and Mar was Alexander Stewart, earl of Mar, a knightly condottiere who is one of the more colourful figures of medieval Scottish history. He was evidently more capable and less wastefully savage than his father, the infamous Wolf of Badenoch, but the two had much in common. In his youth, Alexander had harried the North East at the head of a gang of Highland bandits. As we have seen, it was he who had scandalously abducted and married the countess of Mar, after first arranging her husband's deposition and subsequent death in his own castle dungeons. Shortly afterwards, he took over her lands and title. The countess died three years later, having issued a public proclamation that she had surrendered her title voluntarily. Time and wealth eventually mellowed the new earl of Mar and, by a combination of ruthless methods and a zest for all the trappings of the age of chivalry, he kept the peace and won the fealty of the north eastern lairds. He was a great hero to his contemporary, the Scots historian Andrew Wyntoun, who describes him as 'honeste, habill and avenand': honest, able and elegant in person and behaviour.[8] Mar seems, like his contemporary, King Henry V, to have turned away from his former self.

At Christmas in the year 1410, Mar entertained a large company of north eastern lairds and clergy at Kildrummy Castle. Among those present were Robert Davidson, the Provost of Aberdeen, Gilbert Greenlaw, bishop of Aberdeen, Henry de Lichtoun, rector of Kinkell, and a host of knights including Mar's brother, Sir James Stewart and his close crony, Sir Alexander Irvine of Drum. It is probable that preparations were made at this gathering for the defence of Aberdeen on the anticipated invasion of the lord of the Isles.[9] We know from lists of those present at the battle of Harlaw that a great many, if not most, of the great families of Buchan, Mar and Angus obeyed Mar's levy which suggests that the recent Stewart seizure of the two north eastern earldoms had been accepted. Since the late 1330s, the province had seen little large-scale warfare, as opposed to the usual incessant feuding between rival families, and most of those present who had military experience had gained it in foreign wars. Sir James Scrymgeour of Dundee, Irvine of Drum and Mar himself had seen military service in Flanders, where the latter won 'gret renown thare horounyt all his natiown'.[10] It was on the armour-plated shoulders of these comrades-in-arms that the defence of the earldom chiefly depended.

Some indication of the general unreadiness of defence in the North East can be gained by looking at Aberdeen's own contribution to the Harlaw campaign. Provost Robert Davidson, 'a man brave and bold who prospered in all things'[11] was yet another close personal friend of Mar, with whom he shared some shady business interests, including organised piracy. He was to organise and lead the Aberdeen contingent but, despite the impending threat of pillage and sack hanging over Aberdeen, records show that only thirty six citizens were 'chosen to go forth against the cateran', out of a population of at least 3,000. Presumably only a small minority had had any military training. While it is possible that some of the company took with them the servants from their households, the general state of preparedness of Aberdeen was lamentable and urgent reforms were made to the burgh's defences after the battle.

During the spring and early summer of 1411, the North East sprang to arms. From scattered hints in the sources and in the Harlaw ballads, it seems that the lairds remained on their own lands throughout this period to guard all possible approaches across the hills to Mar. The Forbes, for instance, probably stood watch over the 'high road' to Donside at the Rhynie gap, and we know that Irvine remained on his own estates at Drum until the day before the battle. Donald of the Isles had evidently decided to take the most direct route to Aberdeen, however, via the King's Highway from Inverness through the Enzie, Strathbogie and Garioch. According to the north eastern ballads, all of which are strongly partisan in tone, the Highlanders pillaged, looted and burned their way towards Aberdeen. The only contemporary evidence however is a claim for damages sustained by lands owned by Lindores Abbey. One should allow for an element of exaggeration in the ballads— one can imagine refugees arriving at Aberdeen with terrifying news of the unheard size of the Highland army: 'there are fifty thousand Heilan' men a-marching to Harlaw!'

Assuming that Donald did not delay overlong in the rich farming country of Strathbogie and Garioch, Mar can have been given only three or four days notice, once it became clear that Donald was taking 'the Low Road' to Aberdeen. Although we do not know what contingency plans Mar had made, judging from events he intended to gather his forces at a pre-arranged rendezvous within striking distance of the enemy, and to follow this by an assault on their position at dawn on the following day. This bold strategy had been used in other medieval battles, notably at Stamford Bridge where the last Saxon king, Harold, had surprised and routed a Norwegian invasion force by such means. In Mar's case, the rendezvous was the royal burgh of Inverurie, which lies at the junction of the Don and Urie and guards the river crossings and approach road to Aberdeen. Mar's standard was probably raised at the old wooden castle at the Bass of Inverurie. There he was joined by the sheriff of Angus and the feudal levies of the North East under their respective knights and lairds. Sir Alexander Irvine, hastening up from Drum Castle, paused, according to tradition, on a hillside in Skene, where he looked back for the last time on the ramparts of his castle and forward to the battlefield on which he and so many others were to perish. The more far-flung detachments did not arrive until battle had already been joined. Among the late arrivals was Sir Alexander Forbes, the guardian of Rhynie gap, if Dr

Douglas Simpson's interpretation of an otherwise obscure passage in the best known Harlaw ballad is correct.[12]

The evening of 23 July leaves the earl of Mar marshalling his troops around the Bass of Inverurie for a dawn attack on the morrow, with detachments still coming in from Donside, Garioch, Deeside and the Mearns. In the meantime, Donald of the Isles had reached Harlaw. His Highlanders chose a strong position on which to camp on the elevated plateau two miles north of Inverurie. To the west of this position, the land drops steeply down to the marshy vale of the Urie, whilst the eastern flank is guarded by the equally wet defile of the Lochter burn. In 1411, the plateau was a bleak and stony heath, crossed by the track of the King's Highway to Aberdeen. Three ancient settlements stood about a mile apart along the road: to the south, the farm-toun of Balhalgardy; in the centre, 'the town of fair Harlaw', in fact another farming settlement with byres and cattle-folds; and, to the north, the posting

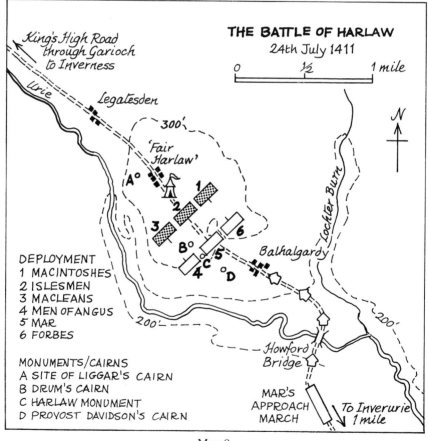

Map 9.

station of Legat's-den.[13] Somewhere in this general area, the Highlanders lit their camp-fires and lay down in their plaids and skins. The only possible approach to their camp was along the long and toilsome slope from the south and so certain were they of the natural strength of their camp that they evidently omitted to post any sentries.

At cock crow on the fateful day, 24 July, Mar's company broke camp and crossed the Urie by the wooden bridge that had spanned the river since 1235. His force must have numbered several thousand, but its precise size is unknown. Mar, possibly aided by the earl of Buchan, though most accounts omit him, ordered his men into two divisions. The vanguard was given to the men of Angus and the Mearns, under Sir James Scrymgeour, constable of Dundee, and Sir Alexander Ogilvy, sheriff of Angus. The main battle was commanded by Mar himself, together with the Earl Marischal and the earl of Erroll. Most of the north eastern knights present—the Irvines, Setons, Leslies and Leiths—fought under Mar's banner. Family traditions give prominent place to their own representative at Harlaw. Sir Alexander Forbes is said to have commanded a wing and he takes the starring role in one of the ballads. The Leslies claim that their laird was Mar's Master of Horse; the Irvines that theirs slew Donald's greatest champion and that his death was mourned more than any other. Many of the great houses, such as the Irvines and Keiths, had been at each others throats for years but, in the face of the common enemy, their differences were temporarily laid aside. Judging from a contemporary headstone in the nearby Kinkell Church, the wealthiest knights were clad from top to toe in plate armour, probably with a squire or two in attendance, but others retained the well-worn mail shirts of their ancestors, as Forbes, for instance, is said to have done. The battle seems to have been fought entirely on foot, with the two Lowland divisions forming dense 'schiltroms' of spearmen as at Falkirk and Bannockburn. Mar may have kept a division of horse in reserve; archers seem to have been absent. Reid Harlaw was to be an infantry 'slogging match'.

According to the early battle poem, the Highlanders were taken unawares by Mar's bold attack:

> And thus the martial Erle of Mar
> Marcht with his men in richt array,
> Befoir the enemie was aware,
> His banner bauldly did display.

Unless the Highlanders were sleeping very soundly indeed, it is difficult to see how this could be so, for they commanded an excellent view over most of Mar's approach from Inverurie. More probably, if the statement in the battle poem is to be taken at its face value, many of Donald's men were absent, foraging and looting about the Garioch countryside. 'The alarm once given', Douglas Simpson relates, 'the Highland host, we may well presume, would pour out of their camp like angry bees disturbed in their byke'.[14] The MacDonald battle song divides the Highland army into three divisions. Hector Roy MacLean of Duart, otherwise known as 'Red Hector of the

Battles', commanded the place of honour on the right wing at the head of his clan, as well as holding an overall command as Donald's 'general'. The clan chief of the MacIntoshes, Callum Beg, who led the left wing, was given grants of lands in Glengarry from Red Hector as recompense for accepting a lesser position.[15] The main battle was commanded by Donald himself with his own kin together with that of John of Harris and Roderick of Lewis.

The vanguards of both armies clashed near the summit of the ridge on which the present Harlaw monument stands. The clans charged with wild yells forcing the massed spears of the Angus men to give ground, 'three acres breadth an' mair'. The clans suffered fearful casualties, ill-protected as they were but, the ballad tells us, they 'laid on us fu' sair' with their heavy 'lang swords'. The royal standard of Scotland dipped momentarily as its hereditary bearer, Sir James Scrymgeour, was cut down. Part of the force sought refuge in a cattle fold at Balhalgardy as the storm of battle swept by. Mar's own division hurried forward and, by prodigious efforts, the line was held.

Reliable details of the rest of that bloody day are lacking. The sources agree that the fighting was 'hot and fierce'. Major thought that 'no battle with a foreign foe, and with so large a force, was ever waged that was more full of jeopardy than this'. Boece had heard that Mar was inept in his deployment of fresh forces, who kept arriving throughout the day, by hurling them into the battle immediately and sustaining unnecessarily heavy casualties. The Harlaw poem gives a sense of the military monotony of what was probably a confused press of exhausted men:

> With doubtsome victory they dealt
> The bludy battel lasted lang;
> Ilk man his neighbour's force there felt,
> The weakest aft-times gat the wrang;
> There was nae mows there them amang
> Naething was heard but heavy knocks:
> That echo made a dulfeu' sang
> Thereto resounding frae the rocks.

Little generalship can be discerned at the battle of Harlaw, but this might be due to the nature of the sources rather than that of the participants. It seems to have been a soldier's battle in which the bravery of the individual was more important than strategy. The forces engaged were equally matched and morale must have been high on both sides to sustain so long and fierce a conflict. Major is, as usual, the best informed of the commentators;

> The civilised Scots slew (Donald's) army commander, Maclean, and other nine hundred of his men, and yet more were sorely wounded. Of the southerners, six hundred lost their lives ... but in so much as very few escaped without a wound, and the fight lasted long, it is reckoned as hot and fierce.

When the sun cast its last red gleams over the piles of dead, the situation was stalemate. The Lowlanders had held their ground but the Highlanders were undefeated. The Highland battle song claims that Mar and Erroll posted in

13. The effigy of Sir Gilbert de Greenlaw, killed at Harlaw and buried in Kinkell Churchyard, near Inverurie.

haste to Aberdeen, pursued by the MacDonalds, while some of the 'civilised' Scots, who had hidden all day in the cattle fold, crept out at night to rob the dead. By the next morning, however, the clans were on their way home. Their losses, which included Red Hector, had been heavy. Perhaps the surviving clan chiefs had decided that the plunder of the Lowlands was not worth any further sacrifice. Boece, writing over a century later, makes a simpler suggestion: both sides retreated under cover of darkness, each imagining themselves to be defeated. At any rate, Aberdeen was saved from destruction and the Highlanders had gone.

The Lowlands had paid a heavy price for the deliverance. The coronach sounded for many a Lowlander who had 'left to the warld thair last gude nicht'. Their names ring out like a roll call of the north eastern chivalry: Robert Davidson, the only provost of Aberdeen to die in defence of his town, Mar's nephew, Sir William Abernethy of Saltoun, Sir Thomas Ogilvy, Sir Alexander Straiton, Sir Robert Maule, Sir Thomas Murray, Sir James Scrymgeour, Adam de Skene, William de Tulideff and a host of 'other gentlemen of lesser fame'. It is said that no less than six sons of Sir Alexander Leslie were carried feet first back to their sorrowing father's nearby castle of Balquhain.

Among the most notable losses was Sir Alexander Irvine who is said to have fought an epic duel with Red Hector MacLean by the end of which both lay dead:

> Gude Sir Alexander Irving,
> The much renownit Laird of Drum,
> Nane in his days was bettir sene,
> Quhen they war semblit all and sum;
> To praise him we sud not be dumm,
> For valour, witt and worthyness,
> To end his days he ther did cum,
> Quhois ransom is remeidyless.

It is said that the successors of Irvine and those of Red Hector exchanged swords long afterwards, to mark an end to the ill feelings between them.[16]

In the year following the battle of Harlaw, the defences of Aberdeen were overhauled thoroughly in the event of any future attack. Mar, naturally enough, became the burgh's first Captain and Governor, a post subsequently held by the son of that Alexander Irvine who had died at Harlaw. Aberdeen was divided into four municipal wards, each under the supervision of a magistrate 'sworne to the defence of the toun'. Arrangements were made for a regular call-up of arms, and the introduction of compulsory arms drill and archery. The 'near run thing' at Harlaw seems to have rattled the complacency of Aberdeen which had prospered in the productive years of Mar's long peace.

Although Harlaw is famed in ballad and song as few other Scottish battles are, it was anything but decisive. Regent Albany was able to recover the earldom of Ross without opposition the next year, but it is doubtful whether his writ was worth much in those remote regions. In 1415, Euphemia Leslie resigned the earldom into Albany's hands and Albany promptly bestowed it upon his son, the earl of Buchan. Donald retained his original possessions but made no serious renewed attempt to seize Ross before his death in about 1423. Harlaw was seen as a national deliverance by the Scottish government of the time—an ominous early sign of the division of Scotland into two nations—Lowland and Highland, Teuton and Gael. The heirs of those slain at Harlaw were exempted from feudal taxes on their succession to the estates, a concession usually reserved for those who were bereaved in wars against foreign foes. This two-nation view of Scotland fuelled the legend of the battle and distorted the real cause of the dispute. On the other hand, the losses at Harlaw were so severe, and its outcome so indecisive, that both sides were deterred from future adventures of the same kind. The real significance of the battle can best be summarised in the words of Professor Ranald Nicholson:

> The battle showed that the forces of the two sides were, for the time being, too finely balanced for the one to prevail against the other. But the battle also raised to a higher pitch the antagonism between Lowlander and Highlander. The time for tolerance or easy assimilation had disappeared, but the time for a wholesale attack upon Gaelic culture and upon the separatist political tendencies of Gaeldom had not yet arrived.[17]

Harlaw today

The battlefield of Harlaw is easily reached by taking the B9001 from Inverurie and turning left down a minor road signposted to the Harlaw Monument. The monument crowns an elevated position, looking west across the Urie valley to where the Mither Tap of Bennachie juts from the skyline like a fang. This fine panorama is unfortunately marred by a row of pylons. The battlefield, known as the Pley Fauld, can be surveyed from the monument. The ground is remarkably level and square fields of barley enclosed by drystane dikes occupy the former moor. The gradual slope to the south from the plateau and the steeper fall westwards to the river Urie can be seen from the monument and the strength of Donald's position is apparent.

There are a number of features of interest associated with the battle. The most obvious is the Harlaw Monument itself, designed by Dr William Kelly and financed by the City of Aberdeen on the 500th anniversary of the battle. Finally unveiled in 1914, it is specifically dedicated to the memory of Provost Davidson and the thirty six burgesses of Aberdeen who fought at Harlaw. A squat, roofed obelisk in grey and pink granite, it is one of Britain's largest and most elaborate battlefield monuments. To further mark the anniversary, a pageant was held in Aberdeen on Coronation Day. The event did not meet with universal approval, according to a contemporary newspaper report: 'to those who took an interest in the historical details, the procession was one of great interest ... but a section of the onlookers regarded the procession as merely a grotesque display'.

14. The monument at Harlaw, commemorating the battle of 1411, erected by
the City of Aberdeen on the 500th anniversary of the battle.

'The town of fair Harlaw' has disappeared, but the well by Harlaw House is said to be that of the former ferm-toun and probably marked its centre. Stone whorls of the type once used on spinning wheels have occasionally been found in ploughland nearby. The names of Harlaw and Balhaggarty survive in fourteenth and fifteenth century documents, and their houses and dikes probably played an important part in the battle; the ballad picture of the battlefield as a barren, featureless moor cannot be entirely accurate. There were probably also contemporary monuments to the battle which have since been lost. Sir Alexander Leslie is said to have erected a cross on the battlefield in memory of his six sons. At least two former cairns had associations with the battle; Drum's Cairn (Grid reference NJ 752241) is said to mark the site of the famous duel between Irvine and Red Hector, and Robert Davidson's Cairn (Grid reference NJ 755238), marked the place where Aberdeen's Provost fell. The Provost's Cairn is still faintly visible as a slight rise with a scatter of small stones beside a farm track. Drum's Cairn and at least two others seem to have vanished and one suspects that they have been incorporated into the dikes enclosing the 'Pley Fauld'.

A chance discovery in 1837 revealed one of the pits in which the dead were buried after the battle. A tenant farmer trenching a piece of barren ground between East and Mid Harlaw dug up the bones of twelve human bodies in an area measuring twelve by four feet long and three and a half feet deep.[18] Apart from providing striking confirmation of the traditional site of the battlefield, this discovery also provides ghoulish illustration to one of the ballads:

> An sic a weary buryin'
> I'm sure ye never saw
> As wis the Sunday after that
> On the muirs aneath Harlaw.

Among the artifacts which are still occasionally dug up from the battle site is the head of a battle-axe, now on display in Provost Skene's House in Aberdeen.

A prehistoric standing stone called Liggar's Stane has also been caught up in the folklore of the battle. In its original position near Harlaw House, it was said to mark the spot where a group of women camp followers were buried. The stone has since been moved to the vicinity of the Mains of Inveramsay where it now serves as a gatepost. Another structure, called 'Donald's Tomb', was destroyed in around 1800. It took the form of four upright stones and a horizontal capstone, built in the form of a malt steep at Legatesden.[19] Donald, as we have seen, survived the battle and did not require its services.

To find another reminder of the battle we must leave the battlefield itself and make our way southwards to the little ruined chapel at Kinkell, now a scheduled ancient monument. Within its walls is an upright stone slab, with the figure of an armoured knight inscribed on one side. This is or was the tombstone of Sir Gilbert de Greenlaw and its date and proximity to the battlefield suggest that Sir Gilbert was killed in the battle. Not much is known about him, except that he was the kin of his namesake, Gilbert Greenlaw, bishop of Aberdeen, who was among those present at Kildrummy during Christmas, 1410. The stone slab shows with great clarity the arms and equipment worn by a knight at Harlaw: slightly old-fashioned for its day, the Greenlaw plate armour is reminiscent of the well-known effigy of the Black Prince at Canterbury. It would have weighed about seventy pounds, but was sufficiently well-designed and balanced for Sir Gilbert to move about freely, mount a horse unaided and even break into a slow, lumbering run.

A partial suit of armour housed in Provost Skene's house is stated, wrongly, to be that worn by Provost Davidson at Harlaw. It is in fact a composite suit, cobbled up from bits and pieces of various periods, the earliest of which post-dates the battle of Harlaw by more than a century. Davidson himself was buried before the altar of the chantry chapel of St Ann, in the toun kirk, Aberdeen. His remains were discovered during alterations to the present-day Church of St Nicholas and an effigy of an armoured knight by the wall of the north transept may have been part of his original tomb.[20] The grave of the earl of Mar lies in Greyfriars Church, in Inverness, where he died in 1435, still battling obdurately against the men of the Isles. The battered remains of a freestone effigy on the wall of the ruined church is thought to be his, although the tomb on which it lay has vanished.[21]

Finally, there is the Drum Stone. Situated within a circular protecting wall by the roadside at Auchronie, Skene, this large boulder is inscribed simply 'Drum Stone—1411—Harlaw'. On a clear day, both the tower of Drum Castle and the Harlaw battlefield are visible, and it was at this poignant spot, according to tradition, that Sir Alexander Irvine gave instructions to his family and servants in the event of his death—including arrangements for his son's marriage.

Part III

Battlefields of the Reformation

The sixteenth century saw a transformation in the art of war by the large-scale introduction of firearms and artillery. Scotland already possessed an impressive arsenal of cannon by the time of Flodden (1513) but the infantry still fought as massed formations of spearmen, who were now vulnerable to improved infantry weapons, particularly the short 'bill' and the hand gun. Archery was on the decline everywhere except in the Highlands and the Borders, although bowmen continued to be employed in the north eastern Lowlands well into the second half of the century. Castles continued to play an important but less crucial role since their walls could now be breached by cannon.

The Scots are said to have discovered cannon during a successful raid on an English camp in 1327, when the first 'crakkis of wer' were uncovered before their incredulous eyes. From 1380 onwards, small iron-wrought cannon were a feature of the Scottish armoury and the first two King Jameses took a close personal interest in their development: too close in the case of James II (1437–1460) who was killed when a cannon 'brak in the fyring' during the siege of Roxburgh. Much improved guns wrought in bronze were produced from 1473 onwards after a foundry had been established at Stirling and, later, at Edinburgh, where the famous siege cannon Mons Meg was housed. By the end of the sixteenth century, the mightiest Scottish nobles, such as the earls of Huntly, themselves owned a battery of small calibre field guns which could be towed into the field by horses. The sixth earl used his to great effect at the battle of Glen Livet in 1594, the first of the north eastern battles to employ artillery.

The musket does not seem to have been used to any great extent by Scots soldiers until the mid-sixteenth century. The disastrous battle of Pinkie, during which the old-fashioned blocks of Scottish pikemen were cut to pieces by artillery and small arms fire, showed the power of the hand gun for the first time. The insurgent English forces used mounted Spanish mercenaries armed with an early form of musket known as the arquebus. A contemporary German musket, the *hackbut*, was introduced at about the same time. The lesson was not lost on the Scots, who employed their own 'arquebusiers' from the mid-century onwards. These soldiers were highly trained and comparatively highly paid professionals. They wore only light armour, namely a steel skullcap or 'knapscull' and either a 'corslet' (a steel breast and back plate) or a 'jack' (a knee length padded jacket reinforced with steel plates). Heavier protection was out of the question since they were festooned like Christmas trees with the diverse equipment needed to prime their weapons, notably powder bottles, flasks and lengths of cord or 'match'. Units of arquebusiers were employed in a similar way to later dragoons as mobile, mounted troops who dismounted, preferably behind cover, in order to fire on the enemy. They were also trained to act in concert with pikemen, whose long spears protected them from the enemy horse. Slightly later on, a smaller and lighter version of the arquebus, the carbine, would allow the trooper to fire, perhaps not very accurately, from horseback. From about 1530, European cavalry officers also used 'short guns', later refined into pistols. These early wheel-lock models were very expensive and easily broken, and they seem to have been little used in Scotland until the end of the century.

The development of infantry arms took place at a slower rate than that of powder weapons, but the sixteenth century saw the introduction of the vicious-looking Jedburgh axe, a huge edged and pointed blade attached to an oaken staff; the Leith axe, a double-edged weapon with a hooked blade; and, as a prestige weapon, the famous double-handed sword or 'claymore'. Plate armour was in decline, since not even the heaviest plate could protect a man against arquebus fire from close range. The pikemen, who at the end of the century still outnumbered the arquebusiers by at least three to one, made do with a plate corslet, thigh pieces and a steel bonnet. But the clans, imbued with tradition, continued to fight in the way of their ancestors, the men in their plaids, the chiefs in their mail habergeons. Throughout the century swords, 'Lochaber axes' and bows were the Highlander's main weapons of war.

The Reformation battles of the North East reflect these changes in the art of war. At Corrichie in 1562, the Gordons and their allies were destroyed by arquebusiers, foreign mercenaries employed in the royal forces. Arquebusiers also took part in the battle of the Craibstone in 1571, but in this case they failed to act in concert with their protecting phalanx of pikemen and were thus overwhelmed by the Gordons armed with bows and arrows. The most considerable battle of this period, at least in terms of numbers, was Glenlivet, in which the Gordon earl of Huntly defeated a large but ill-disciplined force of Highlanders by cannon fire and cavalry. The steel-plated rugby scrums of Harlaw had been replaced by mobile, tactical operations, more demanding of skill and discipline but potentially greater in their rewards.

The political side to wars and feuding in the sixteenth century North East was dominated by the Gordons. The rise of the house of Gordon to preeminence was closely linked to the strengthening power of the Scottish crown. Before Bannockburn, the then family of Seton were prominent but minor magnates in Berwickshire, holding the village and estate of Gordon under the earl of Dunbar of whom they were kin. After the desertion of the erstwhile earl of Strathbogie during the Wars of Independence, Bruce granted the patrimony of the Strathbogie estate to Sir Alexander de Seton, probably in order to win the latter over to his cause. He was rewarded by loyal and distinguished service: as newcomers to the North East, Sir Alexander and his successors found it in their interests to co-operate closely with the crown. Thereafter, the name of Seton steadily acquired increasing prestige and influence. In 1357, the Seton laird of Strathbogie was admitted to the Scottish nobility. In 1445, a new title, earl of Huntly, was created by King James II for Seton, who adopted the name of Gordon for his kin and successors. In the first earl of Huntly, the king gained a consistent and active supporter who carried the royal banner against the rebellious earl of Crawford and defeated him in an armed clash near Brechin (1452).

Successive Stewart kings found it politic to establish an overmighty subject in the North East to maintain order and defend it against the 'wild Scots' of the Highlands. In consequence, the earls of Huntly were allowed a considerable measure of independence and they governed the North East like princes. The second earl, who assisted James IV in his campaign against the men of the Isles, was created chancellor of Scotland and the king's principal subject in the lands north of the Mounth, a position also held by his successors. Many lesser north eastern families found it prudent to accept the maintenance of their powerful neighbour, in order to enjoy his protection in an area where the king was seldom present in person. Some even adopted the name of Gordon, in order to demonstrate a spurious kinship (which still fills eight columns of the north eastern telephone directory today).

The Reformation brought far-reaching social, political and, of course, religious change to Scottish society. The fourth earl of Huntly nurtured hopes of a Catholic Counter-Reformation under Queen Mary. Mary spurned his offers of assistance; on the contrary, she secretly agreed to revive and grant the earldom of Moray, currently within Huntly's influence, to her Protestant half-brother, James Stewart, as a counterweight to Huntly's suddenly inconvenient power in the north.

The result was a pitched battle at Corrichie, between Mary's forces under James Stewart and those of the rebellious earl of Huntly. Corrichie was one of those encounters which, although comparatively insignificant in themselves, had a decisive influence on the course of history. It alienated the queen from her most powerful Catholic noble and therefore effectively brought to an end any chances of a successful Counter-Reformation. Social discord did not end on the field of Corrichie however. Mary was deposed, and civil war broke out, ending, despite successes by the Gordons in the North East, in triumph for the Protestant 'King's Party'. The Catholic earls of the North East were nevertheless reluctant to concede defeat. Years of plotting and intrigue lay ahead, and one last triumph at the battle of Glenlivet, when the sixth earl of Huntly defeated a force of Campbells and MacLeans led by the Protestant earl of Argyll. Even Huntly was unwilling to confront the King in person, however, and was eventually forced into exile. A year later, he was pardoned after publicly agreeing to renounce popery. With that significant ceremony, a turbulent chapter of north eastern history came to a close.

CHAPTER 8

CORRICHIE

Murn, ye hei'lands, an' murn, ye lei'lands,
I trow ye hae muckle need,
For the bonnie burn o' Corrichie
Has rin this day wi' bleid.

William Forbes, from
The Ballad of Corrichie, first published 1772.

A skirmish in a remote bog, one late autumn afternoon in 1562, changed the balance of power in the North East and cast forward long shadows into the future. The battle set the seal on the Reformation, and effectively prevented a Catholic resurgence, based in the North East, from taking place. Ironically, the battle of Corrichie was also the culmination of a series of determined actions taken by Mary, Queen of Scots, against a fellow Roman Catholic and one whom many regarded as her natural chief advisor, the Gordon fourth earl of Huntly, the 'Cock of the North'.

Queen Mary's acceptance of the reformed religion, at the commencement of her personal rule in 1560, bitterly disappointed the conservative Catholic peers who were plotting to restore the old faith and their personal influence over the sovereign. The earl of Huntly, the most powerful of them all, had even issued an invitation to the queen to land at Aberdeen and join forces with him. The queen rejected this unrealistic proposal, preferring to be advised by her Protestant half-brother, Lord James Stewart. Indeed, she was even persuaded to elevate James Stewart to pre-eminence in the north at the expense of Huntly himself. Huntly's present power and influence in the North East was as great as that of any of his predecessors for, in addition to his own title, he was also, as the sheriff of Aberdeen and Inverness, the *de facto* earl of the vacant earldoms of Mar and Moray. Early in 1562, the queen revived the earldom of Mar and gifted the lands appertaining to it to her half brother. Nor was this all. A gift of the earldom of Moray was also drawn up,

106

in secret, in favour of James Stewart. Such an arrangement, if it became known to the earl of Huntly, was a virtual invitation to rebellion.

In her determination to advance her half-brother as a counterweight to Huntly's influence in the north, Mary acted with unwonted vindictiveness. She had, however, profound political reasons for acting as she did. For long one of the principal props of the crown, the reactionary earl of Huntly was now a liability in Mary's policy of befriending England by wooing the confidence of English Protestants. Mary had her eyes firmly fixed on the English succession. There may have been other reasons, too, for elevating James Stewart. He had, so far, been instrumental in holding the more extreme Protestant reformers in check and it was prudent that he be rewarded with a dignity commensurate with his influence as the queen's chief councillor. He could also be relied upon to secure more of the northern church's wealth for the crown and he already had connections with the North East through marriage with the daughter of the Earl Marischal.

This was the background to Queen Mary's first and only tour of the North East, in late summer 1562, to show herself to her people. The queen was accompanied by her privy council, including Lord James Stewart, and the industrious English ambassador, Randolph, whose letters are the main contemporary source for the events leading to the battle. The court travelled north under armed escort: the queen's political opposition to Huntly was already curdling into personal distrust. Huntly's prodigal third son, Sir John Gordon, had recently escaped from lawful detention after wounding a rival in the streets of Edinburgh, and was now being sheltered by his father. Sir John saw himself as a romantic champion of the Catholic faith and, by extension, of the queen personally, whom he regarded as a helpless prisoner of the Protestant faction. The latter may well have been the common belief of the north eastern Catholics, but, unlike them, Sir John was willing to risk his neck by plotting to abduct the queen with the aid of his Gordon kinsmen. His state of mind was confused further by an adolescent infatuation for the queen, whom he apparently expected to marry, once the 'rescue' had been achieved. Sir John was probably more than a little crazy but, in the present climate of plot and counterplot, his eccentricities were dangerous.

George Gordon, fourth earl of Huntly, was, by the standards of the day, an elderly man. His public career had had occasional moments of military distinction: he had defeated an English raiding party at Haddon Rig (1542) and commanded the left wing of the Scottish army at the battle of Pinkie (1547) at which he was captured and imprisoned by the English. Created chancellor of Scotland in 1547, he had played his part in the shifting political sands of the succeeding years of the century, but the young Queen's appeasement of the Protestant ruling party had left him in isolation. He does not appear to have been a man of outstanding gifts or energy and he was now ailing and subject to sudden apoplectic fits. Bulky, dour, 'grizzled', in Antonia Fraser's words, 'like a great northern bear',[1] he would probably have preferred to spend his remaining years quietly inside the walls of his beautiful chateau-fortress at Strathbogie, leaving his sons to play the power game on his behalf. Events were to deny him the solace of a restful retirement.

The queen arrived at Old Aberdeen on 27 August and held court in the bishop's palace. The burgh council of Aberdeen was on its best behaviour for this rare event, and the provost presented her with a propine of 2,000 merks.[2] The earl of Huntly, already under a cloud because of the behaviour of his son, was conspicuous by his absence. He was represented by his wife, the countess, who tried in vain to persuade the queen to honour them with a visit to Strathbogie. Instead, Mary demanded that the errant Sir John Gordon be returned to custody, pending an investigation of his seizure of the Findlater estates from the Ogilvies. Sir John was duly delivered, but on hearing that he was to be confined in Stirling Castle under a hostile gaoler (Lord James Stewart's uncle), he escaped once more, this time into open rebellion.

After a few days at Aberdeen, the court moved on in stately progress through the North East towards Inverness. In the banqueting hall of Darnaway Castle, on its high wooded promontory above the Findhorn, Lord James Stewart was formally invested with the earldom of Moray. The earls of Moray were the custodians of Inverness Castle, currently manned by the Gordons, and this was to be the first real test of the new earl's authority. On 11 September the queen's party arrived before the gates of the castle—and found them locked, allegedly on the orders of Huntly's eldest son, Lord Gordon. Huntly hastily sent a message countermanding this order and commanding that the queen be admitted and offered the keys to the castle. The gates swung open and, scant hours later, the Gordon commander of the garrison had been convicted of treason and hanged from the castle walls.

The queen's ill temper was due to the attentions of a mounted party, led by Sir John, which had shadowed the royal progress through Gordon lands in Garioch and Strathbogie. The royal bodyguard kept the Gordons at a respectful distance, but their rebellious defiance increased Mary's sense of outrage. On 18 September Randolph wrote to his master, Secretary Cecil, that the queen held Huntly personally responsible for 'manifest tokens of disobedience, no longer to be borne'.[3] By the time the royal party had returned to Aberdeen on 22 September, Mary was determined to make an example of him: The Queen is 'highly offended ... She will do something that will be a terror to others. She trusts to put the country in good quietness'.

Huntly, still in stubborn retreat at Strathbogie, was sent a peremptory summons. He must surrender the keys of his castles at Findlater, Auchindoun and Strathbogie. Furthermore he must forthwith appear before the privy council to answer charges being brought against him. Huntly answered that he was willing to surrender the first two castles, but not his principal seat at Strathbogie. And he refused to appear before the largely hostile privy council. The countess of Huntly delivered his reply to the court, adding profuse apologies for the harrassment which the queen had endured. But Mary's anger was not abated. 'She believed not a word' of the countess's explanations and 'so declared the same herself unto her Council'. Mary was, indeed, displaying a resolution that few had thought her capable of. 'I never saw her merrier, never dismayed', wrote Randolph, 'nor never thought so much to be in her as I find'. By 12 October, the queen had determined to proceed against the Gordons 'with all extremity'. Huntly and Sir John Gordon were formally outlawed—'put to the horn'—and an armed detachment was sent to Strathbogie to seize the earl and escort him to the queen's person by force. Huntly was given just enough advance warning to escape by a back door 'without boote or swerde', and the escort returned empty handed to Aberdeen.

Huntly's whereabouts between this undignified departure from his own castle and the day before the battle of Corrichie are uncertain. He seems to have escaped to his stronghold at Ruthven in the fastnesses of Speyside. It is probable that he obtained court news in his hiding place through his wife, who remained at Aberdeen and consulted fortune-telling oracles. The only evidence we have to explain the earl's subsequent actions are the wild confessions of Sir John Gordon at his subsequent trial and the reported comments of the queen by Randolph. According to these, Huntly intended to call out his dependants, march on Aberdeen, murder the new earl of Moray and other Protestant councillors, and forcibly marry the queen to one of his sons. Whether or not there is any truth in this, Huntly certainly felt that he had been harshly treated and even the virulently anti-Catholic John Knox admitted that there was some doubt as to whether the queen was acting within her legal rights in outlawing him.

In 1560, Huntly had boasted that he could field an army of 20,000 men. The fortnight separating his outlawry from the battle of Corrichie put this claim to the test and found it wanting. On 23 October those who were at feud with Huntly, included the Forbeses, the Leslies and the Grants, were given royal assent to use force against him despite their feudal obligations. Those diehards who rallied to Huntly against the queen in late October 1562, were mostly members of his own family: his sons, Lord George Gordon, Sir John Gordon and Sir Adam Gordon of Auchindoun, his cousin, the earl of Sutherland, and his Gordon kinfolk, among them the notorious 'Black Alister' of Abergeldie, George Gordon of Blairdinnie and William Gordon of Terpersie.[4] Not all of the Gordon lairds flocked to Huntly's banner, however, and some, such as Gordon of Haddo, joined the forces of the queen. The remainder of Huntly's men were from a broad scatter of north eastern families: Abercrombie of Pitmedden, Douglas of Tilquhillie, Irvine of Drum, Bissett of Lessendrum and Menzies of Pitfodels. Even a Forbes laird had decided, for reasons of his own, to 'come out' on the side of his family's traditional enemy.[5]

Nevertheless, when this 'army of folkis' mustered a dozen miles from Aberdeen on a heath at Garlogie, called Gordon's Moss to this day, on 27 October 1562, they numbered no more than 800 and possibly (since many potential rebels probably took one look and turned tail for home) as few as 500.[6] It was a very poor showing for a great earl, and much less important men would normally have expected to field at least as many. Only the boldest and most partial followers of the Cock o' the North seemed willing to 'partye' him openly against their sovereign's person. The others prudently stayed at home, shuttered the windows and bolted the doors. Huntly's rebellion was a flop. His followers sullenly pitched their tents on the moor; the night air must have rung with argument and recrimination.

The earl of Moray had already taken steps to ensure Huntly's final downfall. Having advised Mary to 'bring Huntly to utter confusion', he sent for reinforcements from the south and cautiously obtained a royal commission absolving him from any charge of levying war on his own behalf. By the time messengers brought in news of Huntly's re-appearance with a tiny following, Moray commanded some 2,000 dependable troops, including trained Lothian pikemen, a strong detachment of cavalry and 120 arquebusiers from Edinburgh. He sent a mounted vanguard of local men ahead, under the command of the earl of Errol, Lord Balquhain and Lord Forbes, to harrass the Gordons and hinder their retreat.

At dawn on 28 October, the day of Corrichie, the troops of Moray's vanguard engaged those of Huntly, and the two sides 'skarmisched' about the rebel camp. If we can believe Knox, who gives us an insight, albeit a prejudiced one, into Huntly's motives, Huntly did not know what to do next. He was being attacked by some of those whose support he had evidently counted on. 'Rightly a long time', says Knox, 'he could do nothing'.[7] In the end, the Gordons made the only possible decision in their circumstances: they would retreat westwards to rough high ground which would favour them and hinder mounted troops and artillery. Three miles to the west lay their obvious objective: a granite spur of rolling heather muir, fringed by birch and pine woods—the Hill o' Fare.[8]

The Gordons' fighting retreat was skilfully conducted. The precise route they took is unknowable but Fenton Wyness conjectures, reasonably enough, that they ascended the defile of the Landerberry Burn and crossed over the vale now called Gordon's Howe in their memory. And so, by early afternoon, they reached a strong, elevated position, among the browning heather, 'at ane place callit Bank-a-fair, utherwayis callit Coruchie'.[9] The eastern part of the Hill o' Fare is formed by a horseshoe-shaped ridge, which rolls around the dog-leg shaped vale or Howe of Corrichie. The summits—Meikle Tap, Greymore, Blackyduds and Craigrath—are broad and relatively dry, but the headwaters of the Corrichie burn rises in a peat bog, which was to play a decisive part in the battle. The precise part of the ridge on which the Gordons chose to make their stand is not known for certain. Douglas Simpson[10] suggests Berry Hill, a steep, conical hill guarding the south eastern approach to the vale. Fenton Wyness places them on the ridge between Greymore and Meikle Tap, at the head of the Landerberry burn.[11] The problems of siting the battlefield are discussed later in this chapter.

In the meantime, the royal army under the command of the earl of Moray, had marched out of Aberdeen, probably proceeding westwards along the route of the present day B9125 and B977.[12] Moray's intention seems to have been to cut off Huntly's retreat by passing around the southern slopes of the Hill o' Fare and entering this upland fastness via the vale of Corrichie. The repeated mention of 'Coruchie' or 'Correchie' in contemporary accounts is the best indication we have of this. Of the battle itself, we have a number of brief, near-contemporary narratives and, for the first time among the battles in this book, an account based on the testimony of eye-witnesses. The English ambassador, Thomas Randolph, had remained in Aberdeen with Queen Mary but had dispatched two servants to accompany Moray and 'see the maner'. That same evening, he was able to dash off a short report to Secretary Cecil, followed by a more detailed letter on 2 November. The latter contains the following passage, which is our most reliable version of the events which took place at three o'clock in the afternoon of 28 October and it is worth quoting in full:

> The Gordons had encamped on the top of a hill, where horse could hardly come to them, and were driven by shot of harquebus into a low mossy ground where the horse dealt with them a good space, at length forcing them into a corner, where by reason of the hill and marsh ground, they could not escape. There were they set upon, and at the shock, the vanguard (either for faintness of heart or other thing suspected) gave back, many casting away their spears ready to run. The earl of Murray and his company being behind them, seeing the danger, came so fiercely on, that he caused them to turn again, and so stoutly set on the enemy, that 'incontynent' they give place, and 120 and 'moe' were taken, and eleven score or thereabout slain—Huntly's whole company was not above 500; some say he (Huntly) fought before he was taken—others the contrary.

> Thomas Randolph.

From his vantage point on the hill top, Huntly must have been given a grandstand view of the royalist army, lumbering towards him along the vale of Corrichie. He was outnumbered by nearly three to one, but had cause to believe that his former vassals, at least, would not fight against their lord. Knox places these words into his mouth:

> This great company that approcheth nighest to us [i.e., the vanguard of north eastern levies] will do us no harm, they are our friends. I only fear yonder small company [i.e. Moray's far from small force] that stand upon the hillside, yon are our enemies.[13]

Moray declined to attack the Gordons where they stood, but brought up his arquebusiers who rode uphill into range to rake them with gunfire. Once they had been driven from their hill top, the Gordons were harrassed by cavalry attacks and forced back into boggy ground below the steep slopes at the head of the vale. Sir John Gordon's horse were overwhelmed by superior numbers and Sir John himself was captured.[14] Having pinned down and cornered the Gordons, the royalist horse awaited the arrival of the foot soldiers to complete the task of annihilating them.

The local levies, under Erroll, Forbes and Leslie of Balquhain, approached first. All accounts agree that they fought very badly, if at all. The Gordons charged at them with sword and target, and the levies at once scattered in all directions, casting aside their weapons as they ran. Randolph, as we have seen, suspected treachery and hints that this precipitate flight had been pre-arranged. Later writers went further. The *Diurnal of Occurrents* suggests that the levies deliberately ran into the massed ranks of Lothian pikemen coming up behind, in order to sow confusion and break up their ranks. Buchanan, a later and less reliable source, adds that they placed sprigs of heather in their

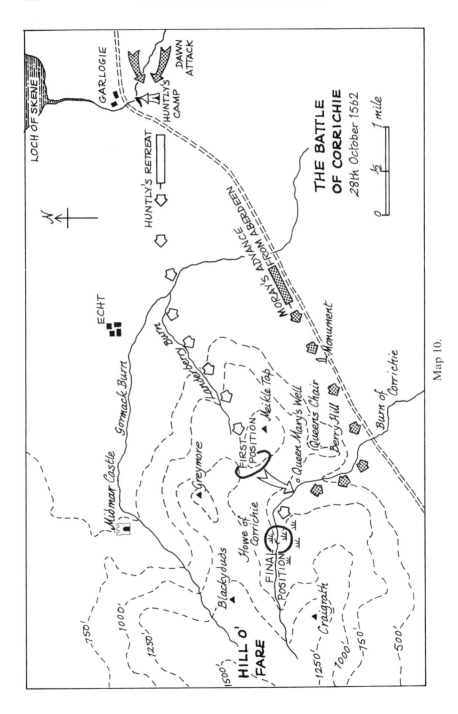

Map 10.

bonnets so 'that they might be known by the enemy'.[15] Oddly enough, the much later ballad transfers these heather sprigs to a band of treacherous Gordons who, 'with traitor Haddo at their heid ... fell on theire britheris an' theire fatheris'. Not much credence need be paid to this story. As Cuthbert Graham has suggested,[16] this ploy was probably concocted to explain to Huntly's Gordon descendents how the invincible Cock o' the North could ever have been beaten at all!

The Gordons regrouped and charged again at the bristling ranks facing them. But the experienced Lothian soldiers 'stuid fermlie still' and beat them off with levelled pikes. The Gordons were 'put upoun their bakkis with speiris', as the *Diurnal* puts it, 'and thairefter fled'. Alas, they fled back into the bog where, floundering amid the peat and bog moss, they were trapped beyond hope of escape.

Further resistance was clearly futile, and Huntly ordered his surviving followers to lay down their arms. Moray gave them quarter. The leading Gordons, '120 and moe', according to Randolph, were taken prisoner, and the bodies of about 200 others[17] lay scattered over the mile or more of blood-stained muirland and bog in Corrichie vale. Moray's own losses were minimal. The battle had lasted for little more than an hour.

The most dramatic event of the day took place during the immediate aftermath of battle. Huntly had surrendered his sword to one Andrew Redpath, of Queen Mary's bodyguard. The stricken earl was placed on a horse and led before his captors, silent, abject, utterly humiliated. What happened next is best described in Randolph's own words:

> withowte ether blowe or stroke ... he sodenlie fawlethe from his horse starke dedde, withowte worde that he ever spake after he was upon horse backe.

The *Diurnal* adds that,

> thairefter he bristit and swelt, so that he spak not ane word, but deceissit.

Huntly had probably succumbed to an apoplectic seizure or a heart failure, brought on by his exertions and the ruin of his hopes. Nevertheless, a rumour spread about the North East that Huntly had been murdered, and that his killer was David Stewart of Inchbreck:

> Then Murray tried to tak auld Gordon,
> An' mony ane ran wi' speid;
> But Stewart o' Inchbraik had him sticket
> An' out gush'd the fat lurdane's bluid.

Huntly's literal fall from his horse symbolised the fall of the house of Gordon. The countess of Huntly's oracles had given an assurance that Huntly would spend that night in Aberdeen. So he did: his body was thrown over a pair of creels and conveyed to the New Town tollbooth, where it was left on the pavement for a time. Accompanying the body, and under close escort, were

Huntly's sons, John of Findlater and Adam of Auchindoun. Lord Gordon and Huntly's cousin, the earl of Sutherland, were also arrested. Most of the rebellious Gordon leaders were warded under various penalties. 'Black Alister', under ward in St Andrews, attracted the huge sum of 5,000 merks, but Gordon of Lesmoir was thought to be worth no more than 2,000.[18] Sir John Gordon's condemnation was a formality, since he had proved incorrigible. According to Randolph, he confessed to having plotted the murder of the queen's councillors, adding, for good measure, that he would also have liked to burn the queen's house down. His elder brother, Lord George Gordon was also sentenced to death, but was granted a stay of execution on Queen Mary's personal intervention and eventually pardoned. He succeeded to his father's estates in 1565 and died ten years later of a fit during a game of football. Sudden fatal seizures seem to have been characteristic of the sixteenth century Gordon earls.

The execution of Sir John Gordon took place in the Castlegate on 2 November with the queen and her court looking on from a window in the tollbooth. Five of his leading accomplices, including Gordon of Blairdinnie, the wealthy laird of Coclarichie, were hanged, but Sir John's high rank merited the privilege of beheading, perhaps by a newly fashionable mechanical contrivance used for the purpose and known as 'The Maiden'. Romance, which loves to linger on such scenes, tells us that the blade was blunt, that Mary wept at the cruel sight, that she had really been fond of the young man all along:

> But now thi day maist waefu' cam'
> That day the quine did greit hir fill;
> For Huntly's gallant, stalwart son
> Wis headit on thi heidin hill.
> Fyve noble Gordones wi' him hangit were
> Upon this samen fatal playne;
> Cruel Murry gart thi waeful' quine luke out,
> And see her lover and liges slayne.

The impartial record of Randolph tells a different story. On the day of the execution, Mary had 'declared how detestable a part Huntly thought to have used against her, as to have married her where he would, to have slain her brother'. The popular belief that the queen wept and was cast down by Gordon's fate has an origin in the untrustworthy narrative of Knox, who asserts that she was 'gloomed' on hearing of Moray's victory at Corrichie. It is impossible to know to what degree Mary's animosity towards Huntly and his kin was the result of the machinations of the ruthless and unprincipled men who filled her court and council. The supposition that she disliked the course which events had taken seems, however, to be based on hindsight, following her break with Moray in 1565. The record suggests that Mary herself took the initiative against the Gordons, although it suited the purposes of Moray and other Protestant lords to egg her on.

The earl of Huntly's humiliations did not end with his death. Under Scottish custom, his body was required to 'hear' the sentence of forfeiture passed, and 'see' its armorial bearings being struck from the roll of heralds. It was therefore embalmed with 'vinegar, aqua vitae, powders, odours and other necessities',[19] dressed in sack-cloth and propped upright in its coffin during the hearing in Parliament in May, 1563, where it was solemnly declared guilty of treason and its estates seized by the crown. Not until the Gordons were restored to their estates and royal favour in 1565 was the body finally laid to rest in the family vault at Elgin Cathedral.

Corrichie today

Until quite recently, the battlefield of Corrichie remained much as in 1562— heather muir, scrub and bog. Alas, this is true no longer—the vale and the hillside over which the battle was fought have been planted with pine, larch and spruce, although the crest of the hills is still open grouse muir. The bog where the Gordons were trapped and surrounded is marked by a stand of Sitka Spruce. The straight, regimented stands of trees marking the positions of Moray's troops rather resemble contemporary infantry formations, although doubtless of a more ordered and regimented kind than the army of 1562. The contours of the land can still be seen but once the trees have grown up, this battlefield will be more difficult to appreciate.

A twelve foot high granite pillar was set up by the Deeside Field Club in 1951 to commemorate the battle. It lies on the north side of the B977 and, although it is now surrounded by trees on three sides and easy to miss, it originally stood with the battlefield in the background. Enscribed in Celtic lettering on the stone are the Gaelic words 'CUIMHNICHIBH LA COIRE FRAOICHIDH; Remember the day of Corrichie'. Two further features are marked on the Ordnance Survey map, although both are now difficult to reach. The hollow in a granite crag on the side of Berry Hill is known as the 'Queen's Chair' where, according to tradition, Mary is said to have watched the battle. It provides an excellent view of the Howe of Corrichie but, as we have seen, Mary was not there to appreciate it. At the foot of the hill is a spring called Queen Mary's Well, from which the queen is supposed to have drunk, in the same way as Macbeth is said to have done at his own well in Lumphanan. Four miles to the west of the battlefield, there used to grow a fine old tree called Darnley's Ash, in the grounds of the mansion house of Craigmyle. Tradition has it that the tree was planted by Lord Darnley shortly after the battle, another improbable story, since Darnley was in England at the time and had not yet been considered as a possible consort for the queen of Scots. His ash tree was cut down in 1960, after the demolition of Craigmyle House.

There is a grisly relic of the aftermath of the battle in Provost Skene's House in Aberdeen. On display in the museum is the blade of the Aberdeen 'Maiden', possibly the very one which chopped off the head of the ill-fated Sir John Gordon. It is about the size and shape of a spade and, although it is heavily weighted with lead, it was probably a much less efficient instrument than the one which Dr Guillotine invented in time for the French Revolution.

15.   The monument at Corrichie, commemorating the battle of 1562, erected by the Deeside Field Club. The view from it of the battlefield has been obscured by afforestation.

Its possible victim, Sir John, lies buried in the crypt of the toun kirk of Aberdeen, St Nicholas' Church.

The site of the battlefield

Whilst there is no doubt that the battle was fought in and around the Howe of Corrichie and the hills above it, it is no easy matter to say exactly where. The broad plateau of the Hill of Fare is rather featureless and contemporaries were vague as to the directions taken by the approaching forces. Corrichie appears to have been a running fight rather than a set-piece positional battle. Since the Gordons were finally brought to bay floundering in a bog at the head of the Howe, it is clear that the end point of the battle must have been at the upper end of the Burn of Corrichie, the only substantial marsh in the area. In 1927, G.M. Fraser found a number of grave mounds near the bog on the north bank of the burn at OS 699023. If these are accepted as being the burial place of the rank and file killed in the battle—and it is difficult to imagine what else they could be—they provide firm evidence that this was indeed the place where the Gordons took their last stand. And this is where the Ordnance Survey place their crossed swords of battle. The site of the Gordons' initial stand on the hill top, as described by Randolph and Knox, is more difficult to place. W. Douglas Simpson's suggestion is Berry Hill,[20] but although this is the nearest approximation to an isolated hill in the neighbourhood, it lies well outside the direction which Huntly would have been likely to take and he would have been effectively trapped on its tiny summit. We know that Huntly's hill was one of those surrounding the vale of Corrichie, and that the Gordons were driven by musket fire from its summit into a corner of the vale where the main action took place. My own interpretation of the evidence is that the Gordons halted on the ridge between Greymore and Meikle Tap. The subsequent action was fought in the Howe o' Corrichie, and Moray's main force, approaching up the vale from the south, forced the Gordons back towards the head of the vale. This would seem to fit the time sequence of the battle, which was over in the space of an hour. Alternatively, the Gordons might have attained the crest of Blackyduds and Craigrath on the western side of the Howe. It is possible to refight the battle from this premise, but if Huntly had reached this position, it would have been more sensible for him to continue to retreat westwards since dusk was already approaching and the prospect of escape from a hopeless situation would then have been good. On the evidence one can only suggest probabilities: definite assurance eludes us.

CHAPTER 9

BLOOD FEUDS

Thy swerd is drawin', thy bow is bent
To plaig us in thy ire.
Thy wrythe on us is kindlit bauld
As hoit consumyn fyr.
Hald up thy hand, and spair us, Lord,
Maist hummelie we desyre.
Haif grace to us, we pray.
Nocht for our saikes, bott for thy lufe.
O Lord, O Lord, O gracious Lord,
Lord, turn thy wrathe away.

from a sixteenth century ballad, 'A sinner crying on God for mercy in time of
trouble' attributed to Nicolsoun in *Chronicle of Aberdeen.*

The short but savage civil war of 1571–3 foreshadowed the great events of
'The Troubles' in the 1640s, when Scotland became torn with strife between
those fighting for kirk and covenant on the one hand and those who supported
the prerogative of the reigning monarch on the other. Among the great houses
of the North East, the former faction was represented by the Forbes and
their allies, and the latter by the Gordons. The colourful 'gay Gordons' tend
to be the more sympathetic, partly because the best local accounts of the
religious wars of the sixteenth and seventeenth century are biased in their
favour. Like the Cavaliers in the well-known historical lampoon, *1066 and
all that*, the Gordons seem 'Wrong but Wromantic' whilst the sober Forbes
resemble more the Roundheads, 'Right but Repulsive'. The two opponents
personified conflicting attitudes to the Reformation, and when their hatred
for one another erupted into open violence in 1571, they acted out in miniature
a conflict which was being waged in one form or another throughout Europe.
In his *Earldom of Mar*, Douglas Simpson comments that 'on our narrow
northern stage, a conflict of European import was fought out; and in the

118

provinces of Mar the battles of Tillyangus and Craibstane and the grim fire of Corgarff are seen, not as mere scufflings of feudal rivals, but as details in the super-national conflict between Protestantism and the Counter-Reformation'. On the other hand, it is difficult not to feel, when following the fortunes of the rival houses, that this merciless conflict originated as much from inherited blood-hatred and land rivalry than from any higher aspirations. At times, an onlooker might have been inclined to agree with Don Pedro de Ayala that 'the Scots spend all their time in wars, and when there is no war they fight with one another'.

Civil war became inevitable when, after Queen Mary's enforced abdication in 1567, various factions, including the Catholic fifth earl of Huntly, took up arms on her behalf. The ultimate aim of Catholic reaction, both inside and outside Scotland, was to overthrow the Protestant government and restore Queen Mary as the first step in securing Mary's claim to the throne of England. How far the Gordon gentry and their tenants shared the beliefs of the more fanatical adherents of the Counter-Reformation is hard to say. Gordon resentment had been smouldering since their downfall on the field of Corrichie, ten years earlier. It only needed a spark to set off a renewed war, and, in the lawless days of 1571, the Counter-Reformation provided it.

The battle of Tillyangus

The principal champion of the house of Forbes was 'Black Arthur' of Putachie, a son of the seventh Lord Forbes. He is described from a Gordon source, which had no cause to praise him unnecessarily, as 'a man of great courage, ambitious and readie to undertak anything whatsoever for the advancement and reconciliation of his familie'.[1] Holinshed calls him a man 'of singular wit and of no less readie hand'. Black Arthur Forbes 'mortallie hated the Gordouns', persuading his nephew to 'repudiat and put away his wyff' on the grounds that the unfortunate lady was the earl of Huntly's sister. The action which turned this petty domestic feuding into open violence appears to have stemmed from Black Arthur's own initiative for, late in 1571, we are told that 'the whole surname of Forbes, by the persuasion of Black Arthur, had appoynted both day and place, where they should assemble together, not onlie for their owne generall reconciliation among themselves, bot also to plot something against the Gordouns of the rest of the quein's favorers in these parts'. The meeting place was to be the Forbes family seat at Drumminor Castle, a fortified tower house in the vale of Bogie, beneath the ramparts of the heather-clad Correen Hills.

The Gordons gained secret intelligence of this dangerous gathering. The earl of Huntly was absent in Edinburgh but his brother, Sir Adam Gordon of Auchindoun, was acting as Queen's Lieutenant in his place and he used his authority to assemble his kin and followers at Strathbogie. According to our fullest account of the affair, Adam Gordon, whose implacable hatred of the Forbes made him very much Black Arthur's *alter ego*, straightway set about confronting the Forbes on their own ground, in an operation which has since become known as a pre-emptive strike.[2] A different source asserts that, far from inviting a battle, Adam Gordon wished merely to pass peaceably through the Forbes lands on his way south to join his brother, but that the Forbes opposed his crossing.[3] There may be some truth in both versions: the Forbes' must have been expecting, indeed deliberately inviting, a clash with the Gordons for they had entrenched themselves in a fortified position on the 'Mar road' across the Correen Hills, barring the Gordons' route to the south via the old Suie Road and the Don crossing at the Boat of Forbes. The Forbes' camp lay on or near the White Hill of Tillyangus, a spur of the Correens which slopes gently upwards to around 1,000 feet above sea level. The present day Mains of Tillyangus and the village of Clatt lie on level ground immediately below the hill.

The ensuing skirmish, which has become known as the battle of Tillyangus, probably took place on 10 October 1571, although an alternative dating of 17 October is possible. A contemporary manuscript, entitled *History of the Feuds and Conflicts among the Clans*, provides a crisp and reliable narrative of the battle and can be allowed to speak for itself:

> The Forbesses, understanding that the Gordouns wer coming against them, intrenched themselves within their campt, which they had stronglie fortified, divyding ther armie in two severall companies, whereof Black Arthor Forbes commanded that which lay nixt unto the Gordouns. Adam Gordoun perceaveing ther order, divyded his men lykwise in two companies, whereof he gave the one to his brother Mr Robert Gordoun, whom he commanded presentlie to invade the one half of the Forbesses army; and Adam himselff, without any stay, feircely set upon that quarter wher Black Arthor was. Thus they began a cruell skirmish. The Gordouns, with great courage, did break the Forbesses trenches, and run desperatelie upon the spears of ther enemies. After a sharp and obstinat conflict, couragiouslie foughtin a long tyme on either syd, Black Arthor Forbes, with divers other gentlemen of his surname and familie, were slain. The rest of the Forbesses wer overthrowen, put to flight, and chased evin to the gates of Drumminor.[4]

Thus ended the fight on Tillyangus brae, with victory to the Gordons. The Gordons appear to have assembled a force large enough to overwhelm the Forbes faction, and carried the day by a general assault on their positions. Bannatyne[5] adds one significant detail to the above account, stating that the Gordons' main force had been kept in reserve until most of the Forbes' were engaged, and then launched an 'ambush' from an unexpected direction. This is not corroborated by other sources, but it seems compatible with the above account and is inherently plausible. According to Forbes tradition, Black Arthur heroically defended the rear of his retreating army and being 'a man of remarkable bodily strength and energy', kept his pursuers at bay, until, overcome by thirst, he rashly stooped to drink from a brook. There William Gordon of Terpersie pounced on him and stabbed him to death through a joint in his armour.[6]

Estimates of the total numbers engaged at Tillyangus vary from between 1,300 to 2,000. Bannatyne, who cites the lower figure, adds that the Gordons

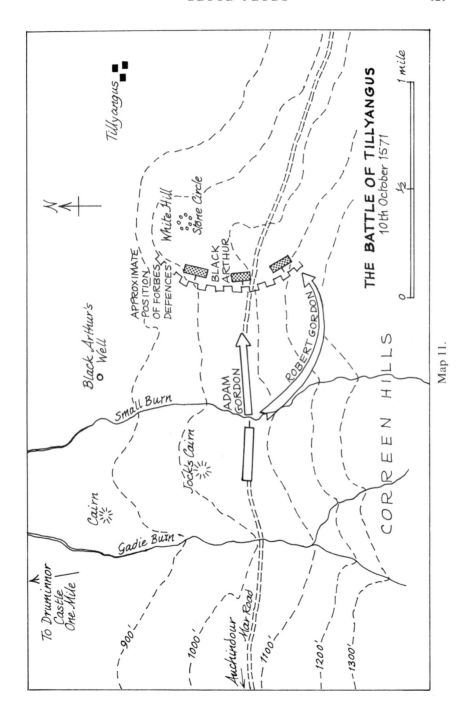

THE **BATTLE** OF TILLYANGUS
10th October 1571

Map 11.

outnumbered the Forbes by 1,000 to 300 but, as secretary to John Knox, he probably wished to place his fellow Protestants in as heroic a light as possible. His further statement that only thirteen to seventeen Forbes men were slain and seventeen taken prisoner, compared with twenty-two Gordons slain, accords ill with the contemporary (and usually reliable) *Diurnal of Remarkable Occurrents* which states that 120 Forbes men were killed during the battle and pursuit which followed.[7] The body of Black Arthur was conveyed across the Correens by his men, where it rested briefly on the hill top which now bears his name before being laid to rest in Forbes Kirkyard in Donside. A two-handed claymore, said to have belonged to Black Arthur, is preserved at Castle Forbes. The Gordons kept quiet about their own losses, but they included John Gordon of Buckie, who was buried with honour in the Kirk of Dunbennan.

The Gordons followed up their victory at Tillyangus by capturing the whole of the Forbes horse and munitions as well as William of Fodderbirse, Lord Forbes' second son. They may even have captured and ransacked Drumminor Castle immediately after the battle,[8] but more probably this action took place some weeks later. The castle seems to have been badly damaged and possibly even partially demolished during the war, for it was

16.   Drumminor Castle, looted and badly damaged by the Gordons after the battle of Tillyangus in 1571.

substantially rebuilt in 1577. Among those who escaped from Drumminor in the nick of time were the elderly laird and his first-born son, the master of Forbes, who rode south to Stirling to enlist the aid of the regent of Scotland, the Protestant earl of Mar. This was to result in a second battle, recounted below.

Three years after Tillyangus, when peace had been more or less restored, a curious postscript to the battle showed that the blood feud still raged. Adam Gordon was by then engaged in military service in France, whence he was followed by a nephew of Black Arthur, also named Arthur, intent on avenging the death of his uncle. He hired a bunch of Parisian ruffians to ambush Adam as he rode past through the streets. In the ensuing scuffle, Adam received a pistol ball in the thigh, but his servants gave chase to the would be assassins and cornered them in an alley way. Arthur Forbes was killed on the spot, but his less fortunate accomplices were arrested and later suffered the appalling death of being broken on the wheel. Adam Gordon survived the episode and managed the not inconsiderable feat of dying in his bed, in 1580. But his tale is not yet fully told.

Tillyangus today

The field of Tillyangus is crossed by an ancient track known as the 'Mar Road' which crosses the northern flanks of the Correen Hills between Lumsden and Suie Hill. It can also be approached by the unmade road from Clatt, leading past the Mains of Tillyangus and Gordonstown. The battle was fought on or below the west on slopes of White Hill, once called 'Gordons' Camp Muir', between the stone circle on the hill-top and the Smallburn. There is no battle monument and the entrenchments of the Forbes camp, which were said to be visible long after the battle, have since disappeared.[9] 'Jock's Cairn', at map reference NJ 519243, is said to mark the burial place of those slain in the battle, and human remains were found at the site of another, now vanished, cairn at NJ 518247.[10] The site of Black Arthur's death was probably the Small Burn, but another claimant is 'Black Arthur's Well', a spring situated between the Small Burn and Gordonstown.

The battlefield lies in attractive walking country. W. Douglas Simpson comments that 'there are few more pleasant places in our Province than Tillyangus' bloody brae. And anybody wishing to grasp the lie of an ancient countryside, steeped in history and prehistory, should walk the length of the old Mar Road from Knockespock westward, past the stone circle (on White Hill) and across the battlefield towards Marchmar'.[11] Unfortunately, commercial afforestation to the immediate south of the Mar Road will ultimately change the character of this unspoiled and attractive area.

Drumminor Castle, now a 'palace house' restored by Margaret Forbes-Sempill in 1960, is privately owned but is sometimes opened to the public.

The burning of Corgarff Castle

During the interval between the battles of Tillyangus and Craibstane, the Gordons harried the Forbes lands, dismantling the fortifications of their houses and sequestering their weapons. Removable goods and cattle were frequently stolen, and those who resisted did so at peril of their lives. At some stage between 1 and 20 November, an event took place which has been called by a modern historian the most atrocious deed in the history of Mar[12] and immortalised in the famous ballad of *Edom o'Gordon*: the burning of Corgarff Castle. This lonely tower-house guards the strategic confluence of the passes of the Don, Dee and Avon. At the time of the incident, it was owned by the Forbes of Towie. According to the best contemporary account, Adam Gordon sent one Captain Ker to order its surrender in the queen's name. The laird was absent, but his indomitable wife, Margaret Campbell, refused to submit. 'Whereof', says our source, 'the said Adam, having knowledge, movit in iyre towartis hir, causit raise fyre thairintill, quhairin sho, hir dauchteris and utheris personis wer destroyit, to the nowmer of 27 or thairby'.[13]

The ballad, *Edom o'Gordon*, adds heartrending but unauthenticated detail. As the smoke rose from the burning house, Margaret's bairns beg her to surrender, but the dauntless lady cries: 'never!'

> I winnae gie up my house, my dear
> To nae sik traitor as he;
> Cum weil, cum wae, my jewels fair,
> Ye maun tak share wi' me

One of her daughters manages to escape down the castle walls on a pair of knotted sheets, but she is spotted by the Gordons and put to death. Too late, cruel Adam Gordon is credited with remorse:

> Then wi' his speir he turned hir owr
> O gin hir face was wan!
> He said, 'You are the first that e'er
> I wist alive again.

Adam Gordon's alleged wickedness and cruelty on this occasion sorts ill with the considerate and generous treatment he offered to his prisoners after the battle of Craibstane and some have laid the responsibility for the atrocity at the door of Captain Ker. It is probable, however, that the burning of Corgarff was only one incident in this brutal, internecine warfare. Lord Forbes' assessment of damages to the properties of his own house and those friendly to him included the theft of goods, the poaching of cattle, the wrecking of policies, plantings and orchards and sundry other damage. He adds, darkly, that 'sum of thair housiss, wyffis and bairnis being thairin wer alluterlie (utterly) wraikit and brount'.[14] Was this a reference to the Corgarff episode or were similar atrocities committed elsewhere, which history has forgotten?

Today, Corgarff Castle has been meticulously restored by Sir Edmund and

Lady Stockdale of Delnadamph. Thrice committed to the flames during its history, the castle has been extensively modified since its original construction in 1537, particularly after the Forty-five, when much of the interior was gutted and major external alterations were made.

The battle of Craibstane

While the Gordons overran the Forbes lands in the North East after the battle of Tillyangus, the master of Forbes gathered reinforcements in the south. At Stirling, he was commissioned Lieutenant of the North by the Protestant government and offered the command of five companies of foot, including 200 harqubusiers or 'culvering men' and a troop of horse. This substantial force numbering some 700 men was further augmented by a detachment of 100 mounted gentleman volunteers from the Mearns, Angus and the toun of Dundee. This army mustered at Brechin on 16 November and marched north over the Cairn o' Mount into Deeside to begin their task of 'danting and suppressing' Adam Gordon.[15]

In the meantime, Adam Gordon, whose military intelligence seems to have been very efficient, had been apprised of the movements of the would be avengers. His own band had also been reinforced by a detachment sent from his brother in Edinburgh with 'a commandment to offend the Forbeses all that they can'. He now commanded some 1,500 armed men. Adam moved east to Aberdeen, laying waste all the orchards and grainstores of the lower Dee, in order to rob the approaching Forbes army of sustenance.

The Forbes army reached Deeside on 19 November and crossed the river, probably by the ford at Mains of Drum. Here, according to Robert Lindsay of Pitscottie,[16] our most detailed source of these events, the army separated. One company under the son of the Earl Marischal continued the northward march into Gordon lands; the other, under the master of Forbes, was to advance east along the Deeside road to occupy Aberdeen. Pitscottie suggests that Forbes felt that he had been left rather in the lurch by his allies, but, being 'ane manlie man', he nevertheless marched his small company through the night, intending to reach Old Aberdeen by dusk the following day. By early afternoon on 20 November, the tired and hungry company arrived at the Justice Mills on the How Burn, within a short distance of their goal.

The appearance of early Aberdeen, so different from the later Granite City, has luckily been preserved for posterity by James Gordon, minister of Rothiemay, who was commissioned by the town to produce a detailed map in 1661. This shows that the town was approached from the south and west by a single road, the Hardgate, which passed through a field of oats and crossed the Denburn by a Bow-brig before entering Aberdeen via a wide street known as The Green. Shortly before reaching the Bow-brig, the track passed an ancient boulder known as the Craibstane or Crab Stone. Originally a boundary marker of lands granted to the Crab family at about the time of Bruce, the grassy promontory about the Craibstane had since become a popular meeting place, where morality plays were performed on festival days by the town's craft and guilds. As Forbes and his men neared the stone at about four o'clock, an hour or so before dusk, they were intercepted by a large force of Gordons who had marched out from The Green, crossed the Bow-brig and lined up to bar the approach to the town. Although he was outnumbered, Forbes decided to fight, and, in the words of Holinshed's contemporary chronicle, 'a sharp conflict was committed between them' which was 'cruelly fochten for the space of ane hour'. As darkness fell over the brawling field, 'the victorie inclyned to Adam Gordoun'.[17] Pitscottie, whose partisan account favours the master of Forbes, explains that although the Forbes 'faucht that day verie manfullie, so lang as thay mycht', they were finally overcome by exhaustion and hunger, for 'the maister and his small companie beand ryding all that nicht by past and nathir had gottin meit nor drink all that day and so they war forstousit (forsaken) for meit'.

Holinshed, whose chronicle is equally biased, but in favour of the Gordons, provides a further reason for the Forbes defeat:

> The King's footmen (appointed to the Forbes') desirous more hastilie than wiselie to fight, and adventuring further in following of the Gordons than their shot of powder would continue, they went so far that, in the end, being out of reach of defence or help of their company, they were put to fearfull flight by the bowmen of the Gordons, who persued them eagerlie, and continued the battell until night.[18]

The *Diurnal of Occurrents* adds that the Master of Forbes 'and his folkis gaif bakkis and fled, quhom on followit the said Adam and chacit thame four myullis'. Thus the key to the Gordon's victory seems to have been their success in separating the enemy musketeers from their protective phalanx of spearmen, and picking them off with bows and arrows.

We have no precise estimate of the numbers present at the battle of the Craibstane, although there is general agreement that the Forbes were outnumbered. Holinshed states, and other evidence confirms, that Adam Gordon conscripted many of the citizens of Aberdeen 'to make the number of his army seem greater', but the *Diurnal* nevertheless limits his force to some 900 men. We might surmise that other contingents of Adam Gordon's army were still actively engaged in suppressing the Forbes lands and that the force present at Craibstane was understrength. Of Forbes' original army of 800, possibly 500 were present at the battle. Pitscottie probably exaggerates the 'small nommer' of the Forbes compared to the 'gret cumpanie' of Gordons. The *Diurnal* states that a total of 300 were killed from both sides—an improbably high casualty rate—with 200 prisoners taken. Pitscottie says merely that 'sundrie war taine and slaine on baithe the syddes'. A more probable casualty figure of 60 killed on each side is offered by Holinshed, although the only person named was one Captain Chisolme, a professional soldier who led the company of Dundee. The following morning, the provost of Aberdeen donated £10 Scots 'to burie the deid folkis quhilk was gret pitie to sie'.[19] The most important prisoner was the master of Forbes himself, who was locked up for the night in the tollbooth and later held in custody by the

Gordons at Spynie Castle. He seems to have been treated with courtesy and respect.

The hostilities between Gordon and Forbes factions continued thereafter, but the ascendency of the Gordons was not seriously challenged again. After Craibstane, Adam Gordon 'passit to all placeis of the Forbusis and tuik thame perforce and causit thame to be keipit in his name ... and so the said Adam dantownit all the north cuntrie and held justice courtis upone all thame that assisted nocht with him, fra the watter of Dee north'.[20]

The war which Adam Gordon had effectively won for Queen Mary in the North East, came to an end at the general pacification of February 1573, when the earl of Huntly and his party submitted to the authority of the Protestant government. The town of Aberdeen had been occupied by the Gordons since the battle of Craibstane, and its citizens had soon grown sick of the feuds and brawls of the lawless 'clannit men', who made a habit of beating up any magistrate brave enough to intervene. In the end, the council donated 600 merks (£400 Scots) to Huntly in order to be rid of them. This, unfortunately, did not save Aberdeen from reprisals after the war was over. The Regent Morton, in need of ready money, fined the burgh the enormous sum of 4000 merks in 1574, on the pretext that it had supported the rebellious Gordons! Aberdeen, as usual, suffered from both sides.

The site of the Craibstane battle has long been built over and the Craibstane itself shifted from its original position and incorporated into a nearby wall at the top of Hardgate (although there is some doubt whether this is in fact the real stone). A plaque above the stone commemorates both this battle and the later civil war one of 1644, fought over much the same ground. The Gordons most probably occupied the open rise where the Hardgate is crossed by Bon Accord Terrace, and the subsequent fighting would have taken place in the vicinity of Union Glen.

CHAPTER 10

GLENLIVET

They were not many men of weir,
But they were wondrous true:
With hagbuts, pistols, bow and spear,
They did their foes persue:
Where bullets, darts and arrows flew,
As thick as hail or rain,
Whilk many hirt; and some they slew
Of horse and gentlemen.

From the *Ballad of the Battle of Glenlivet.*
Anon., first printed 1681.

The battle of Glenlivet, or the battle of Alltacoileachan as some prefer to call it, represented the final fling of Roman Catholicism as a political force in Scotland. At the same time, the battle was an innovation in terms of the evolution of military weaponry and tactics, for the outcome was decided by artillery. Glenlivet was a dramatic battle and, moreover, a relatively well-documented one, but it nevertheless receives little more than a passing mention in most Scottish histories. The reason is clear enough: it was an isolated episode in the continuing political struggles of the Reformation, and was decisive only in the sense that it led to the exile and enforced apostasy of the North East's leading Catholic nobles. But this would have happened sooner or later anyway. The battle was all sound and fury, signifying nothing.

The battle of Glenlivet had deep and complex roots. The sixth earl of Huntly, who was born in the year of Corrichie, was a Roman Catholic who intrigued actively for the restoration of the faith. Together with his fellow Catholic and political partner, George Hay, earl of Erroll, Huntly continued to command the allegiance of most of his feudal tenants and kinsmen in the North East, many of whom were also Catholics. King James VI pursued a cautious policy towards them, for Huntly and Erroll, through their traditional ties with their kin and dependents, still maintained law and order in the north.

Moreover, James had no personal interest in military matters. Armies were expensive, campaign marches were dirty and uncomfortable and generally led only to renewed feuds and rebellion; better by far to practise patience and conciliation. This did not of course go down well with some of the king's ultra-Protestant ministers and councillors, who branded him in consequence as a coward and a fool.

In 1589, the year after the destruction of the Spanish Armada, letters from Huntly to the king of Spain were intercepted in which the earl expressed regret over the failure of the expedition and pledged his support for like attempts in the future. In the same year, the Catholic earls joined in rebellion, marching towards Edinburgh with their armed followers with the intention of overthrowing the Protestant ruling council. The revolt quickly petered out and James, forced by events to take punitive action, led an army north to Aberdeen. At first Huntly pondered resistance, but finally disbanded his forces at the Brig o' Dee and submitted peaceably. Despite his treasonable actions, Huntly was kept under ward for a few months only before regaining his liberty.

Two relatively uneventful years were followed by further trouble in 1592. In February, Huntly's men attacked Donibristle House on the Forth and murdered Huntly's enemy, James Stewart, the 'bonny earl o' Moray'.[1] Church pulpits throughout the country clamoured for retribution, and, once again, Huntly was briefly imprisoned and then released. In revenge, former vassals of the murdered earl burned Gordon houses in Deeside and killed four Gordon lairds. At the close of that year there followed the mysterious affair of the 'Spanish Blanks'. Letters and documents incriminating Huntly and Erroll were again intercepted on their way to Spain. Huntly's messenger was put to the torture and eventually confessed that the earls had plotted to bring foreigners into Scotland to assist in the overthrow of the monarchy and the restoration of popery. Huntly and Erroll were summoned to court to answer the charge. The king, however, decided against a trial and informed the pair that if they renounced their religion or, alternatively, went into exile, no further action would be taken against them. The earls did neither and so, in autumn 1594, they were excommunicated by the general assembly and their lands declared forfeit. The earls paid little heed. There were dark and mysterious comings and goings in Aberdeen. The town's magistrates, who had arrested three suspected papist spies, were threatened by Huntly with the destruction of the town by fire and sword unless they were promptly released. The magistrates fearfully complied, but when news of this latest affront reached King James he decided that enough was enough.

James summoned his lieges to enforce the forfeiture of the lands of the errant earls and was lent 19,000 merks (about £12,600 Scots) for the payment and equipment of an army. The eighteen year-old earl of Argyll was entrusted with the king's commission to raise the clans in the west, with orders to join forces with the king's men once the latter reached the north. Meanwhile the Forbes and others at feud with Huntly mustered their own forces, ready to assist the expedition when it reached Donside.

Huntly seems to have been a man of mettle and he responded vigorously.

During the late days of September, he scraped together all the forces he could lay his hands on. That anyone was willing to serve him at all, in the face of such peril, is remarkable and eloquent of the strength of the traditional ties of loyalty to the 'Cock o' the North'. But Huntly also offered tempting financial inducements: 40 merks (about £26 Scots) a month for the services of a mounted man and £40 a month if he arrived 'fully furnished'. This was very good pay for those days, and was apparently sufficient to tempt 'sundry borderers and many of those who lately served for the king's guard'[2] into his service. Even Lord Forbes was offered restitution for previous damages in return for his non-participation. By the time Erroll had joined Huntly with his Buchan horse, the Catholic earls commanded some 800 horse and 1,200 foot[3] despite the fact that many Gordon dependents had thought the matter over and decided to stay at home.

The young earl of Argyll had been warned not to tackle Huntly until the king's army had reached the North East. He had raised a large clan army of 6,000 foot 'or thereabouts', mostly his own Campbells with detachments of MacLeans, Grants, MacIntoshes, Clan Gilzean and Clan Gillivray. About half were armed with harquebuses, bows or pikes; the remainder bore a motley collection of 'swords and other mixed weapons after the fashion of the Highland man'.[4] Argyll commanded no sizeable body of regular or mounted troops and possessed no artillery train. 'This army', wrote the English Ambassador, Thomas Bowes, on 24 September, 'thus marching without guard of horsemen, is much scorned in court and thought easy to be over-thrown by Huntly'. Even so, Argyll had determined to move ahead of the king's army to 'hunt Huntly out of the country ... and avenge Moray's murder'. His stated reason for risking the king's enterprise and disobeying his orders was that he 'could not preserve the provisions prepared without loss and offence to his people'. In other words, he had food rations enough to victual his large force for only a short period; he could not afford to delay without risking wholesale desertion. He might have been better served by a smaller force of proven quality. As it was, Argyll approached the North East from Speyside with few experienced captains and a ragged, polyglot army, many of whom were 'raskalls and poke bearers, who led and marched at raggle and in plompes without order'.[5] His evident intention was to invest Huntly's castle at Strathbogie. The king's commission had in the meantime been read in Aberdeen on 27 September, and the levies of the town were ordered to join Argyll, together with the followers of Lord Forbes, Leslie of Balquhain and Irvine of Drum. Fearing the pillage of their lands, the local MacKendowies of Strathbogie promised not to support their laird, Huntly, and had even sent a small and distinctly unenthusiastic contingent of their own to join Argyll.[6]

At first Huntly temporised and attempted to parley with Argyll. On the latter's refusal to negotiate, however, he prepared to resist Argyll's passage, boasting that he would 'rubb his cloake on Argyle's pladd'.[7] The army of Huntly and Erroll, lately reinforced by the last minute arrival of eighty Ogilvy horse, moved from Strathbogie to Auchindoun where they were joined by Sir Patrick Gordon, Huntly's uncle and a veteran campaigner in the late wars. Unlike Argyll's Highland army, Huntly and Erroll's joint force of 2,000 men was well equipped, with a strong contingent of horse and an artillery train of six field guns. Huntly's munificent offers of payment had attracted experienced officers and mercenaries to his service. On hearing of Argyll's whereabouts, the force set out from Auchindoun at dawn on Thursday 3 October and advanced southwards towards the hilly marches between the Gordon lands and Strathavon. Their mounted vanguard reached the pass above Glenlivet at 11 o'clock.[8] There they ran straight into a company of Argyll's skirmishers coming up from the other side and the day-long battle began.

The terrain of the Glenlivet battlefield has altered out of all recognition, and only old maps show it as it might have looked in 1594. Through the rugged scenery of steep, rounded hills and fast-flowing burns, a complex network of drovers' roads crossed between Glenlivet and Glen Rinnes. One of these passed between two hills, the massive Carn Tighearn to the west, and the lower Muckle Tomlair, a spur of Carn a' Bhodaich, to the east. Below these hillsides runs the Allt a' Choileachain burn, passing westwards along a steep wooded valley. In the sixteenth century the slopes were covered with scrub woodland, probably of pine, birch and juniper, but the tops of the hills were bare. There were no settlements on the battlefield except for scattered cattle shielings. Below, in the glens, there were scattered cots and farm-touns but none were significant enough to lend their name to the battlefield.

Our best surviving account of the battle implies that the vanguard of either army ran into each other along the Achorachan-Achinoir road, somewhere near the crossed swords symbol on the Ordnance Survey map. Argyll's skirmishers were taken by surprise. Since his army was strung out in column over several miles of rough hill tracks, Argyll himself, together with all of his 'heavy infantry', the pikemen, were two miles distant as the advance guards clashed. Huntly is said to have been 'well advised of this'. Without the protection of the pikemen, Argyll's men, armed only with harquebuses and bows, were extremely vulnerable to cavalry. Erroll sent a mounted patrol ahead to cut them up and disperse them whilst the guns were placed in position on the hillside, covering the approaches to the pass. Many Highlanders scattered almost immediately, but others took shelter among the scrub vegetation on Muckle Tomlair where they were safe from the horse. Huntly's guns began to roar as further detachments of Argyll's force reached the field, perhaps wondering what was happening. Possibly few of Argyll's Highlanders had ever faced artillery fire before and its effect on their morale was devastating; 2,000 or more of them were in full flight before Argyll's main body of Campbell pikes had even arrived on the scene.

Flushed with success, Erroll led a mounted charge against the Highlanders. But as the small but sturdy horses were spurred uphill, they ran into a hail of enfilading fire from the bowmen and harquebusiers hidden in the bushes. Horse and riders toppled over like nine-pins. Patrick Gordon of Auchindoun was shot from his horse, at which 'the horsemen gave an exceedingly great cry and lamentation, seeking to rescue him'. But, according to Bowes' account of the battle, 'he was well known to Argyll's men, so they sharply assailed

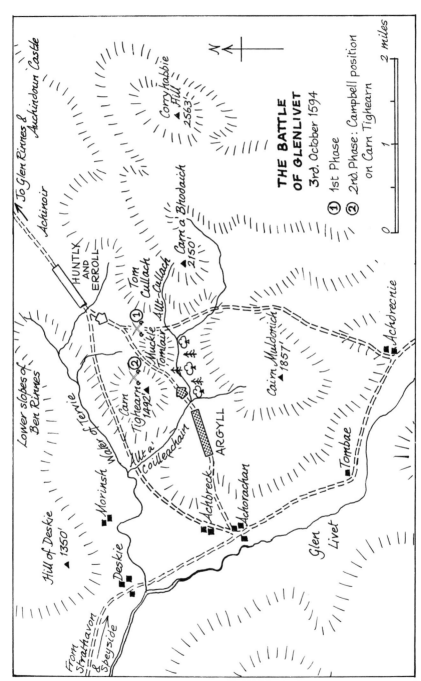

THE BATTLE
OF GLENLIVET
3rd. October 1594

① 1st Phase

② 2nd. Phase: Campbell position
on Carn Tighearn

Map 12.

him and with dirks stabbed him, and afterwards cut off his head'. Erroll himself was struck in the arm by a bullet and in the thigh by an arrow and a rumour spread that he had been killed. Gordon of Gight was 'stricken by three bullets in his body and two plates of his steel coat carried into him ... it is thought he cannot live many days'. Likewise the laird of Cluny was 'hurt on the flank by a bullet', according to one account, 'shott through the cheekes' by another, but 'in hope of life'. Bowes reckoned that out of 100 riders taking part in the ill-fated charge, eighteen to twenty were killed outright and forty to fifty wounded, all of whom, gloated one of Argyll's captains, were 'cheefe and speciall men'.[9] It was a veritable Charge of the Light Brigade of the north eastern gentry.

The tattered and bloody remnants of Erroll's horse reeled back onto the main body of Huntly's army and there was a pause whilst both sides regrouped. During the interval, Argyll at last arrived and took up position on Carn Tighearn, a hillside 'rough and high',[10] flanked by the steep defile of the Choileachain burn. The Highlanders now had the advantage of ground, sun and wind. Fighting resumed at about three o'clock in the afternoon. Argyll played little part and took shelter in a nearby wood, leaving the business to his general, the chief of the MacLeans. MacLean was among the few Highlanders present who 'undoubtedlie played the man'. Most melted away under renewed artillery fire, but Maclean himself, vast and ferocious in his ancient chain mail and 'jack' (a leather coat), led a charge towards the main body of Huntly's force. Wielding his great two-handed Lochaber axe, he slew four or five men as he hacked his way towards Huntly's standard, then, with the spear-point of his axe, 'sticked the horse whereupon the bearer raid', and finally proceeded to cut the unfortunate standard bearer in half before making off with the standard. Donald Campbell is also credited with the capture of a standard.[11]

Huntly's men stood firm, however, and with the low autumn sun now glaring into their eyes, his horse assailed Argyll's hill-top position. Campbell of Lochnell was killed in the fighting together with his brother and 'three or four gentlemen and fifty of the common sort'. In the fierce skirmishes about the hill-top Huntly's own horse was killed beneath him. The Lyon Herald of Scotland, who bore the royal standard, was surrounded by a party of Gordon riders, and fell, pierced with three lances to cries of 'have at the Lyon!'[12] The hill-top position was eventually taken and, while Argyll wept salt tears of shame, the remaining Campbells fled the field. Only the MacLeans retired in good order.

There was no pursuit. According to one account, cited by Bowes, both parties 'severed of ther owne accordis, without the persuite of anye chase'. Argyll's men were given leave to bury their dead on the spot, making hurdles out of bow staves and plaids to carry away the injured. Contemporary estimates of the casualties are, as usual, uncertain and at odds. Argyll is variously said to have lost between 200 and 500 men.[13] Huntly's own losses seem to have been heavy, despite his preposterous letter to the king of Spain claiming to have lost only one man. 'Black Alister' Gordon, the veteran of Corrichie, lost his son George, while Thomas Gordon of Seggyden was killed,

17.   George Gordon, 6th earl and 1st marquis of Huntly (1562–1636). In 1594
his forces defeated forces under the earl of Argyll at Glenlivet.

together with his two sons. At least fourteen 'landed gentlemen of good quality' are said to have lost their lives together with no fewer than 150 horses, an indication of the ferocity of the fighting.[14] A contemporary letter attributes the 'greatest losse to Huntlie'.

Glenlivet was a victory of artillery and horse over irregular infantry. One source states flatly that Huntly would have lost had it not been for his cannon. On the other hand, Bowes makes it clear that nobody expected Argyll's army of foot to win a battle on its own without the support of cavalry, and one of Argyll's own men admitted that he 'was in no wise minded to fight'. The bad news reached the king's party, on their way north to Aberdeen, on 7 October. James was reportedly furious at the loss of his standard bearer.[15]

As at Corrichie, rumours grew of treachery in Argyll's ranks to explain his poor showing. Certainly the unwilling contingent of MacKendowies of Strathbogie had deserted Argyll in the heat of the action and gone over to the other side, and perhaps other reluctant warriors followed suit when they saw who was likely to win. The blackest treachery was attributed to Campbell of Lochnell who had been implicated in the murder of the earl of Moray, and who, it is alleged, secretly intended to lead the vanguard away in flight. He had even arranged that Huntly should direct his artillery fire at the 'yellow standard' where Argyll stood. But the plan went astray, and it was Lochnell himself who was killed, 'as God would have the traitor punished'. The same writer also accredits the MacIntoshes and Grants with treachery. None of this is corroborated by other contemporary accounts of the battle, however, and the stories about yellow standards and wholesale treachery sound suspiciously like attempts to sugar the bitter pill of defeat.

After the battle, Argyll retired southwards along Strath Avon. Since his baggage had been abandoned and looted by the Gordons, he was unable to victual his men and all but 600 MacIntoshes were dismissed. Eventually he reached Stirling where he 'sent for his friends and forces in the lowland, for he will no more trust the highlandmen'.[16]

Huntly, who was prepared to fight on the next day if necessary, released his force, except for 500 mounted troops, and retired to Strathbogie, leaving the more seriously wounded of his party to recover from their injuries at Auchindoun. He evidently planned to occupy Aberdeen and hold it against the king but, whereas Argyll and the hated Campbells were fair game, many of Huntly's company were unwilling to 'partye' the earl against the king himself. In consequence, the 'Gowk's storm', as Huntly had derisively labelled the king's expedition, was not contested. King James reached Aberdeen, borrowed powder, masons and tools, and moved on to Strathbogie. Huntly's beautiful Renaissance castle was systematically demolished under royal supervision as were those of George Gordon at Newton and Erroll at Slains. Huntly and Erroll crossed the seas into exile shortly afterwards, while the vengeful Campbells over-ran their lands.

Eighteen months later, the earls returned in secret to negotiate the return of their lands in return for their abandonment of the Roman Catholic religion under the terms of their earlier agreement with the king. In June 1597, an elaborate ceremony took place at the Cross in Aberdeen's Castlegate during which the earls were received back into royal favour and received absolution at the pulpit for their 'defection and apostasy'. At the session house, a peace pact between Gordon and Forbes was drawn up, 'berrying all quarrellis and deadlie feadis betwix thame twa'. Both parties signed the document and there, in the presence of the King's Commissioner and the bishop of Aberdeen, the earl of Huntly solemnly shook hands with the laird of Forbes. 'These proceedings', remarks Gordon Donaldson, 'marked the extinction of Roman Catholicism as a political danger'.[17] It was also an appropriate ending to more than thirty years of plot, counterplot and war in the North East.

The site of the battlefield

The earliest accounts of the battle say that it was fought 'on the hill of Ben Rinnes' or, more precisely, 'six miles above Auchindoun beside Ben Rinnes'.[18] Calderwood names the encounter the 'Battel of Glenrinnes' and a contemporary manuscript, 'a field called Auld Auchainachie'. We know, in addition, that Huntly had marched from Strathbogie and past Auchindoun, whilst Argyll was approaching Auchindoun from Badenoch. Pooling this information, the site of battle must have been at the head of Glen Rinnes, near the pass which guards the approach from Strathspey to the Gordon lands of Auchindoun and Strathbogie. There are no good maps of this neighbourhood dating back to the time of the battle, but the settlements recorded on the county map of Gordon of Straloch (1654) and the drover's roads on the maps of Taylor and Skinner (1776) were very probably present in 1594. The confusing details of topography given in contemporary accounts of the battle imply that the action took place on and around the head of the hill-pass leading from Achorachan in Glenlivet to Achinoir (now Achmore) above Glen Rinnes. There are three flat-topped hills here, Carn Tighearn, Muckle Tomlair and Tom Cullach, and the main action, as interpreted in this chapter, swung from the latter two hills at mid-day to Carn Tighearn in the afternoon.

The early references to Ben Rinnes require some explanation, since the summit of this hill lies at least four miles away from the suggested battlefield. The probable reason is that these witnesses decided to name the battle after the best-known local feature, and one, moreover, which dominates the neighbourhood. There were no nearby settlements large enough for the purpose. One is reminded of the battle of Hastings, which took place at Senlac Stream in uninhabited country, but which was named after the one nearby town which everyone had heard of.

The battlefield of Glenlivet has been afforested and cast into deep gloomy shade by dense ranks of spruce and pine. In consequence, one can no longer easily explore this site, although the original drove roads still exist as forestry tracks. One of these passes along the Allt a' Choileachain to the battlefield, which the Ordnance Survey mark on their maps. The original appearance of the site is described in the *New Statistical Account*:

The battle of Altachoylachan or Glenlivet (was) fought ... upon an inclined plain near the Glenrinnes border of Inveravon parish, terminating in a flat ridge which descends rapidly to the burn of Altachoylachan, and flanked on the south by a somewhat precipitous shoulder of the contiguous mountain (Carn a' Bhodaich). About three quarters of a mile from the scene of action, a small knoll on the east bank of the stream Coulalt (Allt Cullach), commonly called Lord Auchindown's cairn, two thirds of it swept away by the flood of 1829, marks the place where Sir Patrick Gordon of Auchindown is supposed to have died.

PART IV

Battlefields of the Civil Wars and Jacobite Risings

The civil wars in the North East were of brief duration but exceptionally bitter and destructive, even by the standards of the earlier battles of the Reformation. For the first short war in spring 1639, traditional rivalries asserted themselves, with the Gordons and their allies supporting King Charles I and episcopacy, while the Forbes, Frasers, Crichtons and others supported the National Covenant and presbyterianism. This conflict was therefore very much on the 'traditional' pattern, but the later, and far more ferocious, war of 1644–6 was complicated by the appearance of a new element: an insurgent Catholic Irish and Highlander army fighting for the king under the command of the marquis of Montrose. Its appearance split the loyalties of the Gordons and other North Eastern royalists. Some threw in their lot with Montrose; others, led by the example of the marquis of Huntly himself, remained aloof and resentful of the presence of Irish Catholics on their lands.

A detailed account of the causes of the Scottish Civil War would lie well beyond the scope of this book. The war was the product of a mixture of religious and constitutional grievances which expressed themselves in the National Covenant of early 1638. The covenant, despite its lip service to the institution of monarchy, was in effect an organised rebellion against the crown for it unified the various factions in Scottish politics and abolished episcopacy, introduced by King James VI and strengthened by Charles. The government machinery was too weak to prevent a ground swell of support for the demands of the Covenant. The Scottish nobility had been the main beneficiaries of the dissolution of church lands after the Reformation and most Scots peers were opposed to the rehabilitation of the bishops and the absolute rule of the monarch they represented. This division led to the conflict known by English historians as the 'First Bishops' War' and in Scotland as the outbreak of 'the Troubles'. King Charles could not afford to fund an army of sufficient size to threaten the covenanters, whose unity and urgent sense of purpose resulted in the rapid mobilisation of a militia army and an easy victory over the king's lieutenants. The king's traditional lieutenant in the north, the marquis of Huntly, was taken prisoner and subsequent royalist efforts in the North East proved a fiasco.

The burgh of Aberdeen enjoyed Huntly's patronage and protection and was reluctant to make common ground with the other Scottish burghs and subscribe to the covenant. Aberdeen was therefore occupied by a covenanting army on three separate occasions in 1639 and the compliance of its baillies and magistrates thereafter enforced by a garrison of unruly soldiers. The effective leader of the covenanter forces in the North East in 1639 was the twenty seven year-old James Graham, then earl, and later marquis, of Montrose. Montrose was first among those who had initially supported the National Covenant with great enthusiasm but later became alienated as extremist views took root and more and more constitutional influence was transferred from the king to the Scottish parliament. He also suspected some nobles, particularly Archibald Campbell, marquis of Argyll, of using the aspirations of the covenant in order to advance their own private ambitions.

In 1643, a Solemn League and Covenant was made between the Scottish and English Parliaments. In exchange for Scottish military aid, the hard-pressed English Parliamentarians entered a commitment to introduce a form of church government in England and Ireland along similar lines to the Scottish model. The Scots mobilised and, in January 1644, crossed the border with a vast army of 18,000 foot and 3,000 horse. This effort proved over-ambitious for Scotland, although it succeeded in reversing the tide of the English war in favour of the parliamentarians.

The Solemn League impelled Montrose to take the final plunge and switch his allegiance to the king. The covenanter of 1639 became, in 1644, one of the king's most dedicated and resourceful generals. Montrose was of course one of Scotland's most famous military commanders, whose dashing exploits held a touch of the miraculous about them. His qualities of leadership are incontestable. He forged the fighting skills of the Gael into a potent weapon of victory and managed, for a time, to unite in the service of the king men of mutual hostility and very different cultural backgrounds. Contemporaries pay tribute to his military *savoir faire* and to his personal highmindedness, courage and sense of destiny. Set against this must be placed his tendency, re-inforced by his biographer, Wishart, to take all the credit for the royalist's successes when much was due to other factors. The contribution of his leading subordinates, particularly his Gaelic lieutenant Alasdair macCholla, has often been under-rated. One also has the feeling that there would have been friction had Montrose served under the king's direct command. His successes owed much to the departure of Scotland's finest officers and men to take part in the distant English war. Like all military leaders, Montrose made mistakes. He took incredible risks. His neglect of scouting nearly led to disaster on a number of occasions and was ultimately fatal. His grand strategy of breaking into the Lowlands and then marching into England to join the king was probably never very realistic. His opponents were mostly amateur, conscript armies with little discipline or training, led by inexperienced officers and poor

Map 13.

commanders. The covenanters consistently underestimated Montrose, partly, perhaps, out of religious conviction: God was on their side and Montrose's band of Catholic savages were agents of the devil. God would see to their punishment.

Montrose's 'year of miracles' began in the early autumn of 1644 when, after slipping into Scotland in disguise, he joined with a force of Highlanders and Irish Catholics and raised the king's standard at Blair Atholl. For a year this predominately Gaelic force turned Scotland upside down, winning victory after victory for the king. Mobility, fortitude, discipline and high morale were among the hallmarks of the royalist army. So, also, was its cruelty. Although Montrose was personally chivalrous and humane, his army took no prisoners, except those worth ransoming, and his victories all too often ended with a hideous butcher's bill of massacre which made any accommodation with the Lowlanders less likely.

Three set piece battles were fought in the North East in 1644 and 1645. The circumstances of each were different, but together they demonstrate Montrose's skill and versatility as a general and not a few of his weaknesses. The first, the battle of Justice Mills or Aberdeen, was won by an outnumbered force, weak in cavalry and on inferior ground; it ranks as one of Montrose's most brilliant victories, although it was marred by the subsequent sack of the city. Fyvie, which followed soon afterwards, was a defensive battle which Montrose brought upon himself by his poor scouting. Perhaps for that reason, it is customarily classed as a minor encounter. The battle of Alford, the best known of the three, was exceptional in that it was primarily a cavalry battle and because Montrose for once commanded more men than his opponent and was able to choose the ground on which to fight. The war in the North East cost the lives of several thousand Scots and left a legacy of bitterness towards the Highlanders. Its long-term result was to widen the divide between Scotland's two nations, Highland and Lowland, and set them further along the collision course which led to the tragedy of Culloden.

Weapons and warfare in the Civil War

The main infantry arms during the Civil War were the musket and the pike. Since the days of Corrichie and Glen Livet, the performance of the musket had improved in range and at close quarters could now pierce all but the thickest armour plate. It was still, however, a heavy and cumbersome weapon, capable of firing no more than two or three rounds a minute and not very accurately either. The musket butt was reinforced with steel, so that it could, at need, be used as a club. In addition to his firing piece and a forked pole to rest it on, the musketeer had to carry a variety of extra kit including a bandolier of powder bottles, a priming flask and bullet pouch and a length of match-fuse. The leather bottles each contained enough powder for a single charge. They were prone to catch fire and, when empty, tended to rattle noisily in the wind. Indeed, wind and rain made it difficult to use the musket at all, for the match fuse, a cord soaked in saltpetre, would stubbornly refuse to light. Not surprisingly, with all this paraphernalia to carry, the musketeer wore little or no body armour.

The musketeer was trained to act in concert with the second type of foot soldier, the pikeman, whose job it was to defend him from the enemy horse. Pikes varied between twelve and eighteen feet in length and ended in a narrow steel point. Tall strong men were recruited to carry them. The pikeman wore partial armour, consisting of a helmet or 'pot', a breast and backplate or corslet, with tassets to protect the thighs, and leather gauntlets. Contemporary descriptions suggest that most Scots wore a thick leather 'jack' or 'buff-coat', and rarely bothered with plate armour. Pikemen were considered socially superior to the musketeers and at the time of the Civil War there were roughly two pikemen to every three musketeers.

Higher still on the social scale was the cavalryman—in the North East, this tended to be anyone who could afford the pasture and winter feed for a war-horse. The rider would normally be armed with a sword and a supply of wheel-lock pistols. Scots cavalry also included old-fashioned lancers, in effect mounted pikemen. Detachments of Scots lancers fought at Marston Moor and appear to have been present at the battle of Aberdeen. There were also light cavalry or dragoons armed with a small musket, the arquebus, or the still smaller carbine. By the time of the Civil War, the armour of cavalrymen had been reduced to a helmet and breastplate or simply the buff-coat; the full armour one sees in portrait paintings of the period was usually reserved for ceremonial occasions.

Finally there was artillery. Guns of the period varied from the huge siege guns or 'cartows' of Dunnottar Castle, each weighing one and three quarter tons and discharging roundshot of twenty seven pounds to a range of up to 1,700 yards, to the much smaller 'minions', 'sakers' and 'falcons' of around three to five pounds in calibre. Only the smaller pieces were normally employed in the field although the great 'cartows' were used with notable success at Megray Hill and the Brig o' Dee in 1639. Each gun had a crew of about three men. Transporting large guns was a perennial problem on Scotland's rough roads, and this limited their value in the campaign of speed and mobility chosen by Montrose.

The most successful generals of the Civil War were those who could combine the separate arms of pike, musket and horse to their best advantage. Some of Scotland's best generals had fought as mercenaries in continental armies during the Thirty Year's War, a testing ground for new techniques in warfare. The traditional way of deploying infantry was to mass together a large number of pikemen flanked by musketeers, in a formation known as the tercio. The musketeers were taught to fire in ranks, and to shelter beneath the extended pikes when attacked by cavalry. The Swedish king and soldier of genius, Gustavus Adolphus, revolutionised the art of war by breaking up the unwieldy tercio into much smaller units of battalion strength. His musketeers, ranked in threes, were trained to fire in a single devastating salvo at close range. His pikemen would then move forward to attack the disorganised ranks of the enemy. Such techniques required discipline and long experience but, as Gustavus proved on the field of battle, they won victories. Gustavus' military ideas profoundly affected the thinking of men like Montrose.

The cavalry arm was also due for overhaul. Hitherto, cavalry units had been trained to approach the enemy at a trot, then halt, half-turn and fire their pistols in ranks. This tactic, known as the 'caracolle', was often ineffective due to the short range of the pistols and the difficulty of aiming accurately from horseback. Gustavus reintroduced the less gentlemanly method of shock action. His troopers would hold their fire until the last moment and then drive into the disorganised enemy ranks at the point of the sword. He attached units of musketeers to the cavalry to provide extra fire power and help to soften up resistance. Montrose used this technique at the battles of Aberdeen and Alford. Again, it needed strong nerves, stronger discipline and effective leadership.

By these means, it was possible for experienced soldiers to overcome superior numbers of less well-trained opponents. Many of Alasdair Mac-Cholla's following had fought in the brutal Irish war which preceded the Scottish Civil War, and Alasdair had forged the natural endurance and elan of the Gaelic warrior into a deadly weapon. The chain mail, Lochaber axes and two-handed swords of an earlier generation had been superseded by the more familiar broadsword and targe. Under Alasdair, the wild 'Irishes' and Highlanders charged forward in dense masses, yelling as they ran and planting terror in the heart of the bravest opponent. Against conscripts and less than well trained troops they proved irresistible.

CHAPTER 11

THE FIRST BISHOPS' WAR

O woful Abirdene! by thy sins this heavie scourge is laid upone thee bye all the burrows in Scotland—much to be bemoaned and lamented.

John Spalding, *Memorialls of the Troubles*

The cock of the north

Some of the earliest fighting of the Civil War took place in the Scottish North East during the first half of 1639. As the prospect of war drew closer, following the National Covenant of 1638, King Charles hoped to capitalise on the North East's traditional ties of loyalty in his forthcoming struggle with the covenanters. By secret arrangement, he was to send reinforcements to the marquis of Huntly in order to enable the latter to strike southwards, as part of a three-pronged assault on the Lowlands. In practice, the king could not afford to fund an adequate force from his own means. The covenanters therefore managed to mobilise before the king, whose grand strategy quickly fell to pieces through poor co-ordination, low morale and lack of funds. Huntly and the north eastern royalists were left alone to aid the king as best they could; their struggle against hopeless odds was therefore essentially a private one recalling the civil wars of the previous century. As Scotland had enjoyed an unprecedented forty years of peace, so landowners and their followers had had no opportunity to develop military skills at home when in 1639 they began to prepare for conflict. On the continent, however, many thousands of Scots had served as mercenaries in the Thirty Years' War. Many veteran officers now returned to Scotland as civil war offered opportunities for employment at home, and provided an officer corps for the covenanters' armies: only a few joined the royalists.

All over the North East during 1639, clandestine groups were meeting, plotting 'their awin bussineis'. When several hundred covenanters, including the master of Forbes, James Crichton of Fendraught and Lord Fraser, met at Turriff in February 1639 in order to select commissioners to represent them in Edinburgh, the marquis of Huntly, whose family seat at Strathbogie stood a bare dozen miles to the south west, rightly saw it as a threat to his prestige. He was advised by Sir George Ogilvy of Banff, a political hot-head, to take immediate steps to intimidate the committee into cancelling their meeting. Unfortunately, George Gordon, the second marquis of Huntly, was one of the least gifted holders of that title. Cold and aloof by nature and self-confessedly not a natural leader of men, he was not made for revolutionary times. Although unswervingly loyal to the king, he proved too indecisive to realise his master's great expectations. On this occasion, however, he allowed himself to be goaded into making a show of force. A royalist force assembled in Aberdeen and marched out with Huntly at its head to confront the covenanters at Turriff. Unfortunately, Huntly was in an impossible position. Storming the village would merely provoke reaction and lose support for the king; failing to storm it would result in a painful loss of face.

Huntly arrived at Turriff on 14 February to find it defended by a powerful force of 800 men, well equipped with 'buff-coats, swords, corslets, pistols, carbines, hagbuts and other weapons'. It would be impossible to evict the committee without heavy loss of life, and, beset with conflicting advice from his captains, Huntly prevaricated. In the end, he sent Lord Findlater into the church to parley with the earl of Montrose, who now headed the committee. Montrose was politeness itself: so far as he was concerned, Huntly was welcome to enter the town if he had any business to transact, providing that he did not interfere in any way with the covenanter's business. Huntly had to content himself with riding through the main street of Turriff within two pikes lengths of the garrison troops before retiring. The Cock o' the North lost some of his feathers in this bleak encounter, for the public loss of face eroded much of his authority—as Montrose and the covenanters had intended. Thus ended the 'First Raid of Turriff'.

In March, the king's long expected proclamation was read out from the mercat cross in Aberdeen. Huntly was commissioned as the king's lieutenant-general in the north and the activities of the covenanters were declared illegal. This was in effect a declaration of war. The burgh council of Aberdeen had already voted to arm and train a force for the defence of the town, and called-up townsmen were equipped with pikes and muskets from the armoury, and set to work digging a defensive perimeter between Gallowgate and Castlehill. Eleven small field guns from the harbour blockhouse were placed in key positions guarding the approaches to the town.

Montrose, whose gamble at Turriff had paid off, was once more employed as the 'troubleshooter' of the covenanters. His attempts to persuade the burgesses of Aberdeen to make common cause with the rest of the kingdom were unavailing and a large army was therefore dispatched from the Lowlands to occupy the town and enforce its submission. As the covenanter army approached Aberdeen, Huntly had little choice but to withdraw his own much smaller force and leave the town to look after itself. Finding themselves deserted in their hour of need, Aberdeen's defenders laid aside their arms and, on 30 March an army of 9,000 men with Montrose and the Earl Marischal at its head entered the town. This was probably the largest and best equipped force Aberdeen had ever seen, although it consisted mostly of ill-trained conscripts. File after file passed in ceremony across the Green, through Castlegate and out onto the Links to the sound of trumpets and drums. An impressed John Spalding recorded their appearance in detail. Each cavalryman and foot soldier wore the covenanting colours, the blue sash of St Andrew, across his buff coat. Mounted troops led the way, each 'with ane carbine in hand, two pistols by his side, and other two at his saddle toir'. They were followed by massed ranks of pikemen and in the rear the musketeers with their panoply of specialised equipment: 'musket staffs, bandolier, sword, powder, ball and match'.[1] After lunching on the sand hills, the main part of the army marched off to Kintore in search of Huntly, leaving behind a garrison under the earl of Kinghorn to occupy the town. Aberdeen's reluctant soldiers were disarmed and set to work filling in the trenches which, under Huntly's supervision, they had laboured so hard to dig.

In the meantime Huntly had disbanded his force and was negotiating with Montrose. Bereft of any material support from the king, he had little room for manoeuvre in the face of such overwhelming odds and was forced to sign what amounted to a document of surrender. But that was not enough for the covenanters. Huntly and his eldest son, Lord Gordon, were asked to come to Aberdeen for further negotiations. But when they arrived, they were arrested and sent to Edinburgh Castle. For this act of treachery, Huntly blamed Montrose personally, since the latter had at one stage guaranteed his safe-conduct.[2] Huntly never forgave and never forgot, and the now permanent rift between these two leading nobles was to gravely damage the royalist cause in Scotland in the years to come.

The trot of Turriff

The capture and imprisonment of the marquis and his eldest son left the Gordons and their allies with no obvious leader to turn to. None of the natural substitutes were suitable. Huntly's brother, Adam, 'his braines being craickit', was useless for the task while his only available son, Lord Aboyne, was regarded as too young and too much tied to his mother's apron-strings.[3] In the end, the leading royalist gentry agreed to sign a 'band', as the covenanting lords had done, 'in defence of his majestie's royall prerogative; and nixt, for the dewtie, honour and service they owe to the house of Huntly'. All present solemnly inked their quills and signed the pledge and a force of 2,000 men was gathered in arms to resist the covenanters.

For the past few months, covenanting forces had been making surreptitious attempts to disarm royalist strongholds. In February, Frasers and Mackenzies had raided Inverness castle and seized for their own use arms and ammunition deposited there by Huntly, the nominal sheriff. Early in May, Hays of Delgatie and Keith of Towie-Barclay broke into their royalist neighbour's tower-house of Balquholly (now Hatton Castle) and made off with the stockpile of muskets, powder and ball in the armoury, storing them for safekeeping at Towie-Barclay. The newly-formed royalist 'band' decided to dispatch a force under Colonel ('Crowner') Johnstone, a professional soldier and son of a former provost of Aberdeen, to recover the stolen arms. Johnstone, described as 'a brave and valiant' man, was one of the few leaders in the North East to emerge from the Bishops' War with distinction. Taking with him four brass cannon from Strathbogie he laid siege lines about the walls of Towie-Barclay and opened fire. The Towie-Barclay retainers sniped back from the windows and turrets and one chance shot struck and killed a Gordon servant named David Prat, who thus achieved a kind of immortality as the first victim of the Civil War.

Having thus committed themselves to military action, the royalists resolved to avenge Huntly's humiliation at Turriff by storming that town and evicting the covenanters. The covenanting garrison had been reinforced recently and now numbered some 1,200 men under Hays of Delgatie, Keith of Ludquhairn

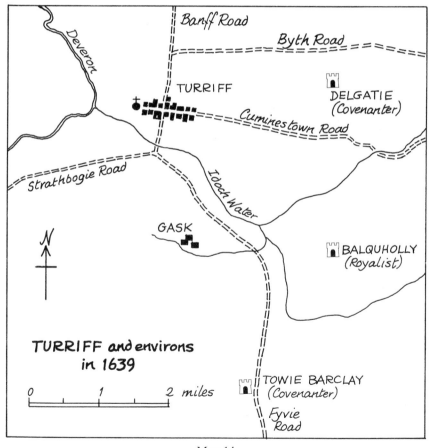

Map 14.

and the latter's son, Sir William Keith. Crowner Johnstone, still engaged in the seige of Towie-Barclay, was given six companies of foot and a squadron of horse, totalling perhaps 800 men in all, and ordered to take the town in the name of Huntly and the king.

Johnstone marched his force northwards by night along the Banff road, so as to be in a position to launch a surprise assault at dawn on 13 May. A night march is a difficult manoeuvre to undertake by inexperienced troops but Turriff's elevated view over the surrounding countryside would betray the approaching royalists to the enemy sentries during daylight hours. Another consideration was Turriff's strong natural defences, guarded from the south and west by the steep slopes above the Deveron and Idoch Water. If Johnstone's bold plan failed and he found the covenanters prepared and waiting for him, a drawn-out and costly battle might result.

The action which did take place is known as the 'Trot of Turriff'. We are given three contemporary accounts of the skirmish, all by royalist sympathisers. Their evidence is conflicting, but it is clear that Johnstone was successful in taking the covenanters by surprise, and that they consequently had no time to marshal their superior force before the assault took place. Aberdeen's famous chronicler, John Spalding, paints a vivid picture of the prevailing confusion after the alarm had been raised in the pale light of the early summer dawn by a sleepy sentry.

> The Coventeris, quhairof sum war sleiping in thair bedis, uther sum drinking and smoaking tabacca, utheris sum walking up and down, heiring this feirfull noyss of drumis and trumpettis, ran to their armes and confusedlie to array and recollectis them selffis.[4]

According to another contemporary, Patrick Gordon of Ruthven, the covenanter officers managed to form some of their men into line behind makeshift barricades, but most of their force were still milling into the main street as the Gordon bugles and drums sounded and their cannon fired an opening salvo. A round or two of musket fire, followed by a spirited push of pikes, drove the covenanters back into the town.

> This charge they gave with such undaunted courage and resolution, as the main body of the foot battalion gave backe, and loseing their ground, could not be keepe in order, altho Delgatie, Ludquhaird and his sonne, Sir William Keith, all these three streive to incourage them, first by faire persuasione, and then by threttings, to reallie them, but all in vaine.[5]

Most of the covenanter foot fled westwards into open country and Johnstone forbade pursuit, lest the mounted covenanters should regroup and attempt to counter-attack. For a few more minutes street fighting continued, centred on the house of the earl of Erroll, from which musketeers continued to fire from the upper windows. The cannon were brought up to face the house, and after they had roared three or four times, the last defenders surrendered. With their enemies in flight, the royalists turned to the pleasant task of ransacking the houses of known covenanters. Thomas Michell, the minister of Turriff, was discovered hiding inside his church at the western end of the street, 'disgwysed in a womans habite ... lurkinge above the syling of the churche, whilst the souldiours wer discharging volleyes of shotte within the churche and piercing the syling with ther bullets'.[6] Like the other inhabitants of the town, Michell was forced to sign the King's Covenant.

There seem to have been few casualties during the affray, which suggests that there was little hand-to-hand fighting. James Gordon, minister of Rothiemay, recorded that two covenanters and one royalist were killed, the latter having been shot accidently by one of his fellows. Several others were wounded and the lairds of Skene and Echt were taken prisoner.

With hopes and ambitions soaring after their little victory, the royalists turned south towards Aberdeen, plundering covenanter's estates as they went. There they were joined by the young Lord Lewis Gordon at the head of one thousand Highlanders, including the Farquharsons of Deeside and the Gordons of Glenlivet, armed with ancient muskets, swords and even bows and arrows.[7] Lowlanders of whatever sympathy had good reason to dread such an invasion, but the Gordons were still hesitant to escalate the war further by striking southwards into the Mearns, lest harm should befall the hostage marquis of Huntly. And while they dithered, Montrose, the Earl Marischal and the northern covenanters reoccupied Aberdeen on 25 May.

This time, the town was treated more severely. A fine of 10,000 merks (£6,666 Scots) was levied and some property was pillaged. Aberdeen's street dog population was put to the sword since some royalist wags had demonstrated their feelings towards the occupying forces by dressing the animals in ribbons of covenanting blue.[8] Montrose was, however, able to resist the demands of those extremists among his colleagues who demanded that the whole troublesome town be burned to the ground.

Events now began to escalate rapidly. The best part of the covenanter force was suddenly recalled to deal with the worsening situation further south and, soon afterwards, James Gordon, Viscount Aboyne, accompanied by the earls of Glencairn and Tullibardine, sailed into Aberdeen harbour bearing the King's Commission. At last royalist North East had a figurehead behind whom the king's men could rally. Aberdeen was once more in royalist hands, and the king's grand design could at last begin.

The hill and the bridge

Viscount Aboyne commanded about 2,500 men including a rather reluctant contingent from Aberdeen 'who never wer burdenit with like bussines befoir'. It was not a very happy army; the wild Highland caterans and the Aberdonians hated each other. Furthermore, one Colonel William Gunn had been wished on Aboyne by Charles I—his sole contribution to the northern royalists. The appointment of Gunn as military advisor proved a disaster. Indeed this officer was so spectacularly incompetent that the puzzled Gordons afterwards credited him with treachery. Unfortunately, Gunn had a great influence over the young and inexperienced Aboyne. The royalists do not appear to have formed any clear strategy: most of them had risen in arms simply to avoid being disarmed by the covenanters and forced to sign the covenant.[9] With Gunn's help, Aboyne seems to have cobbled up a vague plan to lead his raggletaggle army southwards, but his objectives are unclear.

On 14 June, the army crossed the Dee and, after a days march, camped at Muchalls Castle. The country folk fled before them with all their 'best goods' to the safety of Dunnottar Castle. Resuming their march early the next day, the royalists halted on a heath two miles north of Stonehaven. Aboyne and Gunn decided to offer battle to the covenanters at Dunnottar, under the Earl Marischal and Montrose, and their troops were marshalled in battle order. The vanguard was given to a company of 100 gentlemen volunteers with red hankerchiefs tied to their lances, while the foot were placed in the centre with Gordon horse on either flank. Wisely, Aboyne decided to separate the Highlanders from the rest of the force, and placed them at the rear. As the men were being deployed into ranks, the first of a series of disasters struck. Whilst priming his musket, a foot soldier carelessly dropped a burning length of match onto a large heap of gunpowder. The resultant explosion caused 'his owne great hurt and (also) many of the bystanders, who wer thereby miserably scortched faces and clothes: some had ther eyes neer lost'.[10] A worse mishap soon followed. The wind changed and the three royalist supply ships which had followed the army south were forced to bear off seawards, taking all their cannon and much powder and shot with them. This failed to deter Colonel Gunn, who ordered a general advance to the brow of Megray Hill, within cannon shot of Stonehaven. What he hoped to achieve there must remain unknown; he and Aboyne went off for a late breakfast.

The royalist troops were soon made uncomfortably aware that the covenant troops marching out of Stonehaven towards them had brought the two brass 'cartows' of Dunnottar—twenty pounder siege cannons, each weighing three-quarters of a ton—as well as several smaller pieces of ordnance.[11] The royalists had no reply to these since their own artillery was literally at sea. Colonel Johnstone interrupted Gunn's breakfast to ask for permission to engage the enemy advance guard with a troop of horse. Consent was grudgingly given, and Johnstone impatiently led a small detachment of horse towards Stonehaven. At the little fish toun of Cowie, he encountered a superior patrol of mounted covenant troops and, after an exchange of pistol fire, was driven off. Montrose and the Earl Marischal assembled their 1,200 foot and horse at the base of Megray hill, with their artillery in a forward position. The hapless royalists, standing motionless on the hill-top, were sitting ducks. The cannons roared and the Earl Marischal 'stentit his cartowis and ordinans just in thair faces and began most furiouslie to play upone the army'. Fortunately for the royalists, the covenanter's guns were firing uphill and had difficulty in setting the range: 'Some balles went over them... some fell short and but one lighted amongst them, whereby some were hurt and some slaine, but not many'.[12]

That was nevertheless enough for the Highlanders at the back, who hated and feared 'the musket's mother' above all things. They broke and ran, pausing on their way home to lay waste the Earl Marischal's lands in Strachan, where they 'took horss, nolt [cattle] and scheip to the wrak of the countrie people'.[13] With his army dissolving before his eyes, Aboyne sounded the retreat and the remains of the unhappy force wandered disconsolately back to Aberdeen. Casualties were light, but few royalists could have retained much confidence in their leaders. Most of them would probably have agreed with James Gordon, minister of Rothiemay, that the rout of Megray Hill was 'so ridiculously and grossly managed that in all the warre, nothing can be recounted lycke it'.

By the time Aboyne reached the Brig o' Dee, little remained of his erstwhile army except for 180 Gordon horse, a company under James Grant and a handful of foot. In pursuit were Montrose and the Earl Marischal who, strengthened with contingents from Angus and Dundee as well as by the Forbes and the Frasers from the North East, now commanded 2,000 foot soldiers and 300 horse. They also brought with them their powerful artillery train. Aboyne hoped to hold the Brig o' Dee against the covenanters long enough to raise fresh troops. The baillies of Aberdeen had raised a scratch force of 100 Aberdonians to support Colonel Johnstone in the defence of the Brig. It was arranged that they should stand guard in twelve-hour shifts of fifty men at a time.

The bridge was then, as now, an imposing structure, spanning the river in seven ribbed arches of granite. Above each pier was a recess for the safety of pedestrians, and at the southern end there was a large stone port or gatehouse, crowned with a pair of turrets. The defences were further strengthened by a trench and barricade of 'faille and thatch' rapidly thrown up in front of the gatehouse. The river was swollen by rainwater, and impassable for cavalry for many miles upstream. To take Aberdeen, the covenanters had first to storm the bridge.

The royalists were not kept waiting long. Just before sunrise on 18 June the covenanter horse passed over the hill of Kincorth on the south bank of the Dee and engaged Aboyne's cavalry outposts in front of the gatehouse. The musketeers manning the bridge defences took up their positions. As Montrose's main force began to arrive, Aboyne withdrew his cavalry across the Dee where they dismounted and took cover. Montrose deployed his troops out of musket range on the higher ground south of the bridge, and placed his artillery well forward to bear down on the defences. Then both sides settled down to shoot it out. Once again, the two 'veray feirfull' cartows roared, hurling their twenty pound shot against the masonry of the gatehouse. The defenders gave answering fire with four small field guns transferred from the town, but 'which did littill service'. The Aberdeen musketeers managed to put up quite a creditable defence. Throughout the long June day the continuous crackle of musket fire was punctuated by dull blasts from the cartows and the whine of ricochetting musket balls; smoke and dust clouds swirled around the gatehouse as flying chunks of earth and masonry blew into the river.

The spectacle of the battle attracted crowds of spectators from Aberdeen, who were soon hard at work serving the defenders with refreshments:

> Women and servants wer become so couragiouse that, after two or three hours
> service they, misregarding cannon and muskett shotte, went and came to the
> bridge with provision and necessairs for ther friends and relationes.[14]

Thus encouraged by their friends and relations, the defenders successfully
repelled an attempt to storm the bridge by two companies of Dundee foot
and drove them back, 'seconded with the whooping and hallowing of such as
wer looking on'. By the end of the days fighting, the men of Aberdeen still held
the bridge. The accuracy of the shooting on either side may be judged from the
day's casualties: two. One townsman, John Forbes, had been shot dead through
the head; one other had been injured, 'rakleslie schot' in the foot.[15]

For the first time in his brief military career Montrose was being worsted
and he did not like the experience. During the brief hours of darkness he
moved his cannon closer to the bridge and levelled them against the gatehouse.
He need not have worried. Early on the morning of 19 June, fifty of the
Aberdonian defenders of the bridge—half their total force and almost the
entire 'shift'—decided to quit the battle for the time being, in order to
accompany the body of the late John Forbes back to the town and attend his
funeral in the toun kirk. Spalding, in a restrained understatement, remarks
that this was 'veray unwyslie done'. And so the bridge was manned only by
a skeleton defence when Montrose renewed the assault. This time his cannon
fire was much more accurate, but at first Johnstone and his men 'wonderfullie
stood out and defendit the bridge albeit cruellie chargit both with cartow and
muskat schot in grete aboundans'.

Montrose decided to attempt to draw Aboyne's horse away, in preparation
for a frontal assault on the bridge. He ordered his own horse to move
westwards along the south bank of the Dee and make a pretence at crossing
the river. The Dee could not possibly be forded and it must have been a fairly
obvious ruse, but Colonel Gunn rose to the occasion once more and ordered
the whole of the royalist horse to keep pace with the enemy on the south
bank of the river. As they emerged from shelter and galloped frantically
away, Montrose played his guns on them. A well-aimed cannon ball won
John Seton of Pitmedden a place in the ballads: 'he was shotte deade, most
pairt of his body above the saddel being carryd away and quashed by ane
canon shott'.[16] His family coat of arms thereafter depicted a heart dripping
blood.

Once the royalist horse had disappeared over the horizon, Montrose
opened up a tremendous fire on the bridge. Great chunks of granite masonry
flew off the shattered turrets of the gatehouse and finally an entire wall gave
way. The gallant Johnstone was 'half buryd in the ruine and broke his lig'.
At this critical moment, the covenanting vanguard under Major Middleton
stormed the barricade. Johnstone, realising that further resistance was hopeless, gave the order to retire: 'Do for yourselves, and haste ye to the toun'.
By four o'clock in the afternoon, covenanting colours were flying from the
bridge. By the time Gunn, Aboyne and the royalist horse reappeared, blown
and sweaty after their futile chase, the bridge had already fallen. They took
one look and made off without a blow being struck.

The casualties of the battle were remarkably light: Spalding claims that only four Aberdonians and one covenanter were slain,[17] although 'sum others' were wounded (and he may have omitted any non-Aberdonian casualties). Spalding was very proud of the performance of the Aberdeen musketeers: 'it is said our Abirdeins men wes praisit evin of thair enemeis for thair service and reddie fyre'.

When the covenanters entered Aberdeen for the third time in less than five months, the townsfolk must have expected the worst. To his credit, Montrose once again refused to commit the burgh to the flames, this time with considerable difficulty, and also managed to restrain his army from wholesale pillage. This merciful gesture was later to be held against him by the mad Mullahs of the covenant. The covenanters were quartered in the city for three days and the town was fined another 7,000 merks.[18] Those who had taken part in the defence were rounded up and thrown into the town tolbooth, bound 'in disgraceful manner', where they received 'neither meat, drink, nor candle nor bed'.

A day or two later, a ship sailed into the harbour bearing the news that the war was already over. The covenanters and King Charles had reached agreement at the Pacification of Berwick, and a truce had actually been signed before the battle at the bridge. Montrose released his prisoners at once and the covenanter army prepared to march away south on 21 June. The Aberdeen townsfolk breathed a sigh of relief. They must have fervently hoped they had now seen the last of Montrose. Alas, a much more serious encounter awaited them, five years hence.

As for Colonel Gunn, he made his way to Berwick and delivered *his* account of the battle to the king in person: the gallant Gunn had led 300 royalists to victory over the covenanters, had shot holes in Montrose's hat and had singed the hair of the Earl Marischal.[19] After this triumphant report, he fades from history.

The Brig o' Dee today

The bridge, which was already a venerable object in 1639, is of course still with us today, albeit in modified form. Plans for a stone bridge at this point on the river had first been discussed in 1384, when a public fund was established for the purpose, but not until 1459 was a master of works appointed and even then the plan fizzled out. Council deliberations seem to have been quite leisurely then, even by today's standards. In 1509, Bishop Elphinstone, the founder of Aberdeen University, took an active interest in the project and supervised the design of the bridge but another twenty years went by before the construction work was completed in 1527, under Elphinstone's successor, Bishop Gavin Dunbar. The master-builder was one Thomas Franche, later master-mason to King James V. The contemporary coats of arms of the king and the two bishops are still to be seen inscribed in stone between the seven great arches of the bridge.

The port or gatehouse, with its turrets and watch tower, was constructed at the southern end of the bridge in 1595 and it was this structure, rather than the bridge itself, which bore the brunt of Montrose's guns. The port was removed in 1773 and no trace of it now remains. It is interesting that there are no visible marks of the battle on the bridge today. The arches of the bridge were partly rebuilt during major repairs between 1719 and 1723 and, in 1842, the bridge was widened from its original sixteen and a half feet to twenty-eight feet, to cater for the heavier traffic now flowing into the town. The parapets of the bridge are comparatively modern. Despite these alterations, the structure of the bridge is fundamentally unchanged and it is still as splendid a battle monument as one could desire; the addition of a commemorative plaque to the brave Aberdonians of 1639 would not be out of place.

The rising ground above the south bank where the covenanting army observed the battle was long known as Covenanter's Fauld and cannonballs have occasionally been ploughed out of the ground. After the Second World War, the field was built over, and the housing estates of Kincorth now cover the ground. Modern streets such as Covenanters Drive, Faulds Crescent, Pitmedden Crescent and Montrose Drive are reminders of the battle.

CHAPTER 12

JUSTICE MILLS (OR ABERDEEN)

Loving Friends ... [I] require you render and give up your town, in the behalf of his Majesty; otherwise that all old persons, women and children, do come out and retire, and that those who remain may expect no quarter.

I am as you deserve,
                    MONTROSE.

The period between the Pacification of Berwick in June 1639 and the early autumn of 1644 was theoretically a time of peace for the burgh of Aberdeen, but these five years were probably among the most miserable in its history. From May 1640 to February 1642, Aberdeen was garrisoned by covenanting troops, whose 'daylie deboshing, drinking, nicht-walking, combating and sweiring' were a source of continual complaint. The Calvinist severity of the church courts re-enforced the prevailing gloom. After the departure of the garrison in 1642, the city was left to its own devices for a further two years, but the troops returned in 1644 after a brief and abortive occupation by royalist forces under the marquis of Huntly that spring. By this time, the townsfolk were subdued into unwilling obedience to the covenant. Like most comparatively prosperous Scots, they hoped to sit out 'the Troubles' without further destruction to their property and livelihoods.

The precarious peace was shattered in the late days of August 1644 when the marquis of Montrose raised the king's standard in Atholl. With a small and threadbare army of Catholic Irishmen and Highlanders, he routed the covenanters of Perth at the battle of Tippermuir, on 1 September, and captured the town. After Tippermuir, Montrose's first objective was to secure the principal northern towns for the king. He first marched on Dundee but, finding that well-defended city too difficult to attack, struck north towards Aberdeen where he probably entertained hopes of a more friendly reception. Since Huntly's spring rebellion, the iron hand of Kirk and Covenant had lain heavily on Aberdeen and the North East. After the Sunday sermon on

8 September, the ministers of the Kirk called for a muster to arms of every able-bodied man in the North East between sixteen and sixty. Around 2,500 men reported for duty from the four wards of Aberdeen, many of them 'harllt out sore against their willis to fight aganist the Kingis Liuetennant'.[1] They were armed and sent out to the Links for drill under the command of Major Arthur Forbes. Their moral fibre was stiffened by reliable covenanting officers and a regiment of foot from Fife, which had garrisoned the city since the spring. Their reaction to the news of the massacre of the covenanter foot at the battle of Tippermuir is, unfortunately, unrecorded.

Montrose gained few recruits as he passed northwards through the Mearns. The Ogilvies came in at the head of a squadron of horse but most visitors to his camp spoke him fair, promised their support, went home and, in one writer's words, 'shut their doors until the royalists were far away'.[2] On 11 September, the royalist army reached the Dee. The Brig o' Dee was held against them and, perhaps with memories of the trouble he had had with the bridge five years earlier, Montrose turned west, fording the river near the Mills of Drum and enjoying the hospitality of Sir Thomas Burnett at Crathes Castle, before continuing the march towards Aberdeen the next day. The army camped by the Twa Mile Cross in what is now the suburb of Garthdee. As the royalist soldiers cleaned and primed their weapons, and the rabble of womenfolk and camp-followers prepared meals over the camp fires, the harvest moon rose as 'reid as blood, two houis befoir his tyme'.[3] The onlookers must also have recalled that the next day was Friday the thirteenth and likely to be unlucky for some.

On the following morning, Montrose set about observing the customs of war. Approaching the town from the south west, he sent a herald and a drummer boy under flag of truce to bear his declaration to the city fathers. This hastily scrawled message, a draft of which still survives, summoned the town to surrender. Its substance was brief and to the point:

> Loveing freindes,
>   Being heir for the maintenance of religion and liberty and his Maiesties just authority and servility, thes ar, in his Maiestis name, to requyre yow that immediatly upon the sight heirof yow rander and give up your toune in the behalf of his Maiestie. Otherwayes that all old persons women and children doe come out and reteire themselffis, and that those who stays expect no quarter.
>   I am as you deserve, MONTROSE.

Montrose may have expected the town to surrender and declare for the king; and left to themselves, the provost and baillies would probably have done so. The envoys were conducted to the house of Alexander Findlater by the Green, where they found the provost and his officials assembled, but with the commanding officers of the covenant forces also present and breathing down their necks. While the herald and drummer boy were given refreshments, the provost penned a diplomatic but firm reply, of which, as chance has it, a draft has also survived.

18.   James Graham, 5th earl and 1st marquis of Montrose (1612–50). Victor at Aberdeen and Fyvie in 1644 and Alford in 1645. This engraving was taken from the account of his deeds by his chaplain, George Wishart, first published (in Latin) in Holland in 1647.

Your lordship must have us excused that will not abandonne and render our
toune so lightly, seeing we luik we deserve not censure as being guiltie of the
breatche of any of the afforesaidis poyntis.. bot have beine ever knawin to be
most loyall and dewtiefull subjectis to his maiestie and be Gods grace sall to
our lyves end stryve to contenew so ...

    Your lordship's as ye love us, PROVOST AND BAILLIES OF ABIRDENE.

The drummer boy was tipped a piece of silver and the pair were escorted
back to their lines bearing the town's reply. The polite charade was suddenly
shattered when an unknown musketeer coldly levelled his piece at the drummer boy and shot him dead. The assembled local militia might well have
gasped in horror. The flag of truce had been dishonoured and, if defeated,
they could now expect little mercy from the enemy. Spalding records Montrose's own reaction: 'fynding his drummer agenes the law of nationis, most
inhumanelie slayne, he grew mad and becam furious and impatient ... charge-
ing his men to kill and pardon none'.

    The battle of Justice Mills, also variously known as the battle of Aberdeen
or the 'Craibstane Rout', was fought at the approaches to Aberdeen, between
Justice Mills on the Howburn and the haugh of the Denburn, land which has
long since been built over. We can get an idea of its original appearance from
the map of James Gordon, minister of Rothiemay. Aberdeen was not a walled
town, but was protected on its western approaches by the steep declivity of
Corby Heugh, which was crossed by a single Bow-brig. The road to the town,
known as the Hardgate, was surrounded by tilled land which, on the day of
the battle, bore a ripe crop of oats. The Hardgate rose up a slight eminence
called Clay Hill before crossing the Heugh into the town, and it was on this
rise the covenanting officers formed their men into line. One or more 'cot-
touns' with walled kailyards stood between the hill and the marshy valley of
the Howburn below, and these were manned as strong points by the covenanters, with detachments of pikemen.

    The covenanter army was composed of about 2,000 foot and 500 horse.
Only five days had passed since the muster and, although troops had been
recalled from their garrisons in the country, it is probable that the majority
of the foot were from the garrison and town of Aberdeen. They might have
been better employed manning the gates and other defences of the town as
had been done at Dundee. The garrison had been strengthened by mounted
gentlemen volunteers including Lords Fraser, Crichton of Frendraught and
Forbes of Craigievar. With greater reluctance, Lord Gordon had also obeyed
the levy, but he took his time about it and only eighteen Gordon horse arrived
in time for battle, under the command of his younger brother, the impetuous
Lord Lewis Gordon. The commander of the covenant forces was Lord Bal-
four of Burleigh, by virtue of his position as president of the northern
Committee of Estates. His military experience was limited and his troop
dispositions that day are not entirely clear. The mounted Frasers and Crichtons evidently formed the left wing with Lord Lewis' small squadron on the
right. The mass of foot, armed with muskets and pikes, stood in the centre
while several light cannon were placed in front of the foot. Poor co-ordination

and lack of leadership on the part of the covenanters were to influence the outcome of the battle.

By contrast, the royalist army, which was drawn up in front of the Howburn, was smaller but more experienced and commanded by officers of quality. In the centre, Montrose had placed his three foot regiments of MacDonalds and Irish, led by Alasdair MacCholla, a charismatic giant who was already a living legend among the Gael (often wrongly referred to as 'Colkitto', through confusion with his father). His flank was guarded by small squadrons of cavalry, each supported by 100 musketeers, following the precepts of the Swedish King Gustavus Adolphus. The horse on the left flank were commanded by Colonel James Hay and Nathaniel Gordon, the latter a tough soldier of fortune and a former lieutenant of the marquis of Huntly, who found himself facing some of his Gordon kin on the opposite side of the burn. The right comprised the Ogilvy horse under Lord Airlie and Colonel Sir William Rollo,[4] whilst Montrose and his staff officers took up the classic position of command behind the centre of the front line. A few light cannon captured at Tippermuir were placed along the royalist front, pointing uphill towards the covenanting line. Altogether Montrose commanded some 1,500 foot and 70 horse. Before the battle began, at around 11 o'clock, each man plucked a handful of oats from the surrounding fields and stuck them in their bonnets in order to distinguish friend from foe.

The battle of Justice Mills was fought on one of those damp, overcast autumn days so common on the North East coast. The musketeers must have worried about their powder getting wet and refusing to fire. Spalding recalled that as the covenanter cannon began to roar, 'thair raise ane heighe and michtie wynd out of the wast-south-wast in the bak of the enimy and face of oure people quhilk wes to oure preiudice'. The gun-smoke billowed back towards the covenanter gunners, smarting their eyes and obscuring their view of the field. After the opening exchange of artillery fire, there followed a succession of unco-ordinated attacks by the covenant horse. The first was led by Lord Lewis Gordon who, supported by a score of his fellows, trotted down the hill and fired a series of pistol volleys 'in caracole'—the old-fashioned method of half-wheeling and firing in ranks from the saddle. This manoeuvre was at once stately, noisy and superficially impressive but the experienced royalist officers knew that distant pistol shots from horseback nearly always miss their mark. After using all their pistols the Gordons wheeled and trotted back up the hill. The covenanter left flank under Lords Fraser and Crichton, who refused to associate themselves with the Gordons, now advanced in their turn. According to Gordon of Ruthven, our most detailed source for the battle, they were equally ineffective:

> The right winge of the Royalistes was twyce charged by the lord Fraser, who shewed himself like a brave and valiant gentleman, with whom was the lord Crichtone, but they were repressed, not being seconded with the horsemen tymely; for the barrones of the name of Forbese, with those of Buchan, stood of, not for want of good will to fight, but for want of experience, not knawein that it was there tyme to charge; and this errour came chiefly for want of a general commander, whose ordoures they should obey.[5]

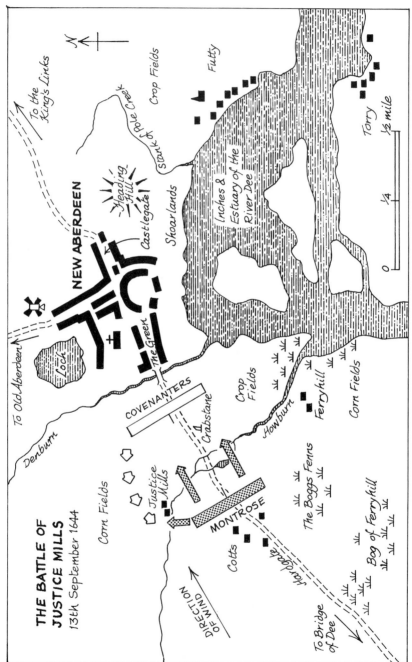

THE BATTLE OF
JUSTICE MILLS
13th September 1644

Map 15.

The Frasers and Crichtons were met by close-range volleys from the royalist musketeers which sent them reeling back in disorder, chased by the Ogilvy horse. In the fighting, Sir Thomas Ogilvy and the earl of Kinnoul were unhorsed and Sir John Drummond wounded by a blow on the head.

Burleigh made no attempt to support the embattled covenanter horse for he was engaged in a complicated plan of his own. Detaching a force of 100 horse and 400 foot, he ordered them to work their way around Montrose's left flank, under cover of a sunken path (probably Justice Mills Lane)[6] hidden behind the rising ground. Making their way around the hollow containing the mills and their ponds, the column passed out of sight of the main battle until they emerged to the rear of Montrose's foot, who had, in the meantime, advanced further forward. Had they fallen on the backs of the royalist soldiers there and then, it is conceivable that this flank attack might have won the day. As it was, they succeeded only in capturing Montrose's stationary cannon and otherwise stood irresolute on the slope of the hill, wondering what to do next. While the covenanters hesitated, one of Montrose's officers, a Captain Mortimer, smartly formed his band of musketeers into line to face them and kept them at bay with a steady, blistering fire. Perceiving the danger to his flank and rear, Montrose transferred 100 musketeers from his right and, led by Nathaniel Gordon, the royalist reinforcements 'joyneing with the few horse they hade, ascends the hill, and routes them, and cutes all there foote in pieces'.[7]

With fierce fighting now taking place on both flanks, William Forbes of Craigievar took advantage of the confusion to launch an attack against the royalist centre. Charging down the hill at the head of his troop of horse, he was astounded to see the veteran Irish foot regiments opening their ranks, allowing the horse to pass harmlessly between them. Forbes and his men were simply 'swallowed up'. As they strove to control their horses, the Irish musketeers turned and fired a volley at their backs. Forbes' men fell like skittles, and the laird himself was pulled from his saddle and made prisoner. This classic infantry response to a cavalry charge required discipline and training, and the credit for its success is probably due to Alasdair MacCholla. Such professionalism was foreign to the amateur army of the covenanters and must have sapped the morale of their remaining horse for this was their last attack.

In the meantime, the Irish regiments were becoming restless under the ceaseless but inaccurate fire of the covenant artillery. In one of the best-known incidents of the battle, an Irishman had his leg nearly severed by a cannon ball. Pulling out his dirk, this stalwart is said to have cut away the remains of the mangled limb, cheerfully remarking that, since he was now useless for the infantry, perhaps the marquis would make him a cavalryman. Tossing the amputated leg to a friend, he added, 'bury that, lest some hungry Scot should eat it'.

With all of their attacks thus blunted, Burleigh and his fellows seem to have run out of steam. Montrose, recognising that the crucial moment of the battle had come, took the offensive. The yards and cot-touns along the Howburn were cleared of the last pockets of resistance and the royalist drums and trumpets sounded a general advance. Casting aside their pikes and muskets, Alasdair's Irish and Highlander regiments swept uphill at a run, with target and claymore. The wavering line of Fife levies and Aberdeen militia, many of whom had 'never been tryed in a day of battell befor', barely had time to advance their pikes and discharge a ragged volley of musket fire before the yelling caterans were upon them. For a few minutes, the ridge of Clay Hill was occupied by a chaotic mass of struggling men, as Highland claymores sliced through wooden pikes and then through muscle and bone. Then the entire covenant line crumbled, and knots of men were throwing down their weapons and fleeing back towards the town. The Aberdeen militia tried at first to retire to the Bow-brig in good order, but the panic was infectious and quickly seized the whole line. Their banner, so proudly borne at Harlaw, was flung away and trodden underfoot. The battle had lasted less than two hours.[8]

Most of the covenant horse got away. For the lairds and gentlemen volunteers who had retained their steeds, their 'general resolution to recover their loss gave way to the private care of each one's safety, which brought them all to a timely flight, although they stayed till they saw the most part of the foot cut off'.[9] Burleigh himself spurred his way towards the Don and thence northwards to his lands in Buchan. For the foot, it was a different story. One source says that the more experienced Fife regiment managed to retire towards the Dee in good order, but that Alasdair detached 400 Irish to seal off their retreat and surround them. Most were killed or taken prisoner.[10] The Aberdeen townsmen had only one thought—to rejoin their families and homes and bolt the doors. Many never returned. The Hardgate was covered with scores of their bodies as they were overtaken by the fleet-footed Irish and cut down. The wounded were finished off with dirks.

Gordon of Ruthven was quite clear in his own mind over what had caused the covenanter's defeat:

> Wee may trewlie say that God, Who would have it thus, send amongst them the spirit of division for punishment of oure sinnes; for the horsemen, being almost composed of lordes, barrones, and gentlemen of qualitie, ware all divided in severall opiniones, for want of a head, whose opinion and order they ought to have followed.

Montrose had promised his troops the sack of Aberdeen. There were no city defences for the defeated forces to hide behind and the Gaels spilled into the cobbled streets, 'hewing and cutting down all maner of man they could overtake within the toune, upone the streites or in thar houssis'.[11] Well-dressed victims had the clothes torn from their bodies so as to preserve them 'onspoyllit' before their owners were dirked. The town's prison or 'correction house' was broken into and the inmates freed. Women unlucky enough to be caught were raped on the spot or sent to the royalist camp for a new life as army kitchen maids or servants. On Aberdeen's Black Friday, writes Spalding, an eye-witness, nothing could be heard 'bot pitifull howling, crying, weiping, murning, throw all the streittis'. An Irish officer exulted: 'The riches of the toun ... hath made all our soldiers cavaliers!'

19. View of Aberdeen from the south west in the mid-seventeenth century, from an engraving at the foot of James Gordon's map of Aberdeen. The viewpoint is near the Crabstane, which was the scene of the conflict of 1571. In 1644 Montrose's victorious army broke into the burgh from this direction after their victory at the Battle of the Justice Mills.

Not all of the royalist forces were of this mind and many remained outside the town that night, where sanity still prevailed. Montrose did not enter Aberdeen until the following day, when he is said to have been dismayed at the destruction and chaos he had let loose. Nevertheless, he set about requisitioning clothing and provisions for his men from whatever was left of Aberdeen's governing body. The burgh records show that the clothing manufacturers in the town's Correction House provided cloth and stockings for his men, four suits for Irish officers and more elaborate attire for Colonel Sibbald and Montrose. By ordering clothing for his men, Montrose may have intended to safeguard the independent weavers and tailors of the burgh for 'utherwayes they wald not be able to saiff the boothes of the toun unplunderit altogidder'.[12] He also ordered the city baillies to set about cleaning up the streets and burying the dead. The evidence suggests, however, that some of the wild Irish, not yet sated by their bloody debauch, roamed the streets inflicting terror all that weekend. On the following Monday, Spalding saw 'two corpis cariet to the buriall throw the Oldtoun with wemen onlie, and not ane man amongst them, so that the naiket corpis lie onburiet so long as this lymmaris (Irish) war ongone to the camp'. After staying in the town at Skipper Anderson's house on Saturday night, Montrose realised that the only way to restore a semblance of order in Aberdeen was to move his army a safe distance away. After a rather hollow proclamation from the mercat cross that he had come to restore the king's subjects to obedience, he shifted his entire force to Kintore.

Modern opinions have varied on the relative enormity of the sack of Aberdeen. One recent biographer of Montrose regards it as 'one of the most unforgivable atrocities of the Scottish war'.[13] Another finds it 'hard to feel that the pillage of Aberdeen was by any contemporary standards a very wicked or dishonourable business'.[14] Contemporaries were, in fact, shocked by it and in direct consequence Montrose won few royalist recruits from Aberdeen and the North East. It was a cruel irony that Aberdeen, the most reluctant town to sign the National Covenant, should in the end have to pay the heaviest price in blood for the covenanting cause. That this price had been extracted by Montrose, the covenanter general at the Brig o' Dee only five years before, deepened that irony.

How many died during the battle and the subsequent pursuit? Our only reliable figures relate to the townsfolk of Aberdeen. The burgh records state that 'eight score' of their citizens were killed while Spalding, who made a special effort to compile a comprehensive list of the dead, perhaps for a roll of honour, records ninety-eight names among a total of 118. These include Matthew Lumsden (a baillie), Thomas Buck (the master of kirkwork), Robert Leslie (the master of hospitals), and so on, through an entire cross-section of seventeenth century town life: merchants, advocates, maltmen, fishermen, millers, websters, a student and a gardener. In addition, adds Spalding, 'sum' country people and Fifeshire soldiers were also slain. Many of these died on the battlefield itself or during the pursuit through the fields and cot-touns of the Dee which followed. Eye-witnesses of the sack of Aberdeen recall seeing only 'several' or, at most, twenty to thirty bodies lying in the streets of the town itself, suggesting that the marauders were more interested in loot than in massacre, although that did not lessen the impact of an event which shocked and appalled the whole of Lowland Scotland, royalist and covenanter alike. The Sack of Aberdeen tarnished the reputation of the 'gentle' Montrose permanently. But on the evidence, it would also appear that contemporary estimates of the death toll at 800 or 1,000 were exaggerated. The royalists covered up their own losses, as victors are wont to do. Montrose is variously stated to have lost between seven and twelve men, with a further twenty or so seriously wounded. These figures should be taken with more than a pinch of salt but it is clear that the royalist losses were relatively small and those of the covenanters correspondingly heavy.

Montrose could not linger at Aberdeen. All considerations of public order apart, he had received news that a large force under the marquis of Argyll was fast approaching. The royalists departed, leaving a handful of drink-sodden, renegade Irish still roaming the streets like hungry wolves. Two days later, the covenanters marched into the shattered town. Spalding relates poignantly that when the surviving townsfolk heard of Montrose's departure, 'mony who lovit the king wes glaid of thir newis, utheris of the covenant was no less sorie'.

The battlefield today

The battlefield of Justice Mills now lies submerged under building stone near the heart of the bustling modern city, and it requires an effort of imagination and a certain amount of street walking to appreciate the main features of the battlefield. Justice Mills and their dams have gone, although old photographs preserve their appearance.[15] The Howe Burn is now piped underground, and the slopes and hollows of the pre-industrial town were shaped and levelled during the great urban expansion of the nineteenth century. To see the battlefield as Montrose saw it, we have to turn to James Gordon's map of 1661, which includes a vignette showing the prospect of the city from the Craibstane, which lay on the eastern flank of the city defenders' lines. Fenton Wyness' plaster models of the early city in Provost Skene's House also help to reconstruct the landscape as it was.

What is left of the battlefield today is best explored on foot. By walking up the Hardgate towards the junction between Justice Mills Lane and Bon Accord Terrace, we are following in the footsteps of Montrose. The city defenders' lines probably lay on the top of the slope above the valley of the Howe Burn where the handsome Regency terrace now lies. The strength of this position can be appreciated by looking up towards the terrace from the open ground of the gardens. Until comparatively recently, the fertile ground of these slopes consisted of gardens and allotments, and this appears to have also been the case at the time of the battle.

The Craibstane, which is mentioned in Spalding's account of the battle, is said to be the massive square stone which now forms part of the wall near the junction of Hardgate and Bon Accord Terrace. Its original function was probably a march stone for the lands of Rubislaw, once owned by the Crab family, but at the time of the battle of Justice Mills it stood in a prominent position on the crest of Clay Hill, south west of the town, on a green used for public gatherings. James Gordon's map shows a taller stone resembling a pillar and some believe in consequence that it is the 'lang stane' in Langstane Place which is the real Craibstone. Be that as it may, the stone in the wall by Hardgate, now surmounted by a commemorative plaque, must be close to the original centre of the covenanter lines.

If one walks westwards from Bon Accord Terrace, down Justice Mills Lane to its junction with Holburn Street, one has crossed the city defenders' position from one end to the other as nearly as is possible today. The western limit of the position is regarded as lying somewhere near the swimming baths and the Odeon cinema.[16] Nearby, on Holburn Street, a road sign points to the scene of Montrose's last and greatest north eastern battle: Alford.

CHAPTER 13

FYVIE

A mater mervalous and wrocht by Godis owne fynger, as wold appeir.

Spalding, *Memorialls.*

The survivors of the sack of Aberdeen may well have given an ironical cheer as the covenanters entered the town, five days too late. Archibald Campbell, marquis of Argyll, had a proclamation read out from the mercat cross, declaring the royalists traitors and rebels, and offering a reward of 30,000 merks (£20,000 Scots) for the capture of Montrose, dead or alive. Despite their brace of victories, Montrose and his following were still hunted men. Their one hope was to raise the Gordons, who, with fresh memories of the events of 1639, had so far shown little enthusiasm to aid Montrose. Argyll was equally determined to prevent any such collaboration from taking place.

Burying the cannon captured at Aberdeen and dumping their surplus baggage, Montrose's little force headed for the hills. Here, at home in their natural haunts, Montrose's irregular Highlander and Irish foot regiments could run circles around any enemy by virtue of prodigious route marches. Argyll showed little inclination to chase them. His main concern was to make quite certain that Montrose would gain no recruits, no sustenance and no arms from the Gordons. Coldly, and with a fanatical zeal which was not altogether impartial, he set about ravaging Strathbogie, leaving a subsiduary force based at Drum to perform a like function in Deeside. Argyll's Campbell regiments fell on the Gordon lands with glee, burning and looting corn stores and houses, and seizing those arms and horses which had not already been purloined by Montrose. When Lord George Gordon, who accompanied Argyll, was moved to angry protest against the destruction, he was blandly assured that it was merely a security precaution, and the Gordons would eventually be recompensed for the damage.

Montrose, in the meantime, was in Speyside, living off the land and attempting, generally without success, to recruit from the pro-royalist clans. In the first week of October, his right-hand man, Alasdair MacCholla, left for the west with two of the three precious Irish regiments, in order to find recruits among his MacDonald kinfolk. Left with a tiny force of 800 foot and 50 horse—scarcely more than a raiding party—Montrose decided to have one more go at activating the Gordons.

Once more Montrose approached Aberdeen, frightening the life out of the townsfolk, but the royalists avoided causing further misery to the town and turned instead to Crathes, where Montrose spent another comfortable short stay with his friend, Sir Thomas Burnett. Striking north from Deeside, the royalists revenged Argyll's detrepidations in Gordon country by pillaging and burning covenanter estates. Echt went up in flames, as did the estates of Lords Forbes and Crichton of Frendraught. But the royalist enthusiasm of the Gordon gentry was at a very low ebb. Their lands had been ravaged twice over in 1644, once following the marquis of Huntly's rising in the spring, and now once more by Argyll's Campbells. They were further restrained by the example of Huntly. A more resolute and self-effacing Cock o' the North might have joined forces with Montrose, but Huntly regarded himself as the only rightful king's lieutenant in the north and was too proud, or too pig-headed, to serve under Montrose, for whom he, in any case, still nursed a grudge. As for Montrose, he had written 'Like Alexander I will reign/And I will reign alone', and he meant it. Thus the king's cause languished between the rivalry of his two greatest Scottish subjects, neither of whom could brook a rival. Few Gordons were willing to act in defiance of their feudal superior's wishes, and thus Montrose gained no more than 200 half-hearted recruits from the North East on this occasion.

Without Gordon support, there was little that Montrose could usefully do except to continue to keep one step ahead of his enemies. On 27 October, for reasons which remain unclear, the royalist army moved east to the wooded vale of the Ythan, where the noble Renaissance castle of Fyvie nestles within a loop in the river. Montrose may have received reports that Argyll's army was again moving north and approaching Strathbogie; by slipping away to the east, he might have hoped to elude them. However Argyll's military intelligence was, on this occasion at least, better than his. The royalists camped by Fyvie Castle on the night of 27 October in imagined security. Early the next morning, the muskets of Montrose's outposted pickets sounded the alarm: Argyll was little more than a mile away and advancing on the camp with a greatly superior force. Poor scouting and a faulty appreciation of the enemy's movements on this occasion, as on many others, were a weakness of Montrose's army. But at such times of crisis, Montrose's match-less qualities of leadership were equal to the occasion. Having been forced to stand and fight a defensive battle against heavy odds, Montrose speedily chose a strong position above the Parkburn glen, on the brae east of the castle. The defences of the castle itself were irrelevant. His Irish and Highland soldiers were not trained for siege warfare, nor was the castle large enough to hold them all. Furthermore, Montrose had to fight a campaign of continuous movement; any attempt to hold a castle or town with limited supplies and little hope of relief would be useless. On the other hand, a use was found for

20. Fyvie Castle. Though the castle dominates the scene of the skirmishes in 1644 between Montrose and the covenanters, it evidently played no part in the fighting.

the pewter vessels within the castle. Since the royalists' stock of musket balls had run dangerously low, the Fyvie pewterware went into the melting pot: reconstituted chamberpot saved the life of many a royalist at the battle of Fyvie.[1]

The vanguard of Argyll's army was approaching the south bank of the Ythan as the royalists dug in on the hillside near the castle. 'The ground here was rough and uneven; and there were besides several dykes and ditches upon it which had been raised by the farmer as a fence to their enclosures and made the appearance of a camp'.[2] Montrose's left flank was protected by a wood, probably the heugh of Parkburn (where the place-name 'Old Wood' still survives) and his right by the steep slopes overlooking the castle from the east. In addition, the approach from the 'Castle Dale' was marshy and bisected by the Park burn, making life difficult for the covenanter horse. Montrose evidently kept his own few horse in reserve and probably corralled them behind his lines, somewhere on the plateau near today's Parkburn Farm. All in all, it was a well chosen site, ideal for defence by entrenched musketeers. It needed to be, for Montrose's little force found themselves outnumbered by at least three to one.

As Montrose's Irish musketeers made last minute improvements to their defences, Argyll's assembled army crossed the Ythan, using the wooden bridge, which is marked on a map of 1654. They drew up out of the range of musket shot in the Castle Dale. With 2,500 foot and 1,000 horse at his disposal,[3] Argyll lost no time in launching an attack. He sent in his best assault troops, the tough regiment of the earl of Lothian, supported by a squadron of cavalry. As the covenanters struggled up the rough slope, Montrose's Gordon volunteers threw down their arms and fled. The Irish regiment poured musket fire into the approaching pikes, endeavouring to make every bullet count. The Lothians stormed up through the whins and thickets and their assault broke over the dikes. In fierce hand-to-hand fighting with musket butts, swords and pikes, the Irish were forced back from their prepared positions by sheer weight of numbers. The earl of Lothian wrote that 'at least fifteen or sixteen' royalists were killed, including (and this pleased him particularly) Robert Keith, the royalist brother of the Earl Marischal.[4]

Montrose waited until the Lothian assault had lost its momentum before ordering a counter-attack. A band of Irish foot, held in reserve, charged yelling down the hill and, as usual, they were irresistible. The covenanter horse, hampered by the ditches and dikes, could do little to aid their foot soldiers and, after more stiff fighting, the Lothians were driven back down the slope, leaving the bodies of dozens of their comrades draped over the dikes or sprawled in the trenches. The Irish fell to cutting off the powder flasks—and cutting the throats—of the fallen and replenishing their dwindling supply of shot. The leader of the successful Irish counter-charge is variously stated to have been Magnus O'Cahan, Montrose's most dependable Irish officer, or Donald Farquharson, a popular figure who was evidently accepted by Irishman and Highlander alike.[5]

Thereafter the battle developed into stalemate. Argyll attempted to attack the royalist flank but his advance was checked by accurate Irish musketry and repelled by Nathaniel Gordon's small detachment of horse. By nightfall, the royalist position remained intact, and Argyll withdrew his battered army to camp across the river.

Our main sources are in apparent contradiction for the events of the following day. According to Wishart, the fighting was renewed, but repeated covenant charges failed even to dent the royalist position. Gordon of Ruthven states, on the other hand, that the covenanter army 'was not sein to appear in the fields'. Perhaps our most reliable witness is the earl of Lothian, who himself led much of the fighting at Fyvie. He explains that his men tried but failed to draw the royalists from their prepared positions. On balance, it is probable that Argyll and Lothian changed their tactics on 29 October, and abandoned frontal assault in favour of skirmishes designed to lure the royalists into the open. Their failure was total on both counts for Montrose's veterans did not rise to the bait and stayed where they were. Running short of provisions, Argyll withdrew his dispirited army on the morning of the 30th. Evidently neither he nor most of his men had the stomachs for any more fighting.

Lothian recorded his disgust at the outcome: 'I wish I were disengaged,

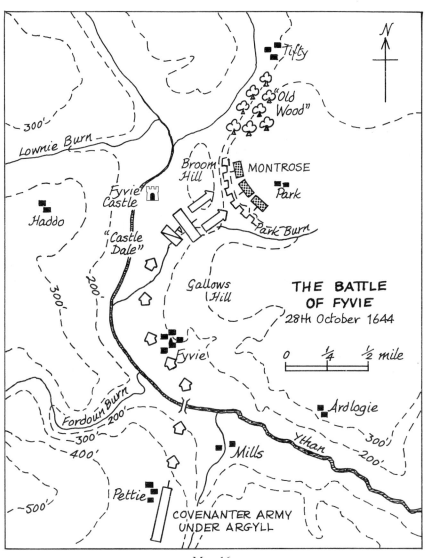

Map 16.

but I must bide it out'.[6] Spalding voices the astonished popular reaction to the news of yet another royalist victory against the odds: 'a mater mervalous and wrocht by Godis owne fynger as wold appeir'. Not surprisingly, the battle of Fyvie soon entered the ballads. A 'Bonnie Lass o' Fyvie', we learn, had fallen in love with an Irish dragoon captain, who was mortally wounded in the battle and died shortly afterwards, whereupon the broken-hearted bonnie lass was left to mourn alone. Whether there is any grain of truth in the story it is difficult to say, but if so it must have been a whirlwind romance for Montrose's men spent only a single night at Fyvie before the battle.

After the battle, Montrose retraced his steps to Strathbogie Castle where, after a minor skirmish, Argyll offered a truce. The experience of Fyvie had temporarily humbled the great Argyll and, after retiring to Edinburgh, both he and Lothian resigned their commissions. The vote of thanks for Argyll's services praised him for 'shedding so little blood'. To a modern ear, this sounds more than a little sarcastic.

With winter drawing in, Montrose retired to base at Blair Castle in Atholl. His greatest successes still lay in the future. Fyvie was a minor affair which has not passed into the canonical six victories of Montrose's 'Year of Miracles', although the royalists probably lost more men there than at Justice Mills. It did however, illustrate one of Montrose's greatest personal qualities: the ability to rescue a potentially disastrous situation and turn it into a victory. It was also an ominous portent of his Achilles heel—the often poor scouting and faulty intelligence which was to bring disaster on his loyal soldiers a year later at Philiphaugh.

Fyvie today

The chief ornament to the battlefield is Fyvie Castle itself, which Sir Herbert Maxwell called 'the crowning glory of Scottish baronial architecture'. The appearance of the earl of Dunfermline's masterpiece has not changed greatly since 1644. Montrose's position probably lay on the slopes between Broom Hill and Parkburn Farm, just north of the defile of the Park Burn. The remains of a field system on the western slope facing onto Fyvie Castle is called 'Montrose's Camp'. It is unlikely that these are the remains of the hastily contrived fortifications put up by the Irish soldiers on the day of the battle, but they may well be the remains of the enclosures mentioned by Wishart and if so they accurately mark the position of the battlefield. Fyvie Castle has recently been acquired by the National Trust for Scotland and is now open to the public.

CHAPTER 14

ALFORD

Like Alexander I will reign,
And I will reign alone,
My thoughts shall evermore disdain
A rival on my throne.
He either fears his fate too much,
Or his deserts are small,
That puts it not unto the touch
To win or lose it all.

From *I'll Never Love Thee More*,
by James Graham, Marquis of Montrose.

The seven months which separate the battle of Fyvie from that of Alford
saw the royalist prospects in Scotland transformed from hopelessness to
expectancy by the genius of Montrose, aided by his 'company of the worst
men in the earth', as the fleeing covenanters liked to call them. They achieved
what was held to be impossible by raiding the fastnesses of Argyll in mid-
winter and slaughtering the Campbells in the snow at Inverlochy. In February
1645 Montrose at last drew out the Gordons: he was joined at Elgin by Lord
George Gordon at the head of 200 Strathbogie horse. Since the destruction
of their lands and property the previous autumn, Gordon's resentment of the
covenanters had sharpened. The news of Montrose's successes encouraged
many of his kin to rally behind the royalist cause once more, although the
marquis of Huntly himself still refused to have anything to do with Montrose.
For the first time, the royalists possessed a respectable force of cavalry and
could break out from the hills. On 9 May Montrose defeated a covenanter
army under Sir John Hurry at Auldearn, near Nairn. For a while he commanded the strongest field army in Scotland, but two factors prevented him
from realising his grand strategy of striking south into the Lowlands. Firstly
many Highlanders had drifted away after the Auldearn victory, anxious
for the safety of their families and homes. Secondly, there was one more

covenanting army in the north which was still undefeated and on which he could not afford to turn his back. This army was led by Major General William Baillie.

Unlike many of his fellow generals, Baillie was a professional soldier. He had served under King Gustavus Adolphus in Europe and in the Scots army in England, where he had fought at Marston Moor. He was an experienced and methodical if not exactly inspired commander. He took over from Argyll as the nominal Commander-in-Chief of the covenanting army in Scotland in late 1644, after the fiasco at Fyvie. He did not relish the task and, as a commoner, was vulnerable to the relentless bullying of the Kirk Ministers and the Committee of the Estates, which often forced him to take actions which his professional instincts knew to be unwise.

During the early summer of 1645, Montrose dogged the covenanters' steps, but Baillie managed to avoid battle; by keeping Montrose in the north, his force was providing precious time for a new army to be raised. His good judgement was not matched by the committee politicians and zealots of the kirk, who continually put him under pressure to attack. Despite their unbroken record of defeat, the covenanters adhered stubbornly to the belief that Montrose's men were scum, mere brigands led by 'James Graham, that viperous brood of Satan'. It was Baillie's duty, as the Joshua of Kirk and Covenant, to purge Scotland of this spawn of Anti-Christ. Victory lay in divine will, not in military considerations. It was in this spirit that the covenanters now committed two fatal blunders. They forced Baillie to give up 1,000 of his best troops for an irrelevant raid into Atholl, in return for 400 raw recruits. And they supposed, against plentiful evidence to the contrary, that with the temporary absence of the dreaded Alasdair MacCholla and some of the Irish, Montrose would wish to avoid a fight. These miscalculations led to the battle of Alford.

On hearing of the sudden departure of the best part of Baillie's infantry, Montrose broke camp at Corgarff Castle and marched north. On 27 June, he caught up with Baillie at what is now the town of Keith. Baillie's foot took up a strong defensive position on a hilltop overlooking Strathisla, flanked by horse and guns. Montrose declined to attack under such unfavourable circumstances, and the following day the royalists withdrew south towards the Don. To the Committee men of the covenant this was clear proof that Montrose would not fight without Alasdair, that he was now in retreat and that Baillie should therefore go after him and bring him to battle. This is what Montrose wanted them to think. After two days march, Montrose crossed over the Correen Hills via the old Suie road and reached the Howe of Alford, fording the Don at the Boat of Forbes, where the Bridge of Alford stands today. Here, he found what he was looking for: a battlefield. Above the ford and the marshes of the Don valley rose a low ridge known as Gallows Hill. Montrose saw the possibilities of such a position. Whilst the royalists made camp for the night of 1 July, by the tiny kirk-toun of Alford, Montrose reconnoitred the banks of the Don east and west of the ford. Having satisfied himself that the Boat of Forbes was the only place where the pursuing covenanters could cross the river, Montrose retired to bed, probably spending the short summer night at Asloun Castle.[1] Alford was the first battle in which Montrose was able to choose his own ground and his position was a very strong one. The boggy flats by the Don gave little room for an enemy to manoeuvre and the royalist rear was protected from a flank attack by the hollow of the Leochel Burn and a 'marsh intersected by ditches and dikes'.[2]

Baillie's army approached the Don on the morning of 2 July to find the rearguard of the royalist army standing to arms on the crest of Gallows Hill. Montrose had kept the bulk of his army out of sight behind the hill: he was inviting attack. From Baillie's viewpoint, the prospects seemed quite favourable. By crossing the Don and sending his horse on ahead he might outflank the retreating royalists and pin them against the river. His professional instincts might have caused him to hesitate, but, with his more precipitate colleagues, particularly Lord Balcarres, the cavalry commander, urging him on, Baillie cast aside any doubts and his army began to ford the Don.

Montrose waited until Baillie's horse and part of his foot were across the river and thus committed. Then the royalist drums began to beat and the main body of the army formed up on the crest of the hill in battle order. Balcarres' three squadrons of horse, which had already advanced about half a mile from the ford, were hastily brought to a halt. The unhappy covenanters

21.   View north from Gallows Hill of the battlefield of Alford, 1644.

now realised, too late, that Montrose was not retreating after all. He had instead forced them to fight on unfavourable ground and now he had them on toast.

Baillie ordered his troops to form a line with their backs to the Don marshes, falling into position as they crossed the ford. His foot were marshalled into ranks, three deep, and they entrenched themselves as well as they could behind the dikes and enclosures at the edge of the bog. Balcarres' three squadrons of horse stood where they had been given the order to halt, rather in advance of the left flank of the covenanting infantry, whilst the smaller cavalry rearguard drew up on the right. Baillie's army numbered a little under 2,000 foot and 600 horse.[3] Not much could be expected of the former. Ill-trained levies as most of them were, Baillie cannot have set much store by them. His main hope lay with Balcarres' horse, reputedly the strongest cavalry regiment in the kingdom.

For the first and only time in his year of miracles, Montrose faced an enemy with near-equal strength. He was actually superior in infantry with over 2,000 foot but possessed only 260 horse.[4] His line of battle stretched over a frontage of about 800 yards with the foot in the centre and the flanking cavalry squadrons strengthened, as usual, by companies of musketeers. The foot were the usual polyglot mixture of Irish, Gordon and Highlander regiments—MacDonalds, MacPhersons, MacLeans, Farquharsons and Atholl men—led, in the absence of Alasdair, by Eneas MacDonald of Glengarry.[5] They were ranked in files, six deep.[6] Lord George Gordon commanded the horse on the right, facing Balcarres, while his brother, Lord Aboyne, led those on the left. Montrose could, for once, afford the luxury of a reserve of foot which he placed in the hands of his twenty year-old nephew, the master of Napier. Montrose took up his customary position by the royal standard, behind the centre of the front line, with a cluster of staff officers around him. This same army had time and again defeated forces of two or three times their number. On superior ground with roughly equal forces, there could be no real doubt as to the outcome this time.

Montrose probably intended to wait and see if Baillie would attack him. As often happened, however, the battle began in an unrehearsed and unexpected way. The royalists spied a great cloud of dust on the Suie road in the rearguard of the covenanter army. Word went about that the dust hid a great herd of cattle, all stolen from Gordon lands during the spring and summer. With thoughts of their starving families and ruined estates foremost in their minds, the right wing of the Gordon horse charged downhill in a body. Balcarres spurred forward two of his three squadrons to meet them. The two forces crashed into each other at a point close to the present day cemetery, and seconds later 500 horses were locked together in a confused, dusty melee. Fighting to control their thrashing, maddened steeds, the cavalrymen wildly fired their pistols and carbines in all directions. They were crushed so close together 'that none could advance a foot or a nail's breadth but over the body of his foe, whilst retreat was impossible, so great was the crush of men pressing on behind'.[7] In their midst was Lord Gordon, who had sworn to bring back General Baillie 'by the neck'. The supporting royalist musketeers

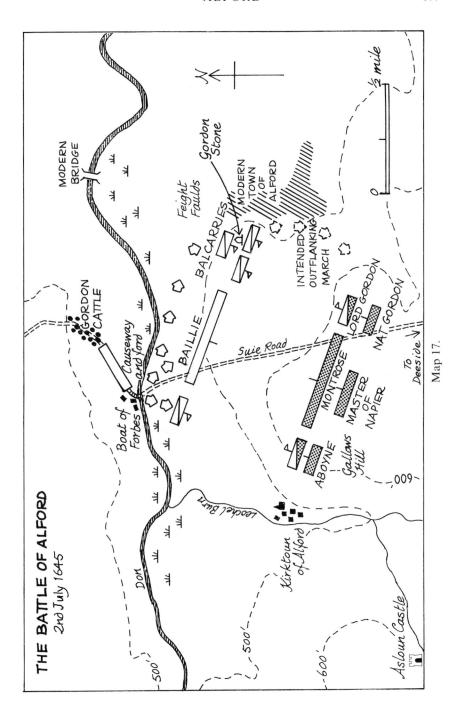

THE **BATTLE** OF **ALFORD**
2nd July 1645

Map 17.

under Major Nathaniel Gordon hung helplessly on the periphery of the fighting, barely able to tell friend from foe. Finally, Gordon told his men to discard their muskets and go for the underbellies of the covenanter horse with their dirks.

By this time, the Gordon horse were in difficulties. Baillie had kept a third squadron of horse back in reserve and, properly used, they might have posed a serious threat. Unfortunately for Baillie, matters went astray. We have his own words for what happened:

> ... the third (squadron) appointed for reserve, when I commanded them to second my Lord (Balcarres) and charge the enemies horse in the flank, they went straight up in their comrades reare, and there stood untill they were all broken.[8]

In the meantime the cavalrymen had run out of ammunition and were attempting to seize each other by the head and beat each other's brains out with their pistol butts. Nat Gordon's musketeers had bravely waded in, dodging the flying hooves, and were now engaged in the cruel business of hamstringing the covenanter horse and slicing open their bellies. Covenant troopers, falling or being pulled from their saddles, were crushed by the screaming horses or stabbed by the Irish. Soon Balcarres horse were forced to give ground and the less bold took safety in flight.

On the royalist left, Aboyne's horse charged downhill 'with a fearelesse and hardie resolution'.[9] Here the opposition was more quickly despatched and the enemy horse were soon in flight. Those unlucky enough to be unhorsed or left floundering in the bog were knifed by the following Irish foot who, according to Gordon of Ruthven, performed their task 'with too little compassion and too much crueltie, no quarters being granted'.

Montrose was now ready for the coup de grace. He unleashed the clans, and once more the wretched Lowland levies were subjected to the experience of a Highland charge. The Highlanders poured down the hill in a mass and seconds later were clubbing and hacking their way over the dikes and breaking the thin covenanter line. At the same time, part of the Gordon horse on the left wheeled and charged the covenant foot in the rear thus enveloping the enemy in the flank. General Baillie, who was, by this time, preparing for flight, gives us one last piece of technical information:

> Our foot stood with myself and behaved themselves as became them, until the enemies horse charged in our rear, and in front we were overcharged with their foot ... For they having six in file, did overwing us, who to equal their front had made the half ranks advance, and so received the charge at three deep.

The infantry battle, as opposed to the long pursuit, was of brief duration. In the first moments of close hand-to-hand fighting, confusion reigned. Alasdair MacRanald recalled that for a time he was unable to strike a blow, being unable to distinguish friend from foe.[10] By the time Napier's reserve joined the battle, however, there was 'little to doe'. Most of the covenant levies broke and ran within minutes, but isolated groups put up a surprisingly brave fight. Montrose's own standard-bearer was wounded, and some of his pony boys and camp followers, rushing down the hill to join in the plunder, were killed in the very moment of victory.

It was victory indeed, but it soon turned sour. Someone hurriedly rode up to Montrose bearing the dread news that Lord George Gordon was slain. Spurring in to charge the Balcarres' horse one last time, he had been shot in the back as he 'advanced to farre among his flieing enemies'.[11] The Ballad of Alford suggests that he was shot accidentally by one of his own men:

> There cam a ball shot frae the west
> That shot him in the back;
> Altho' he was our enemy
> We grieved for his wrack.
>
> I canna say twas his own men,
> An' yet it cam that way;
> In Scotland there was not a match
> To that man where he lay.

Lord Gordon's death made a tremendous impact on the royalists, not least on Montrose himself who had enjoyed the young man's company for the few short months they had been together. The Gordons regarded him as a 'preux chevalier sans reproche'. Gordon of Ruthven devotes three pages to his praise—more than he devotes to the entire battle.[12] His panegyric, beginning with 'that heauine darling sparke of treue nobilitie, that miracle of men ... too rich a jewell to adorne so unhappie ane age' is eloquent of the Gordons' sense of loss, if a trifle cloying for twentieth century taste. Gordon's death was a serious political, as well as personal, loss for Montrose, since he was the one man, save his father, who could rally the Gordons to the royalist cause. His surviving brothers were more impulsive and less reliable.

The death of Gordon triggered off another massacre. The fleeing covenanter foot were pursued eastwards by vengeful Gordon horse who gave no quarter. At Feight Faulds, at the western end of the present-day village, they were cut down in scores and the Buckie Burn was said to have flowed red with blood. Groups of fugitives were hunted down and killed up to four miles from the battlefield and the last stand of those who could run no further was made at Blaudy Faulds, in the parish of Tough. According to Gordon of Ruthven, 1,600 covenanters perished at Alford—over three-quarters of their entire infantry. As with most of Montrose's battles, such figures are unreliable: since bodies were scattered over several miles, it is unlikely that they were ever counted. Edward Cowan's conservative figure of 700 dead[13] might be nearer the real total; but whatever the precise number of casualties, Alford was one of the bloodiest battles ever fought in the North East. Baillie himself escaped to the south along with Balcarres, the latter rather knocked about and minus his helmet. Montrose's own losses were light: Wishart claims that only three royalists were killed at Alford, which is preposterous. Gordon of

Ruthven says seven, including the lairds of Buchollie and Keith, who were killed in the melee along with Lord Gordon.

The battle of Alford is said to have been 'couragiously foghten on both sydes for a long tyme',[14] but the main action probably lasted little more than an hour. The pursuit lasted all afternoon and into early evening. With their shadows lengthening in front of them, the royalists marched away from the battlefield to Cluny Castle where they camped. On 3 July, Montrose, accompanied by a small escort, rode to Aberdeen for the last time, bearing the body of Lord Gordon. He was buried in St Machar Cathedral alongside his mother.

Covenanting reaction to the battle of Alford held a despairing note. 'We pray the Lord to discover the cause of his great wrath, manifested by the continued heavy judgement of pestilence and sword, and why our forces there have received defeat even these five times from a despicable and inconsiderable enemy', wrote the Scots commissioners in London, shamed by the contrasting success of their parliamentary allies in England. Baillie offered to resign his commission but was refused even that dignity. Instead he was obliged to accept advice in future from a committee comprising most of the surviving defeated generals of the Scottish war.

After Alford, Montrose reigned alone in northern Scotland. He had destroyed five armies in less than a year, each time leaving hundreds of bodies of his fellow Scots 'like clothes a-bleaching ... stretched on hillsides, ignoble of aspect'. Now at last he could strike south and secure the whole of Scotland for the king. It was while in Aberdeen for Lord Gordon's funeral that he heard the shattering news of the battle of Naseby. Suddenly everywhere, except in Scotland, the king's forces were in retreat. King Charles himself intended for a while to join Montrose, but the presence of parliamentary and Scottish armies in the north of England made the enterprise too hazardous. In early August, Montrose's army, strengthened by fresh regiments of Highlanders and cavalry, marched south and out of the North East. There was one last great battle to be fought and won at Kilsyth in the Lowlands, and Scotland would at last lie at Montrose's feet. A month later, all his aspirations would be scattered to the winds at the battle of Philiphaugh. The 'cruell' but brave Irish would be shot or hanged by covenanter fanatics and their womenfolk butchered in cold blood. Montrose himself, forced into exile in 1646, would four years later follow the marquis of Huntly and the king he had served so faithfully to the scaffold.

Alford is exceptional among north eastern conflicts in that it was essentially a cavalry battle. The Gordons decided the issue by overcoming Balcarres' horse, after which the rest of the covenanting army more or less fell to pieces. The battle cannot be counted among the more 'miraculous' of Montrose's victories, since its outcome was never really in doubt. But Montrose's personal qualities of generalship before the battle were indisputable: he succeeded in luring the enemy into a position where the opening moves of the battle would overwhelmingly favour the royalists. That is the objective which every general ultimately aims for, and the strategy used at Alford has its parallels in El Alamein and D-Day.

The site of the battlefield

Every student of the civil war owes a great deal to the pioneering work of S.R. Gardiner,[15] whose researches included a careful field examination of most of the major battlefields. His battlefield reconstructions have often formed the basis of later works on the subject, and some of them have rarely been seriously questioned since.[16] One of his less successful battles was Alford. He was misled by the site of the present village, which is a product of the railway and did not exist in 1645. This led him to assume, wrongly, that the old ford of the Don was by the present-day bridge at Montgarrie, and this gave him a great deal of trouble when it came to finding the hill and marshy hollow referred to in Wishart's narrative.

Gardiner's reconstruction of the battle was corrected by Douglas Simpson in 1919.[17] Simpson had a better local knowledge than Gardiner and he was able to show that the old Suie road crossed the Don a mile west of Gardiner's site, at the Boat of Forbes, where the Bridge of Alford now stands. The tiny seventeenth century kirk-toun of Alford stood by the Leochel Burn, behind the royalist lines. Montrose's officers may have had billets there, although the ballad states that the army camped at Asloun, a mile further south. From this position the details of the battlefield described by Wishart fall easily into place. The ford is dominated by Gallows Hill, and the marsh in Montrose's rear would refer to the hollow of the Leochel Burn. The attempted flank march of the covenanters skewed the battle lines north west-south east, with Baillie's command centre somewhere near the present-day crossroads. The Gordon Stone, which marked the place where Lord George Gordon was killed—one of Gardiner's chief difficulties—is then in the right place, and the battlefield no longer poses any serious problems. Until recently the Ordnance Survey's crossed swords symbol lay on the old Gardiner site but this has now been corrected.

Alford today

The battlefield lies in quiet farming countryside, immortalised in Charles Murray's Hamewith poetry, with fields running down to the Don over gently rolling hills. From a vantage point on Gallows Hill, we have to go through a process of subtraction to see what Montrose would have seen. We must eliminate the present village of Alford, the main roads A980 and A944 and the old railway. We must replace the pastures and crop fields by the Don with peat moss, damp rough grazing and a network of ditches and dikes. The landscape would have seemed a great deal less tame in 1645. Gallows Hill itself lies close to the old village of Alford, which then consisted of a handful of cottages, a smithy and a kirk. The hill was probably open common grazing, for the royalist cavalry evidently had an unencumbered run down the hill. The bogs by the Don must have trapped many a covenanter; the skeleton of a man in complete seventeenth century armour plus his horse was found by a peat digger 100 years after the battle.

The battlefield is more readily explored today than most others in this book. The crossroads stand close to the centre of the covenanter's position, where heavy fighting took place. The view from the minor road between Greystone and Gallowhill gives an excellent impression of the lie of land, and this is the view which Montrose himself would have seen. Haughton House Country Park, administered by Grampian Regional Council, lies behind the covenanter's lines, and was probably crossed by fleeing covenanter infantry and horse. It is one of the few areas of public land on north eastern battlefields. There is little to remind us of the battle today, except perhaps (by association) the modern cemetery. The fate of the one battlefield monument, the Gordon Stone, is a sorry one. The *Old Statistical Account* mentions a 'large stone on the field of battle, which is still pointed out by the country people'. A rough boulder, apparently without inscription,[18] it stood at the edge of a field and marked the place where Lord George Gordon is thought to have fallen. As the modern village of Alford gradually expanded westwards, however, it was seen fit to use the site as a rubbish dump. The stone and its surroundings were walled off with corrugated iron and buried under a mound of refuse. The approximate location of the stone is still known; evidently it had failed to meet the criteria for ancient monument status, and hence legal protection, since it lacked an inscription. Its burial took place some years before the law made planning permission necessary for village rubbish dumps. It could still perhaps be dug out and removed to a safer place, but its function as a marker stone to a hallowed place would then be lost. The scurvy treatment meted out to the only Alford battle monument contrasts sadly with that of Montrose's preceding victory at Auldearn, where the National Trust have erected a plaque showing a plan and description of the battle at the best viewpoint.

CHAPTER 15

INVERURIE AND THE '45

On 19 August 1745 Prince Charles Edward Stewart raised the standard of his father at Glenfinnan. In sharp contrast to the rising of the '15, thirty years before, few of the leading peers of the North East received the news with any show of enthusiasm. Most of those who were not entirely hostile to the Stewarts regarded it as a 'mad project' and sat successfully on the fence throughout the '45. The most active north eastern Jacobites were the younger men, lairds of small estates and the cadet branches of the great houses. There were, however, a few exceptions. The old spirit still burned in the heart of John Gordon of Glenbuchat, now aged 68, and although 'so old and infirm that he could not mount a horse unaided', he straightway crossed the breadth of Scotland to meet the prince and returned with his Commission as Major-General. Lord Pitsligo, aged 67, also joined the rebellion, albeit reluctantly and out of a sense of duty. Both men set about raising levies on their estates in Banff, Strathdon and Strathbogie, and their example was followed by many of the lesser lairds and gentry.

The two most active recruiters for the prince were both men of comparatively small estate. Francis Farquharson of Monaltrie, near Ballater, was an able and 'sweet-tempered, agreeable lad' of 35, known as 'Baron Ban' because of his fair hair. He levied enthusiastically in Deeside and was dismissed for his pains from his office as Commissioner by his uncle, the laird of Invercauld. Farquharson was commissioned by the prince as colonel of the Deeside battalion which included not only men of his own name but also those Burnetts, Gordons, Inneses, Irvines, MacGregors, Menzies and Duguids who felt impelled to serve the prince. The second key figure in the rebellion was James Moir of Stoneywood, 'a man of little note or interest, and of no great genius', but who yet managed to raise a battalion of 200 volunteers from the neighbourhood of Aberdeen by sheer persistence.

The common people of the North East, in so far as their opinion mattered at all, were at first inclined to favour the Jacobite cause, since they had been promised freedom from the Malt Tax. The ruling elders of the town of

Aberdeen, on the other hand, mostly supported the Hanoverian government. On hearing news of the rising, Aberdeen was placed in a 'posture of defence'. Guns were mounted to cover the harbour and its citizens organised into twelve companies of infantry with an artillery detachment. However these precautionary measures came to nothing. On 11 September, Sir John Cope, general of the government forces in Scotland, commandeered all of the town's cannon and small arms, for, he said, if the arms should fall into rebel hands, 'the toun would lay themselves obnoxious to the government and be made answerable for such conduct'. And so, after Cope's departure to the south four days later, Aberdeen lay undefended.

On 25 September a band of 100 Jacobite horse and foot led by the duke of Gordon's factor, Sir John Hamilton, entered Aberdeen. Reputedly a 'very haughty' man of reduced means, Hamilton had been busy proclaiming the Old Pretender as King James VIII in every market place between Strathbogie and Aberdeen. His party gathered around the mercat cross in Castlegate, where the proclamation was read out by the Jacobite sheriff-depute, with the Provost and Baillies of the burgh in enforced attendance. There followed a famous and rather ludicrous incident. The provost refused to join in the toast of loyalty to King James, whereat Hamilton angrily seized a goblet of wine and poured it over the helpless provost's face and down his chest. By this and other 'very insolent' actions, Hamilton made himself thoroughly unpopular but, happily for Aberdeen, he left soon afterwards to join the prince.

In October the Prince won over the young and impetuous Lord Lewis Gordon, son of the duke of Gordon, and sent him to Aberdeen as his lord lieutenant for Aberdeenshire and Banff. Lord Lewis' appointment signalled an intensified and much more ruthless recruiting drive. The tenantry of Strathbogie and Deeside were threatened with the burning of their homes and the destruction of their farms, and in a few cases this threat was actually carried out: this, comments our best-informed source, 'soon had the desired effect, for the burning [of] a single house or farm stack in a Parish terrified the whole, so that they would quickly send in their proportion'.[1] By such means, Lord Lewis pressed another 800 or so men into service. The recruits were accoutred in the Highland fashion of 'plaid, short cloaths, hose and shoes' and armed with a broadsword and (if they were lucky) a musket.

The Jacobites were as short of money as they were of men. Aberdeen was ordered to pay a year's cess (a tax based on the rentable value of owned land) but this was later compounded for a single payment of £100. A levy was also conducted by means of circular letters demanding the delivery of £5 or an able-bodied man for every £100 of valued rent. This demand was backed up by an order threatening fire and destruction on those who refused to pay. On the whole, however, the levy was unsuccessful—Aberdonians have ever been reluctant to part with their money. We are told that 'none but some very timourous people paid' and the Jacobites lost many sympathisers into the bargain. Moreover, the anti-Jacobite majority on the Aberdeen council now began to speak confidently of government aid from the north.

The source of the expected aid was Inverness, where Lord Loudon and Duncan Forbes of Culloden had collected together a small army of Highlanders who remained faithful to the House of Hanover. Aberdeen had secretly requested aid and Lord Loudon intended to comply. Unfortunately, in their keenness to obtain relief, the Aberdonian messengers had under-represented the true strength of the rebel army in the North East. In conse-quence, the relief force which Loudon dispatched on 17 December was smaller than the task actually required. The force consisted of two columns which were to march by separate routes through Banff and Aberdeenshire and converge at Inverurie, from whence they were to enter and occupy Aberdeen. Lord Loudon would eventually follow with the remainder of his army. The main column was led by the Skye chief, Macleod of Macleod, with 400 men at his back, mostly recruited from his own clan. Macleod had been among the first chiefs to be sounded out by the prince before Glenfinnan, but had refused to 'come out' and had later committed his clan to the support of the government. The second relief column had been detached from Lord Lou-don's own regiment, and consisted of around 300 Munros, Grants and Mac-kenzies, under a professional soldier, Captain George Munro of Culcairn. The prominence given to Inverurie in Loudon's orders was no accident. This ancient royal burgh lay on the principal route from Inverness, through Garioch to Aberdeen, at the crossings of the Don and the Urie. Its importance had been appreciated by Bruce during his Buchan campaign and by the earl of Mar on the eve of Harlaw. Now Inverurie was to become the scene of the last pitched battle to be fought on north eastern soil.

The progress of this government expeditionary force was at first uneventful. On reaching Elgin, Macleod received information that a small force of rebels under Gordon of Avochie and Gordon of Aberlour had taken possession of the Spey crossing at Fochabers, but they fell back towards Aberdeen as Macleod approached and the government troops crossed the river without incident. Macleod moved rapidly on through Cullen, Banff and Old Meldrum, reaching Inverurie on 20 December 1745. There he was joined by Munro of Culcairn whose column had swept through Keith and Strathbogie, similarly forcing their rebel garrisons to retire to Aberdeen. Macleod managed to quarter most of his own men along the main street of Inverurie, but some of his company and the whole of Culcairn's had to find billets in scattered cots and ferms along the Urie up to one and half miles away. This was their first serious mistake of the campaign. A well-informed contemporary commented that

> there was no wordly necessity for this, as the town of Inverury (later) contained two regiments of the Duke's (of Cumberland) army for some weeks without a man of them going a stone's cast from it.[2]

Once the two columns had joined forces, Macleod seems to have deferred to the professional soldier, Culcairn, in matters of military judgement as he 'did not pretend to understand military matters'. Unfortunately Culcairn's judgement was, at least on this occasion, faulty. He refused to allow advance guards and patrols to be sent out of the town, on the grounds that the surrounding countryside was hostile and outposted troops would be in danger. As a result, his subsequent knowledge of the rebel's troop movements was nil, while the Jacobites were able to control the traffic on the roads from Aberdeen and prevent would-be defectors and spies from joining Macleod. A trickle of gentlemen volunteers nevertheless managed to reach Inverurie by various circuitous routes, of whom the most notable was Sir Archibald Grant of Monymusk, who brought news of the landing of French reinforcements to the rebels in Aberdeen. This intelligence probably influenced Culcairn and Macleod's decision not to march on Aberdeen immediately as planned, but to remain in Inverurie until they were more certain of the situation. In the meantime, their new volunteers included such local notables as Mr Forbes of Echt, Mr Thomson, supervisor of excise, and Mr Chalmers, principal of King's College, who arrived accompanied by his professor of Humanity and a number of students. Alas, Macleod had no spare arms and they were reduced to manufacturing home-made spears out of bits of iron.[3]

Unbeknown to the beleaguered force in Inverurie, a substantial Jacobite force now occupied Aberdeen. Around 300 Gordons of the Strathbogie battalion had come in to join the 200 local men under Stoneywood and the 800 or so levies raised by Farquharson of Monaltrie and Lord Lewis Gordon. 200 men from the Angus and Mearns militia were also present and, most important of all, 150 recently arrived French picquets under experienced officers. Some of these had evidently been detached for other duties, but a force of 1,200 or so remained to deal with Culcairn and Macleod. Lord Lewis and his advisors decided that this was more than sufficient to enable them to take the initiative. Firstly, however, they sent a fifth columnist ahead to Inverurie to infiltrate the Macleods and reap confusion and despondency. This strategem came close to success:

> As this fellow had (the Gaelic) language and was the Macleod's namesake and countryman, they readily listened to him, and it was taking among them like lightning, till the fellow was found out and apprehended, but the impression still stuck to them, till Macleod drew them all out, and very particularly showed them the roguery.[4]

At nine o'clock on the morning of Monday, 23 December, the Jacobites marched out of Aberdeen towards Inverurie. Their force was divided into two columns, one of which would approach Inverurie directly along the King's High Road through Kintore, while the other would cross the Don and approach the town from the east along byways. It was an ambitious plan, difficult to put into effect for its execution depended on taking the enemy fully by surprise and the attacks had to be simultaneous. Furthermore both columns had to take the frightening risk of fording a river in full view of the enemy, the direct column across the Don and the flanking column across the Urie. The flanking column was the larger. It consisted of 900 men, nominally under Lord Lewis, although, our best source assures us, 'Major Cuthbert, a French Officer, did all the business'.[5] This force comprised Stoneywood's and Monaltrie's regiments, the Mearns militia, two companies of Lord Drummond's French regiment and a few gentlemen volunteers raised by one Mr

Crichton. The smaller column consisted of the Gordon Strathbogie battalion, commanded by Major Gordon, another French officer, and Glenbuchat's nephew, Gordon of Avochie. Neither column took with them any artillery, apart from 'two old rusty cannon they had taken from the ships', and which did not, in the event, arrive until the action was over.

Elaborate precautions were taken to guard the approach routes, and advance patrols were sent out to prevent spies from reaching Inverurie and revealing the Jacobite plan of attack. Since the flanking column had much the greater distance to cover, the smaller force halted along the high road at Kinellar and concealed themselves in the churchyard, while their advance party arrested the minister of Kintore and occupied some of the roadside houses. In the meantime, Lord Lewis had posted scouts in the fir plantations of the earl of Kintore around Keith Hall, on the high ground rising east of the Urie, in order to keep an eye on troop movements in Inverurie. They were reassured by what they saw: apparently the government troops were not alert to their peril, and the vital ford of the Urie had been left unguarded.

This deplorable inaction on the part of Macleod and Culcairn is explained by John Daunies, in a letter to the bishop of Aberdeen.[6] They had, we learn, no reason to fear attack, since they assumed that Lord Lewis and the other rebels were preparing to march south to join up with the prince. 'But therein', adds Daunies, 'were they deceived'. In fact Culcairn did rather half-heartedly send out at least one patrol over the weekend and had, as a result, gained some knowledge of the rebels' numbers but he was still completely in the dark as to their intentions. In the early afternoon, the Jacobite scouts around Keith Hall were spotted, 'and [were] pointed out to Culcairn and Macleod as looking very suspicious, yet by some fatality they neglected to send up and see what they were doing'. Shortly afterwards, as the early winter dusk set in at about four o'clock, the pair of inept commanding officers received the greatest shock of their careers: a large force of rebels was reported advancing downhill from Keith Hall and was already within a quarter of a mile of Inverurie. Lord Lewis Gordon had arrived.

Confusion reigned. A sentry fired his piece to give the alarm and the Macleods swarmed from their billets into the main street of the town. There was no time to send for the outposted troops. The anonymous author of *Memoirs of the Rebellion in Aberdeen and Banff* takes up the story:

> Macleod, Culcairn and all the officers with the few men they had in the town [actually numbering some 300] got together resolutely, and all of them discovered a great deal of courage on this occasion, nay, to think at all of standing against such superior numbers bespoke no little bravery. And indeed had they thought of sending down a party to line the Church yard of Inverury, and had others rightly posted on a little hill, called the Bass, both of which were within a pistol shot of the Boat and Ford of Ury where the main body behoved to pass, and also on the Ford of Don where Achavy etc, passed, they certainly had done great execution among them in their passages, and if they had not stopped them altogether, would at least have retarded them till the men that were canton'd at a distance had gone up to their assistance ... But the confusion and surprise of the Macleods at the unexpected coming of the enemy

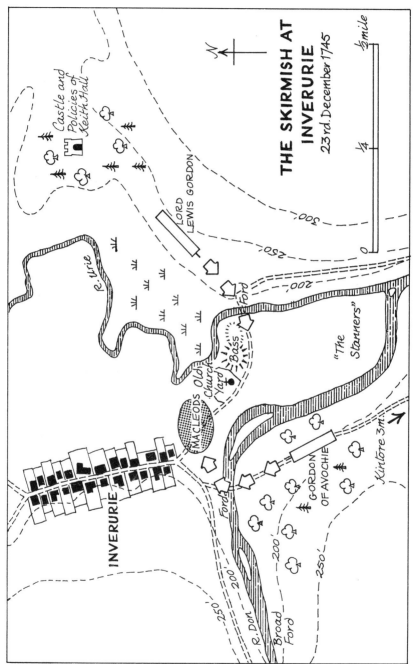

THE SKIRMISH AT INVERURIE
23rd.December 1745

Map 18.

made them neglect all these advantages, and stand on the Rigs on the east side
at the south end of the town, at almost an equal distance from the Fords of
Don and Ury, but at so great a distance as to be able to do execution at neither.

The irresolute Macleods probably did not know which ford to cover for, by
this time, Gordon of Avochie's company had also reached the town and
stood on the far side of the Don. To make matters worse, the Macleods 'who
were none of them disciplined ... had only firelocks and bayonets and wanted
their darling weapon, the Broadsword, which is always their chief confidence'.

A picked party of Jacobites under Major Cuthbert waded across the icy
waters of the Urie, 'very alertly' and under fire from sixty Macleods, and
drew up by the shelter of the Bass and the adjacent churchyard. The gathering
darkness made accurate shooting difficult and only two of the rebels were
wounded. The remainder of Lord Lewis' column behaved rather less heroically: 'many of their common men ran off and skulked by dike-sides till the
action was over and could neither be brought out by threats nor entreaties
till then'. Much the same could be said of the column which had reached the
Don. About fifty or sixty men, led by Major Gordon and Gordon of Avochie,
briskly waded the river under fire and drew up on the nearside bank, but the
rest of their company 'took shelter among the Broom til they saw the event'.[7]

Under a cold, clear moon, the two rebel detachments formed up and
advanced on the Macleods, firing as they went. At first, small groups of
Macleods had ran up to the fords, shot at the men in the water and retired
immediately. Under the close, regular fire of the Jacobites, however, they
began to give way. Most of them streamed back into the town, but one party,
braver than the rest, 'loaded their pieces ... and finding some of their men,
especially the wounded, like to fall in the enemy's hands, they wheeled about
before they were half way up the town, and made another fire, but immediately
ran off'.[8]

The rebels followed:

> (Farquharson of) Monaltrie and (Gordon of) Blelack entered the town; Avochie
> went up the west side to scour the yards from which the Macleods had fired
> and galled Lord Lewis' men in their coming up from the Urie to form agenst
> the enemie. The action lasted but a few minutes after the men were formed,
> and the loss inconsiderable on both sides, night coming on apace; They could
> not be supposed they could see to levell their pieces.[9]

Within less than twenty minutes, Inverurie was in rebel hands and the Macleods were in full flight across the frosty ploughlands at the north end of
the town. Someone cried out that the laird of Macleod had been captured,
at which a party turned and fired one last round at their pursuers, before
disappearing into the night. Before all firing died away, there was a last
farcical incident, related by the *Memoirs* author:

> The Rebels emerging from the north end of Inverury, 'seeing a ridge with a few
> furrows in it, amidst a great deal of unploughed stubble ground, and taking it
> by moonlight for a row of men, they fired once or twice into it very successfully'.

On that wry note, the 'unlucky disaster of Inverurie' was over.

The Munros and Macleods who occupied billets some distance away, had run up towards the town on hearing the commotion, but on seeing that their companions were in flight, they in turn lost heart and followed them into the night. Their commanders' crowning blunder had been to neglect to outpost any officers to lead them to the relief of their comrades. Had they done so, remarks the *Memoirs* author, and 'led them up in a body to meet their friends at the north end of the town and support them, they very possibly might have turned the scale in their favour'.

After the firing had died away over the moonlit town, several bodies lay sprawled and still by the riverbanks and along the main street. The well-informed *Memoirs* states that only five Macleods were killed on the spot 'as was well known, as their bodies were left exposed for some days (before) they allowed them to be buried'. Two more died of their wounds, but all were 'common men'. The Jacobite rebels concealed their own losses, 'but 'tis now generally allowed that they had at least ten or twelve killed, several of these French, but all common men. They had also a good many wounded, among whom was Mr Gordon of Birkenbuss, a gentleman of a small estate, very dangerously'. Local people supposed that a senior French officer had been killed, for one body was placed in a grave by itself 'with several Popish Ceremonies'. John Daunies thought that fourteen had been killed on both sides, and about twenty wounded.

The rebels captured a number of prisoners, many of whom had been wounded and were unable to escape. The sources disagree over exactly how many: the *Scots Magazine* says forty one, John Daunies, sixty and the *Memoirs*, thirty. Apart from ten or twelve 'Humlys' (Highland squatters) who nobody cared much about, they included several officers and gentlemen of note including Gordon of Ardoch, a lieutenant in Munro's company, Forbes of Echt and the hapless Principal of King's College, Mr Chalmers.[10] Another, Maitland of Pitrichy, was captured at Keith Hall where he had taken refuge after the skirmish. The most notable prisoner of all was Macleod's own piper, Donald Ban MacCrimmon, deemed 'the best piper in the Highlands, having had most of the Clan pipers as his scholars, and being looked on by them as a kind of chief'. The taking of MacCrimmon meant considerable loss of face for the Macleods; it is said that 'not a Highland piper would play a tune till MacCrimmon was allowed to be on parole'.[11] Poor man, he was to be shot dead by a blacksmith during the 'rout of Moy', only eight weeks later. Macleod also lost his baggage, and most of it had been looted by the townsfolk before the rebels could get their hands on it.

The retreating Macleods and Munros were not pursued, since the rebels did not wish to push their luck too far. The Macleods and Munros, however, had no wish to renew the fight. Led by their laird, who, despite rumours, had not been captured after all, they 'stopped not a night till they got over the Spey', pausing only for brief rest and refreshment at Rayne and Strathbogie. The counties of Aberdeen and Banff were once again in Jacobite hands.

The aftermath

The gentleman volunteers who had sided with the government forces were lucky not to have had their homes burned in the flush of victory. After Inverurie, the Old and New Towns of Aberdeen had little alternative but to pay their quota of levy money to the Jacobites, which amounted to £500 for the New Town alone. To encourage the town to pay up, a party of wild Highlanders of Clan Chattan were sent up from Dundee, to be replaced later by a still wilder pack of MacGregors: 'they would stop gentlemen on the streets openly, and either take their silver buckles and buttons from them, or oblige them to give so much to redeem them. Without the least provocation they would beat and abuse people...' If the gentlemen gave the least hesitation in declaring themselves in favour of the Pretender, 'they were sure of a slap, and never got away till they sat down on their knees and swore to the Pretender and cursed King George in whatever terms the ruffians pleased'.[12]

True to form, however, the Aberdonians proved extremely reluctant to part with their money and when Lord Lewis, together with the Jacobite garrison and army, departed south in January 1746 to join the prince in Stirling, only half the dues had been paid. Most of the remoter estates in Aberdeen and Banff escaped altogether the awkward knock on the door by Lord Lewis' quartermasters and levy collectors.

For a while, Aberdeen was left without a military garrison. The battle of Falkirk was fought on 17 January, and on 1 February Prince Charles' army began its retreat to the north. One column of the Jacobite army passed through Aberdeen in freezing, stormy weather, but stayed only a short while, and 'had not great opportunity of doing much mischief, though they seemed not at all averse to do it'. Some of the local men stayed behind, however, and made strenuous, but on the whole unsuccessful, last-ditch attempts to raise the remaining levy money. Some of the most recalcitrant debtors were arrested and knocked about, and most of the town's few remaining horses were requisitioned. On 22 February a French ship landed in the harbour to disembark a troop of FitzJames' regiment of dragoons and, on the following day, all the remaining Jacobite troops in the town marched away along the cold, hard road which took them to Culloden.

The government army under the duke of Cumberland was now in pursuit. The advance guard reached Aberdeen on 25 February and the duke himself arrived two days later. Most Aberdonians had been lukewarm, if not hostile, to the Jacobite cause throughout the '45. Nevertheless, the leading citizens, provost and baillies, colleges and clergy, thought it prudent to make a demonstration of their loyalty. The burgesses of the town lined the streets between the duke's entry and his lodgings at Provost Skene's House, where he was waited on by the nobility and gentry of town and country. Various toadying speeches were made and the duke was created a freeman of the burgh. Cumberland remained in Aberdeen for six weeks, whilst his troops captured the principal towns of the North East, mostly without serious opposition. The strategic importance of Inverurie was recognised: the town was occupied by two regiments, and a bridge of boats thrown across the Urie along the line of communication between that town and Old Meldrum. Only at Keith were Cumberland's troops discomforted when a group of Jacobites surprised the town at night and killed or captured most of the garrison.

Those of the government army who remained behind to suffer the rigours of a winter in Aberdeen spited their bad tempers in various acts of petty vengeance. Houses, chapels and meeting places of prominent Roman Catholics and non-jurant ministers were despoiled or pulled down; houses of known Jacobites were plundered; one alleged informer was savagely whipped and another strung up from a tree at the Brig o' Balgownie. The duke himself made very free with his host's, Mr Thomson's, household provisions. On leaving the town, without a word of thanks to Mr Thomson, he purloined the sugar, left behind bed and table linen 'very much spoiled and abused', and was pleased to receive the gift of a stolen tea set belonging to Mrs Gordon of Hillhead. But even so his behaviour was mild compared with the boorish antics of some of his staff officers. General Hawley, who had taken over the house of a luckless Mrs Gordon, deprived her 'of everything except the cloths upon her back'. The duke probably had few admirers left in Aberdeen when he departed on 8 April leaving behind a garrison of 200 men at Gordon's Hospital, lately renamed Fort Cumberland.

The relief was only temporary. On 16 April the Jacobite cause perished forever at Culloden, and Aberdeen was occupied by Fleming's Regiment, who were mostly young men and 'did not at all behave in an agreeable manner'. Aberdeen and the lands around it escaped the wholesale plundering and burning of rebel houses that occurred in Deeside and elsewhere, but the townsmen, whatever their political sympathies, were treated like pariahs. The town's initial goodwill had turned into 'great disgust and heartburning'. Their smouldering resentment came to a head on 1 August when Lord Ancrum, commander-in-chief in the North East, ordered the town's bells to be rung and the houses illuminated to celebrate the anniversary of the accession of the Hanoverian dynasty. Unfortunately, and apparently in all innocence, the town's magistrates ordered only that the bells be rung. This apparent slight enraged a group of soldiers who were sitting about on the cobbled streets, drinking the king's health. One of their officers, a zealot named Morgan, bellowed, 'are you the men to take this kind of insult?', and, staggering up to the nearest unlit window, heaved a cobblestone through it.[13] Soon the streets of Aberdeen were full of drunken soldiers on the rampage, banging on doors and windows, hurling stones at the terrified townsfolk and looting at will. The sheriff himself was accused of harbouring rebels and roughly manhandled. By daylight £130 worth of damage had been done, a considerable sum for those times. The furious magistrates made representations to the lord justice clerk of Scotland, who commented that 'the officers in the army were trampling on those very laws which they so lately [had] defended'. The military authorities maintained that they were not liable to the civil government, although Lord Ancrum was removed from his post as a result of this episode and Morgan placed temporarily under arrest. Six months later, to everyone's unspoken relief, Fleming's regiment left Aberdeen for good. It is said (and it ought to be true) that they marched away to the tune of 'We'll gang nae mair to yon toun'.

Many of the defeated Jacobites of the North East never saw their homeland again. Old Gordon of Glenbuchat watched from his hiding place in the heather as his house at Tomintoul was burned by Hanoverian soldiers, while a similar fate befell his castle in Donside. After numerous sufferings under an open sky with a £1,000 reward on his head, he escaped to the Buchan coast and sailed to Norway. He died in poverty in 1750, without ever returning to Scotland. Lord Lewis Gordon went into exile in France, where he died insane in 1756. John Hamilton, who had been appointed governor of Carlisle by the prince, was hanged after that city surrendered to Hanoverian troops. Others were more fortunate. Lord Pitsligo was attainted in 1746 and forfeited his estates, but was never captured. Francis Farquharson of Monaltrie was taken prisoner after Culloden and condemned to death, but subsequently reprieved. He was held in England until 1766 where he became an expert on farming improvements and put his knowledge to good effect on his return to his estate. He died in 1791, and is regarded today as one of the founders of Aberdeenshire's farming wealth. Moir of Stoneywood escaped to Sweden where he remained until 1762, after which he was allowed to return. Munro of Culcairn commanded a regiment of Highland militia after Culloden and his role in the Inverurie fiasco does not seem to have been held against him. In the fall of 1746, whilst rooting out ex-Jacobites in the bleak hills about Loch Arkaig, he was shot dead by a Cameron, who apparently mistook him for Grant of Knockando. His was one of the remarkably few revenge killings made by the Highlanders after Culloden.

Inverurie today

The modern town lies mostly on the higher and drier ground to the north and north east of the old town. In consequence, much of the battlefield of Inverurie has escaped housing development. The banks of the Urie in particular are still in a natural state, and it requires little imagination to visualise the course of the battle from the top of the Bass. The old church near the Bass no longer exists, but its surroundings are still consecrated ground and are now the burgh cemetery. The 'Rigs' between the Don and the Urie, where the Macleods stood, is now divided between allotment gardens, poultry houses and a sewage works, and crossed by a railway line. The traveller on the Aberdeen to Inverness railway passes over the battlefield on a raised embankment, and is given a bird's eye view denied to the ordinary walker.

The *New Statistical Account* (1843) states that 'musket balls are still occasionally turned up on the field of battle by the plough', but no finds were reported during the deep excavation of part of the site for the sewage works. And, sad to say, no monument exists to mark the site of the last pitched battle fought on north eastern soil.

CHAPTER 16

EPILOGUE. WARD AND WAPINSHAW:
THE DEFENCE OF ABERDEEN

Aberdeen's isolated geographical position made her unusually vulnerable to attack and occupation by unruly armed mobs of Highlanders, to whom it must have seemed like a Babylon of wealth. Because of its isolation, the burgh was obliged to be self-sufficient, particularly in matters of defence, and a degree of 'national service' training and equipment for all able-bodied men was standard practice from at least as early as the fifteenth century, when full records begin. Fordun, a member of the Aberdeen clergy writing in the late fourteenth century, gives us one of our earliest glimpses of the cast of people they thought they were: 'domesticated and cultured, trustworthy, patient and urbane, decent in their attire, law-abiding and peaceful, devout in religious observance though always ready to resist the wrong-doings of their foes'. Fordun leaves out the less attractive aspects of Aberdeen's beleaguered state: the almost xenophobic attitude to strangers and the dour, distrustful manner engendered by isolation and fear. Even at that early date, the 'civilised' Aberdonians formed a marked contrast to the 'wild and untamed' Highland men living scarcely thirty miles from their bolted doors. A high degree of loyalty to the reigning king or queen and the payment of at least lip-service to his representative in the north, the all-powerful Gordon earls of Huntly, were part of Aberdeen's policy of self-preservation.

At times of military call-up, such as at the muster before Flodden in 1513, letters were customarily sent to the sheriffs and read out from the mercat crosses of the main burghs. As in other towns, the baillies and magistrates of Aberdeen were responsible for mustering a contingent of able-bodied men for the defence of Scotland. The size of this contingent grew as the town expanded and prospered. Thirty-six men served their provost at the battle of Harlaw. Twenty spearmen and six fully equipped horsemen were donated for the Flodden campaign in 1514 serving, as was customary, in the earl of Huntly's battalion. No less than a hundred armed men from Aberdeen served

194

in the disastrous Solway Moss campaign of 1542 and thirty out of an unknown number were killed at the equally disastrous battle of Pinkie in 1547. The town also, on occasion, donated a warship with a paid crew towards the king's military expenses. It is not known exactly how many fully armed men Aberdeen could muster in an emergency. Baillie Alexander Skene states that the Aberdeen militia at the outbreak of 'the Troubles' in 1639 consisted of '800 men in good array' with attendent 'military furniture' out of a population of perhaps 9,000, but only 100 seem to have served at the Brig o' Dee in that year. Judging from the record, they were more than capable of facing up to and repelling the undisciplined mobs who occasionally attacked the town, although they were no match for professional soldiers. In the circumstances, their service at Harlaw, the Brig o' Dee and Justice Mills was highly creditable.

We know very little about how Aberdeen organised its defences before 1411, although by that date its citizens had been called out to defend the town on a great many occasions. The close-run battle of Harlaw led to an organised system of quartering and regular training. The town was part of the feudal patronage of its first governor, the earl of Mar, and four magistrates were appointed to supervise arrangements for each of the four quarters of the burgh. These arrangements were often put to the test. Between 1411 and 1560, Scotland was often in a comparatively lawless state, dogged by long royal minorities to say nothing of the intermittent warfare with England. The Aberdonians were called to arms on at least eighteen occasions during this period and sometimes, as in 1530, street fighting resulted in quite heavy casualties.

The defences were based on the time-honoured system of 'watch and ward'. Aberdeen had had no castle since 1308 and had never possessed town walls, but her main streets were guarded by great stone ports or gatehouses which were 'stekit and closit' at night. A further gatehouse guarded the Brig of Dee. In times of danger curfew was kept and squads of up to thirty men patrolled the environs of the town, whilst observation posts on nearby hill-tops were manned. If strangers were seen approaching the town, a sentry would toll the steeple bell of the toun kirk, one resounding clang for every person seen; if the approaching band was a large one, he was given orders to 'knell ay continual'.

The harbour was guarded from at least as early as 1493 by a stone block-house and earthwork equipped with several stone-firing cannon. If needs be, the harbour could be blocked altogether by a boom of iron chains and mast heads strung across the narrows of the Dee between Futty and Torry. The cathedral and bishop's palace of Old Aberdeen had their own separate system of defence whereby guns, horses, and carts bearing arms could be rushed up the cobbled High street at short notice for the protection of 'our masters the canons, and their servants and habitations'. It is no accident that St Machar's Cathedral has strong walls and battlements.

The manufacture of arms within Aberdeen was the responsibility of the Guild of Hammermen, which included goldsmiths, blacksmiths, armourers, saddlers and glovers. Although the highest quality (and most expensive) armour, swords and pistols were imported, the hammermen of Aberdeen were evidently capable of meeting the basic demands of the burgh. An apprentice hammerman had to work seven years at his trade before qualifying as a freeman of the guild, and had first to produce an 'essay' to demonstrate his mastery of the craft. An armourer's essay, for instance, might be a mounted buckler sword together with a mounted rapier, whilst an apprentice gunner would have needed to produce a pistol and a hagbut of quality. A mounted officer with his carbine, pistols, sword, steel gauntlets and saddle stock might require the services of seven or more highly trained craftsmen. The hammer-men, like the masons, were renowned in their day as great drinkers, and contemporary accounts are rife with complaints over their 'visiting and drink-ing, neglecting their due time to come to their work, and to rise early in the morning'.

It was the duty of every craftsman of the burgh to equip himself with the appropriate arms of the day, and to carry them during his watch duties. The penalties for evasion of duty were harsh: the offender risked being banished from the town or having his house pulled down, although minor infringements were later replaced by a fine. An exception was made of 'the poore sort of people quhilk had nather armis nor apparell fitting for musturing', for whom no use could be found. The inspection of arms and drilling exercise usually took place on the Links and was known as the 'wapinshaw' (literally, weapon-showing). In 1522, there was one such muster at a pavilion on Woolmanhill by the 'Play Green', between the Loch and the Denburn. On parade were huge wooden spears, five and a half ells (roughly twenty feet) in length, bows and quivers of arrows and two-handed swords, all, incidently, weapons which were decidedly antiquated by that date. The men were expected to be kitted out in a 'knapshaw' or bonnet, a leather or steel corslet or jack, 'splents' or thigh pieces made of burnished steel and a small Highlander-style targe. Other commonly used military equipment of the time included the short spear or halberd, the 'dense aix' or Lochaber axe and the crossbow.

The second half of the sixteenth century saw the rise of the musket as the principal weapon used in defence of the burgh. We have a detailed account of a wapinshaw on the Links in May 1599, where 'certane young men and nichtbouris of the toun' were given arms instruction by one Thomas Ballan-tyne, who received a rose noble (about six shillings) for his trouble. A roll call was given for each quarter of the town by the appropriate magistrate, and absentees were 'wrettin and unlauit'—a fine of £20 Scots would be their lot unless they could furnish a good excuse. All burgesses of guild and free craftsmen of the burgh were required to own a full stand of armour and to swear to the council that it was 'their awin proper geir'. With the roll call duly completed, the parade marched in procession through the streets to the mercat cross in Castlegate. Leading the procession, behind their nominated commanders, was the company of 'hagbutters' or musketeers with their steel helmets and bandoliers; next the company of pikemen, probably all big men and wearing heavier armour, including a cuirasse or breastplate and thigh pieces; next came a second company of hagbutters followed by a mixed bunch of pikemen, halberdiers and Lochaber axemen. Bringing up the rear 'in the end and taill', were the independent-minded fisherfolk of Futty. In the market place there was some drill and weapons practice, of the sort which nowadays we might call 'a mock battle', and finally the business was brought to a close by the senior magistrate present who gave a solemn warning to all and sundry to attend the next wapinshaw.

The years immediately after the Union of Crowns in 1603 saw the formation of a town armoury. Instead of providing his own armour and weapons at a wapinshaw, each 'brother of the guild' now presented a musket and bandolier to the town, whilst every trades burgess presented a pike: a nice social distinction. This was the system which prevailed during the troubled 1630s and 1640s but, with the coming of more peaceful times, these duties were superseded by payments in coin to an Arms Money fund used to purchase muskets and powder. A vestige of the muster system still remained in force. During the first Jacobite rebellion in 1689, Old Aberdeen was required to furnish twenty four men who were drilled on the Kings College bowling green at three o'clock every day except on the Sabbath. 1745 saw the last call-out to arms by the Aberdeen Council, but any effect that this might have had on the course of the rebellion was nullified by the action of Sir John Cope who confiscated the entire armoury in case the Jacobites should capture it.

After the '45 and the occupation of the town by Hanoverian troops, a new corps, the Royal Aberdeen Volunteers, was formed for policing and emergency duties under the direction of the lord lieutenant of the county. But now that the 'weak piping time of peace' was no longer interrupted by the sour brunt of war, that sense of urgency which marked earlier times was replaced by an urbane complacency. The auld troubled times were over, and the new age of prosperity resulting from the Act of Union and new improved methods of farming had begun. And so all but a handful of the townsfolk gratefully turned their backs on military exercise. Let the *Aberdeen Journal* of 1797 have the last word:

> Last Saturday morning, there was held, in the Record Office, a meeting of the Royal Aberdeen Volunteers ... to consider the most effectual means of discharging the duty they owe to the public, in case of any emergency which may render their services necessary ...

> It was well observed that it was somewhat extraordinary that in Aberdeen, a city supposed to contain 20,000 inhabitants, so small a number should turn out in its defence; but it is still more strange that upwards of fifty names who had originally subscribed the terms of the association had never taken arms and had never attended a single drill ...

APPENDIX

HOW TO FIND THE GRAMPIAN BATTLEFIELDS

MONS GRAUPIUS Ordnance Survey map 1: 50,000 Sheet 38 (Aberdeen).
1: 25,000 Sheets NJ62 and 72.
Grid reference NJ 680250.

Many authorities now accept that the lost battlefield of Mons Graupius lies below the northern slopes of Bennachie. The recently discovered Roman marching camp of Durno lies between the steadings of Easterton and Westerton at grid reference 699272. Its site is easily reached by a minor road from Pitcaple but the outline of the camp is visible only from the air. The site is nevertheless well worth visiting for its fine view southwards across the battlefield towards Bennachie. An equally fine northward panorama can be obtained from the Pittodrie car park provided by the Forestry Commission, which is signposted from the B9002 and marks the approximate position of the Caledonian front line. Neither view is spoiled by modern developments and both allow the battle to be refought in the imagination.

The forest walk from the Back o'Bennachie (Puttingstone) picnic site passes close to an Iron Age settlement which may well have been inhabited in the first century A.D.

NECHTANSMERE Ordnance Survey map 1: 50,000 sheet 54 (Dundee).
Grid reference: No. 516491.

The crossed swords of battle mark the site of the vanished loch of Nechtansmere which lies in a shallow depression within the fields between East Mains of Dunnichen and the village of Letham. Four minor roads make a complete circuit of the battlefield and the one which ascends Dunnichen Hill gives an impressive Pict's-eye view of the field. A plaster copy of the Dunnichen stone stands in front of Dunnichen church and a monument was unveiled nearby in 1985 to mark the 1300th anniversary of the battle. Visitors to the battlefield should not miss the nearby priory with its pre-Conquest tower at Restenneth or the splendid collection of Pictish cross-slabs at Aberlemno.

MORTLACH Ordnance Survey map 1: 50,000 Sheet 28 (Elgin).
                                    1: 25,000 Sheet NJ 33 (Dufftown).
        Grid reference: NJ 325393.

The old kirk of Mortlach marks the approximate site of battle and is signposted from the A941 and from the centre of Dufftown. The so-called 'Battle Stone' stands at a drunken angle in the centre of the churchyard. From there, the visitor can walk up the public footpath by Dullan Water to the Giant's Chair, which figures in 'traditional' accounts of the battle.

BURGHEAD Ordnance Survey map 1: 50,000 Sheet 28 (Elgin).
                                    1: 25,000 Sheet NJ 16 (Burghead).

The remains of the Dark Age promontory fort together with its ancient well are open to the public at the seaward end of Burghead village. The well is a scheduled ancient monument. The precise site of the battlefield is not known.

LUMPHANAN Ordnance Survey map 1: 50,000 Sheet 37 (Strathdon).
                                    1: 25,000 Sheet NJ 50 (Lumphanan).

The Peel of Lumphanan is a scheduled ancient monument and is open to the public. The original settlement probably lay between the Peel and the present day Church of St Finnan; the modern village to the east owes its existence to the Deeside railway. Local associations with Macbeth include Macbeth's Cairn on Perkhill, Macbeth's Well on the roadside bank near the church and Macbeth's Stone in the arable field facing the Peel. The precise site of the battlefield is not known.

SLIOCH Ordnance Survey map 1: 50,000 Sheet 29 (Banff).
                                    1: 25,000 Sheet NJ 43/53 (Huntly).
        Grid reference: NJ 554391

The battlefield lies among large cereal fields, two miles east of Huntly, and the Ordnance Survey map marks its approximate position. The motte of Torra Duncan, the probable site of Bruce's camp, has been ploughed, but is still visible as a low hump in the corner of a field. The battlefield can be viewed from the roadside of the A96, but there are no public rights of way across it.

BARRA Ordnance Survey map 1: 50,000 Sheet 38 (Aberdeen).
                                    1: 25,000 Sheet NJ 72 and 82.
        Grid Reference: NJ 797268

The approximate site of the battle lies in peaceful, cattle-grazed fields between the A920 and B9170, just west of the town of Old Meldrum, whose buildings dominate the skyline. There is no monument but a panoramic view over the battlefield including Bruce's approach from Inverurie can be obtained from the prehistoric fort on the Hill of Barra. The permission of the proprietor of North Mains should be sought before visiting this viewpoint.

CULBLEAN Ordnance Survey map 1: 50,000 Sheet 37 (Strathdon).
                                    1: 25,000 Sheets NJ 40/50 and NO 49.
        Grid reference: NO 429996.

This battlefield, which lies within the Muir of Dinnet National Nature Reserve, can be explored on foot without difficulty. A car park and tea room by the A97 conveniently mark the most probable site of battle, and a map drawn by the author showing the Douglas Simpson version of the conflict is on display there. 'Earl Davy's Stane' a large glacial erratic boulder, is perched on the hillside above the Vat burn and may be reached on foot by following the Nature Conservancy's geological trail, for which booklets are normally available at the tearooms. A fine view over the surroundings of the battlefield is obtained during the course of this walk, and the approach march of Douglas and Moray around Loch Kinord can be followed.

A modern monument to the battle stands by the A97, a mile north of the tearooms, at Grid reference 435003.

HARLAW Ordnance Survey map 1: 50,000 Sheet 38 (Aberdeen).
                        1: 25,000 Sheet NJ 72 (Inverurie).
    Grid reference: NJ 752242.

The battlefield can be reached without difficulty by taking the B9001 from Inverurie and turning left along the minor road signposted to the Harlaw monument. This imposing edifice dominates the ridge where the heaviest fighting took place. There are no footpaths across the 'Pley Fauld' but the field of battle can be surveyed from the vicinity of the monument. The bleak moorland existing at the time of the battle has long since been reclaimed and replaced by stone-diked arable fields. There is little to be seen, unfortunately, of the former burial cairns. The fine view west towards Bennachie is rather spoiled by electricity pylons.

CORRICHIE Ordnance Survey map 1: 50,000 Sheet 38 (Aberdeen).
                        1: 25,000 Sheets NJ 70 and 60.
    Grid reference: NJ 697025.

Corrichie is rather inaccessible. The modern monument, which stands by the roadside at 733014, is easy enough to find but the Forestry Commission's planted trees, which post-date the monument, have obscured its former evocative standpoint against the backcloth of the Hill of Fare. The same trees now bar ready access to the 'Queen's Chair' on Berry Hill, and a rough and awkward scramble up forest firebeaks is necessary before the summit can be reached. To reach the site of the Gordon's last stand in the bog at the head of the vale, one must face a three mile uphill trudge from the B977 at the Green farm, or an even longer walk along the landrover track from Landerberry. Most of the vale has been afforested with conifers, and the site of the bog has disappeared beneath a frowning stand of Sitka Spruce. The surrounding hill tops are still bare, as they were in 1562. The moorland parts of the Hill of Fare should be avoided during the grouse shooting season and, if in doubt, the visitor should first contact Dunecht Estates Office.

TILLYANGUS Ordnance Survey map 1: 50,000 Sheet 37 (Strathdon).
                        1: 25,000 Sheet NJ 42/52 (Rhynie).
    Grid reference: NJ 525245.

The best way to reach the site of battle is along the contemporary drove road known as the Mar Road which can be reached on foot from the village of Clatt, or from the Mains of Tillyangus. The fighting took place between Smallburn and Whitehill, which is crowned by a stone circle. There is no monument, but this is good walking country despite recent afforestation.

CRABSTANE Ordnance Survey map 1: 50,000 Sheet 38 (Aberdeen).
                                           1: 25,000 Sheet NJ 80/90 (Aberdeen).
        Grid reference: NJ 936056.

This battlefield covers much the same ground as the Battle of Justice Mills or Aberdeen (q.v.) and even shares the same monument.

GLENLIVET Ordnance Survey map 1: 50,000 Sheet 36 (Grantown and Cairngorm).
                                           1: 25,000 Sheet NJ 22/32 (Glenlivet).
        Grid reference: NJ 248295.

Although the site of battle is clearly marked on the Ordnance Survey map, its surroundings have been afforested, and consequently the main features of the battlefield have been obscured. The site can be reached by following the Forestry Commission track eastwards from Shenval on the B909, but the only way of viewing the lie of the land adequately would be to ascend Carn a' Bhodaich which requires the adjacent O.S. map Sheet 37 (Strathdon) and a round journey of nine miles or more. There is no monument.

THE BRIG O' DEE Ordnance Survey map 1: 50,000 Sheet 38 (Aberdeen).
                                           1: 25,000 Sheet NJ 80/90 (Aberdeen).
        Grid reference: NJ 929035.

The ancient Brig o' Dee is still the main river crossing and much of the original stonework survives, although the parapet is modern. Perhaps the best viewpoint of the battle is from the landscaped riverbanks on the south western side of the river. The position of Montrose's forces is now occupied by the housing estates of Kincorth where modern street names like Covenanters Row remind us of the battle.

JUSTICE MILLS OR ABERDEEN Ordnance Survey map 1: 50,000 Sheet 38.
                                           1: 25,000 Sheet NJ 80/90
                                           (Aberdeen).
        Grid reference: NJ 936056.

A brass plaque commemorating both this battle and the earlier 'Crabstane Rout' is set into a wall above the Crabstane itself, near the junction of Hardgate and Justice Mills Lane, just off the west end of Union Street. The Crabstane marks the approximate centre of the defender's lines. Montrose's view of the battle can best be appreciated from the public open space below Bon Accord Terrace.

FYVIE Ordnance Survey map 1: 50,000 Sheet 29 (Banff).
                                           1: 25,000 Sheet NJ 73 (Fyvie).
        Grid reference: NJ 774392.

The probable site of battle lies between the Old Home Farm of Fyvie and Parkburn. Fyvie Castle is now open to the public but there is no battlefield monument.

ALFORD Ordnance Survey map 1: 50,000 Sheet 37 (Strathdon).
                                           1: 25,000 Sheet NJ 51 (Alford).
        Grid reference: NJ 562164.

The crossroads of the A980 and A944 lie near the centre of the battlefield which is correctly marked only on recent editions of the Ordnance Survey maps. A good overall view can be obtained from the minor road leading from Gallowhill, and roads and tracks cross the field in plenty. A bench is conveniently provided on the roadside at Ardgathen. Haughton House Country Park lies to the immediate east of the battlefield. The only monument, the Gordon Stone, lies buried beneath the village rubbish dump.

INVERURIE Ordnance Survey map 1: 50,000 Sheet 38 (Aberdeen).
                              1: 25,000 Sheet NJ 72 (Inverurie).
        Grid reference: NJ 780203.

Travellers on the Inverness train receive the best view of the site of this skirmish of the '45. Although most of the field is still open ground, it is broken up by a modern sewerage works and allotment gardens. For the explorer on foot, the conflict can best be appreciated from the Bass of Inverurie which commands a good view over the approaches to the Urie.

SOURCES AND REFERENCES

PART I. ANCIENT AND EARLY MEDIEVAL BATTLEFIELDS: REFERENCES

1. For example, the Franks Casket, a lively and intricate ivory Northumbrian carving dating from the early eighth century—the time of Bede.
2. Sueno's Stone at Forres portrays Scots warriors and probably dates from the late tenth century.
3. *The Orkneyinga Saga*, translated from the Icelandic by Jon A. Hjaltalin and Gilbert Goudie (Edinburgh, 1893). I have used the Longfellow-influenced rhythms of this sanguine translation, but a modern edited version is that of H. Pålsson and P. Edwards, *Orkneyinga Saga: The history of the Earls of Orkney* (London, 1978).
4. *Orkneyinga Saga.*

CHAPTER 1. MONS GRAUPIUS: SOURCES

The only primary source for the campaign and battle of Mons Graupius is Tacitus, whose *Agricola* has been translated many times and is currently available as a Penguin Classic, ed. H. Mattingly and S.A. Handford (Harmondsworth, 1970). The work was written in around 98 AD, fourteen years after the battle, and Tacitus probably derived much of his information from Agricola himself. To that extent he must be considered reliable, but the book is far from ideal for our purpose. It is, by design, a eulogy of its austere hero, with an underlying political message, and it is aimed at Tacitus' contemporaries in Rome, not at posterity. His lack of detail and rhetorical style makes life difficult for those who wish to understand how and why the Caledonians were defeated.

Tacitus could probably have given us most of the information needed to site the battle in a few strokes of his pen. Instead, Scottish historians from Hector Boece onwards have struggled with the threadbare details of geography which Tacitus has grudgingly handed on to us. The early sites suggested for the battle are discussed, and dismissed, by O.G.S. Crawford in his *Topography of Roman Scotland North of the Antonine Wall* (Cambridge, 1949), which proposes Raedykes near Stonehaven as the best contender. The case for Knock Hill, at the Pass of Grange, is discussed in a paper by A.R. Burn, 'In search of a battlefield: Agricola's Last Battle', *Proceedings of the Society of Antiquaries of Scotland [PSAS]*, 87 (1953), 127–33. The case for Duncrub, Perth, is set out by R.W. Feacham in 'Mons Graupius = Duncrub?', *Antiquity*, 44 (1970), 120–4.

The case for Bennachie was first advanced by J.K. St Joseph in 'The Camp at Durno,

Aberdeenshire and Mons Graupius', *Britannia*, 9 (1970), 171–87, and elaborated in his chapter in *Bennachie Again*, ed. A.W.M. Whiteley (Baillies of Bennachie, 1983) 78–90. St Joseph's discovery of the Durno camp has renewed academic interest in the controversy. His conclusions were criticised by W.S. Hanson in 'Roman Campaigns North of the Forth-Clyde Isthmus: the Evidence of the Temporary Camps', *PSAS*, 109 (1970), 140–50. A whole issue of *Scottish Archaeological Forum* (No.12, 1980) was recently devoted to the campaigns of Agricola. Of particular relevance are L. Keppie, 'Mons Graupius: the Search for a Battlefield', 79–87 and G. Maxwell, 'The Evidence of the Temporary Camps', 25–54. In his article in *The Deeside Field* (1984), 'From 83 to 1983: on the trail of Mons Graupius', A.A.R. Henderson suggests that the battle was fought in the far north of Scotland, in Sutherland or Caithness. A book devoted to the subject of Mons Graupius by G.Maxwell, *The First Battle of Caledonia: the Search for Mons Graupius*, is currently in preparation.

The subject of the location of Mons Graupius seems far from closed, although the majority of general text books since 1978 have plumped for the Bennachie site. An indispensible rod for anyone fishing in these troubled waters is the *Ordnance Survey map of Roman Britain* (4th edition, Southampton 1978).

CHAPTER 1. MONS GRAUPIUS: REFERENCES

1. Brian Dobson, 'Agricola's Life and Career', *Scottish Archaeological Forum*, 12 (1980), 1–13.
2. Quotations taken from the *Agricola*, 10.
3. Details derived from the Ordnance Survey's map, *Roman Britain*, which includes a reproduction of Ptolemy's map.
4. Tacitus, *Agricola*, 77.
5. Ibid., 80–1.
6. O.G.S. Crawford, *Topography of Roman Scotland North of the Antonine Wall* (Cambridge, 1949). Still an indispensible guide.
7. For a general discussion of early suggestions, see Keppie, 'Mons Graupius: the Search for a Battlefield', Henderson, 'From 83 to 1983: On the trail of Mons Graupius'.
8. *The Statistical Account of Scotland*, xii, *North and West Perthshire*, ed. B. Lenman (Wakefield, 1977), xii, 80–4, 135n.
9. Crawford, *Topography*.
10. Colonel Alfred Burne's *Battlefields of England* (London, 1950) and *More Battlefields of England* (London, 1952) are still essential reading for those who wish to get the most out of an exploration of Britain's battlefields, although some of his conclusions have since been called into question.
11. Maxwell, 'Agricola's campaign: the evidence of the temporary camps', 25–54.
12. St Joseph, 'The camp at Durno, Aberdeenshire and Mons Graupius'. See also his chapter, 'Durno, Bennachie and Mons Graupius', *Bennachie Again* (1983), 78–90.
13. Local authors have discussed the site in detail e.g. J.C. Watt, *The Mearns of Old* (Edinburgh, 1914) and A. Watt, Highways and Byways Round Stonehaven (Aberdeen, 1984).
14. Feacham, 'Mons Graupius = Duncrub?'
15. Burn, 'In Search of a Battlefield'.
16. St Joseph, 'Camp at Durno'.
17. W.S. Hanson, 'Roman campaigns North of the Forth-Clyde Isthmus'.
18. Keppie, 'Mons Graupius'.
19. Henderson, 'From 83 to 1983'.

20.   Keppie, 'Mons Graupius'.
21.   Duncan Mennie, 'The Battle o' Bennachie'.

CHAPTER 2. NECHTANSMERE: SOURCES

The early sources for the battle of Nechtansmere are in complete contrast to those of Mons Graupius. In the case of Nechtansmere there are at least a dozen more or less contemporary sources, but all are tantalisingly brief. The best known of them is Bede's *History of the English Church and People*, trans. Leo Sherby-Price (revised edn., Harmondsworth 1968). The other near contemporary sources are best listed:

'Life of St Wildred' by Eddius Stephanus, in *The Age of Bede*, trans. J.F. Webb and D.H. Farmer (Harmondsworth, 1983).

Historia Brittonum, in *English Historical Documents 500–1042*, ed. Dorothy White-lock (2nd edn., London, 1979).

Annals of Ulster, in *Early Sources of Scottish History 500–1286*, ed. A.O. Anderson (Edinburgh, 1922).

Annals of Tigernach, in *Early Sources of Scottish History 500–1286*.

Fragment of Duald mac Firbis, in *Early Sources of Scottish History 500–1286*.

The Anglo-Saxon Chronicle, trans. G.N. Garmonsway (London, 1953)—and in Whitelock, *English Historical Documents*.

Two Lives of St Cuthbert, ed. B. Colgrave (Cambridge, 1940). Bede's 'Life of Cuthbert' is also printed in *The Age of Bede*.

Simeon of Durham, *Historia Regum*, ed. T. Arnold, (Rolls Series no.75, vol.ii, 1885)

The campaign and battle were reconstructed by F.T. Wainwright, 'Nechtansmere', *Antiquity* 22 (1948), 82–97. The early Pictish kings, including Bridei, are analysed in M.O. Anderson's *Kings and Kingship in Early Scotland* (Edinburgh, 1973). A very readable general account of Pictish Scotland, which includes a section on the battle, is Isobel Henderson's *The Picts* (London, 1967). *The Problem of the Picts* (Edinburgh, 1955), a series of essays edited by F.T. Wainwright, also provides useful information and A. Smyth, *Warlords and Holy Men. Scotland 80–1000 AD* (London, 1984), provides interesting new insights on the period. Again, the Ordnance Survey's *Map of Britain in the Dark Ages* (2nd edn. with corrections, Southampton 1974), covering the years between 410 and 870 AD, is valuable. An excellent booklet about the battle was written by G. Cruickshank, *Nechtansmere 1300: A Commemoration* (Forfar and District Historical Society, 1985) to mark its 1300th anniversary. A book on the subject by Mr Cruickshank is currently in preparation.

CHAPTER 2. NECHTANSMERE: REFERENCES

1.   This curious entry is found only in the bilingual Canterbury 'F' chronicle, which was not composed until after the Norman Conquest. Its significance is unknown, but it was evidently intended to be an ominous portent, rather like the comet of 1066. The plague of blood was the first of the plagues of Egypt described in Exodus. An unusually large concentration of the microscopic alga, *Haemato-coccus*, imparts a rusty red colour to water, and has been suggested as a possible explanation for 'blood plagues'.

2.   'A Vision of Nechtansmere', *Scots Magazine*, January 1980.

3.   Bede, *History*, 185.

4.   Oswy and Egfrith are spelt as Oswiu and Ecgfrith in many books, in the same way as Alfred and Canute become Aelfred and Cnut. I have sacrificed historical pendantry for the sake of familiarity.

5.   Eddius Stephanus, 'Life of St Wilfred', 152–3.

6. *Anglo-Saxon Chronicle*, (London, 1953), 38.

7. Smyth, *Warlords and Holy Men*, 63–6.

8. 'Siege of Dunfoithir', *Annals of Ulster*, ed. W.M. Hennessy, (Dublin, 1887–1901).

9. Henderson, *The Picts*.

10. Annals of Ulster; Annals of Tigernach, in Anderson, *Early Sources*.

11. Wainwright, 'Nechtansmere'.

12. According to Bede's *Life of St Cuthbert*, a fugitive from the battle arrived in Carlisle only two days later—miraculous, if true. The Norman chronicler, William of Malmesbury, who may have had access to lost northern annals, states that several survivors eventually found their way back to the Northumbrian court. Perhaps they escaped by swimming across the loch and lying low until the fighting was over.

13. Bede, 'Life of St Cuthbert', *The Age of Bede*.

14. Fragment of Duald mac Firbis from Anderson, *Early Sources*. See also Cruickshank, *Nechtansmere 1300*.

15. The three most detailed early accounts of the battle are:

    Bede, *A History of the English Church and People*:
    'King Egfrith, ignoring the advice of his friends ... rashly led an army to ravage the province of the Picts. The enemy pretended to retreat, and lured the king into narrow mountain passes, where he was killed with the greater part of his forces on the 20th of May in his 40th year and the 15th of his reign'.

    Historia Brittonum:
    'Egfrith is he who made war against his cousin, who was king of the Picts, Bridei by name, and he fell there with all the strength of his army; and the Picts with their king victorious, and the Saxons ... never continued to demand tribute from the Picts from the time of the battle, which is called "the fight of Lin Garan".' (*English Historical Documents, 500–1042*).

    Annals of Tigernach:
    'The battle of duin Nechtain took place on 20th May on Saturday; and there Egfrith, Oswy's son, king of the Saxons, was killed (after completing the 15th year of his reign), with a great company of his soldiers, by Brude, son of Bile, the king of Fortriu.' (Anderson, *Early Sources*).

16. *The Statistical Account of Scotland*, xiii, *Angus*, ed. B. Lenman (Wakefield, 1976), 200.

17. *New Statistical Account*, xi, *Forfar and Kincardine* (Edinburgh, 1845), 146–7. An account of the recent history and present appearance of the battlefield is given in Wainwright, 'Nechtansmere', and in his book *The Problem of the Picts*.

18. Cruickshank, *Nechtansmere 1300*.

CHAPTER 3. THE VIKING RAIDS: SOURCES

The sparse contemporary sources of the Viking period in Scotland have been collected in Anderson, *Early Sources of Scottish History*. References to the Vikings in the North East are scattered through the historical and archaeological literature, but most of the sources for the armed conflicts are semi-fictitious in nature, notably the Norse sagas, the writings of Fordun, Boece and Holinshed, and local ballads and folklore. There is a considerable literature on the 'history' of the bishops of Mortlach, founded on the largely imaginary Latin biographies of Boece (Bannatyne Club, 1825). Boece also supplies most of the details of the battle of Mortlach in Lachlan Shaw's *History of the Province of Moray* (revised edn., Glasgow, 1882). The Statistical Accounts contain further information on archaeological finds and folk history, and later local guide books contain brief accounts of the battle apparently based on the above sources. *The Moray Book*, ed. D. Omand (Edinburgh, 1976) is particularly useful for the general history, archaeology and geography of ancient Moray. A general account of this period is I. Grimble, *Highland Man* (Inverness, 1980), published in the Highland Life series by the Highlands and Islands Development Board. This covers the peoples of Moray and the North East in addition to Highland Region *sensu stricto*. The historicity of the ancient bishop's see at Mortlach was investigated by A.D.S. MacDonald and L.R. Laing, 'Early Ecclesiastical Sites in Scotland: a Field Survey', part II, *PSAS*, 102 (1969–70), 129–46.

The only early source for the battle of Burghead is the *Orkneyinga Saga*, a history of the jarls of Orkney, which was probably committed to paper in around 1200. There are a number of modern translations. Sueno's Stone receives its due share of attention in most local history books. For the possible connection with King Dubh, see A.A.M. Duncan's chapter 'The Kingdom of the Scots' in *The Making of Britain* (London, 1984). An interesting article by I. Keillar, 'Sueno's Stone', was published in *Popular Archaeology* (May 1981).

The Ordnance Survey covers the Viking age with another historical map, *Britain before the Norman Conquest, 871-1066* (1973). The blank spaces covering most of the North East are eloquent of our state of knowledge of the period. Finally Smythe's *Warlords and Holy Men* devotes much space to the Vikings and their relationships with the nations of the north.

CHAPTER 3. THE VIKING RAIDS: REFERENCES

1. Details derived from the Ordnance Survey's *Britain before the Norman Conquest*.
2. Annals of Ulster in Anderson, *Early Sources*.
3. Ibid.
4. Smythe, *Warlords and Holy Men*, 191–3.
5. Simeon of Durham, *Historia Regum*.
6. Cited in R.L. Bremner, *The Norsemen in Alban* (Glasgow, 1923).
7. Anderson, *Early Sources*.
8. *New Statistical Account*, xii, *Aberdeenshire* (Edinburgh, 1845), 114.
9. The story is commemorated in verse as *A legend of the Sueno stone*, by James D. Laird (Elgin, n.d.).
10. From the English transcription by Holinshed of Bellenden's metrical Scots translation of Boece (London 1808). Cited with commentary in Shaw's *History of the Province of Moray*.
11. This tradition was described in Shaw's original text of 1827 but the much fuller account of the revised edition, (1882) 136–140, dismisses it.
12. For a fuller account of these matters, see the preface in the Spalding Club edition of Boece's *Registrum Episcopatus Aberdonensis*, ed. J. Moir (1895).
13. MacDonald and Laing 'Early ecclesiastical sites in Scotland'.
14. *Aberdeenshire Journal*, 1 (1908), 42–3.
15. Chamberly Mole, Grampian Regional Council museum services, personal communication.
16. Saga quotations are taken from the translation of *Orkneyinga Saga* by Hjaltalin and Goudie (1893).
17. P.B. Ellis, *Macbeth* (London, 1980).
18. D.P. Kirby, 'Moray prior to 1100', *An Historical Atlas of Scotland c.400–c.1600*, ed. P. McNeill and R. Nicholson (St Andrews, 1975) 20–1.
19. P.B. Ellis, *Macbeth*.
20. A. Dunbar, *Scottish Kings* (Edinburgh, 1906).

21. Most of the early chronicle material in this chapter is taken from Anderson, *Early Sources*, supplemented by *Chronicles of the Picts, Chronicles of the Scots and Other Early Memorials of Scottish History*, ed. W.F. Skene (Edinburgh, 1867).
22. Dorothy Dunnett, *King Hereafter* (London, 1982).
23. See Scottish Development Department's leaflet, *Burghead Well*, (1981).
24. Keillar, 'Sueno's Stone'.
25. Duncan, 'The Kingdom of the Scots', 139–40.
26. Translation of *Heimskringla* in Anderson, *Early Sources*, ii, 216, 236.
27. A.A.M. Duncan, *Scotland: the Early Middle Ages* (Edinburgh, 1975).
28. *Orkneyinga Saga*. The saga writer's statement that King Malcolm IV was 'nine winters old' may have been a slip for 'nine winters as king'. He was about twelve at his accession to the throne.

CHAPTER 4. MACBETH AND LUMPHANAN: SOURCES

As with Nechtansmere, there are at least a dozen early sources which tell us something about the life and death of Macbeth, but the sum of the information they provide is miserably small. The contemporary or near-contemporary Scottish sources have been collected by Anderson, *Early Sources*. These are: Marianus Scotticus; Chronicle of the Kings of Scotland; Chronicle of Melrose (including prose chronicle inserts); Annals of Ulster; Annals of Tigernach; Chronicle of St Berchan.

To these can be added two contemporary English sources, the *Anglo-Saxon Chronicle* and the *Vita Edwardi Regis*, although neither mentions Lumphanan. The Norman chronicle of 'Florence of Worcester' is later in date, but provides some independent information; in its entirety it is available only in original Latin, but relevant selections have been translated and included in *English Historical Documents 1042–1189*, ed. D.C. Douglas and G.W. Greenaway (London, 1953).

Most Scottish histories make use of the more elaborate but mostly fictitious Macbeth stories originating in John of Fordun's *Chronica Gentis Scotorum*, ed. W.F. Skene (Edinburgh, 1871) and Andrew Wyntoun's *Orygynale Cronykil*, ed. D. Laing (Edinburgh, 1872–9). Hector Boece's Macbeth was too much even for the Romantic historians to swallow.

The *New Statistical Account*, xii, *Aberdeenshire* (Edinburgh, 1845) provides a compendium of place-names, antiquities and legends associated with Macbeth in the Lumphanan area, which are supplemented by a briefer note in the *Third Statistical Account. The City of Aberdeen* (Edinburgh 1960). Modern accounts of Macbeth are equally divided between introductions to Shakespeare's play and Scottish history books, with the former sometimes providing more detail than the latter. W.F. Skene's detailed analysis of Macbeth's reign in *Celtic Scotland. A History of Ancient Alban* (Edinburgh, 1876–80) has been supplemented by P.B. Ellis' *Macbeth* (London, 1980), which incorporates Saga material.

CHAPTER 4. MACBETH AND LUMPHANAN: REFERENCES

1. Prose chronicle inserted into the *Chronicle of Melrose*. Wyntoun expanded this passage slightly: (it was) 'a time of gret plenty and he wes in justice rycht lawfull'.
2. *Vita Edwardi Regis*, ed. F. Barlow (London, 1962). The author of this source evidently did not know the name of the Scots king, and called him 'Barbarus'.
3. This is one of the few events in early Scottish history to merit an entry in the Anglo-Saxon Chronicle, and may therefore be worth quoting. The fullest account is given by the northern ('D') chronicle, translated by Dorothy White-lock in *English Historical Documents, 500–1042* (2 edn., London, 1979).

1054. In this year earl Siward invaded Scotland with a great host both by land and sea, and fought against the Scots. He put to flight their king, Macbeth, and slew the noblest in the land, carrying off much plunder such as none had previously gained; but his son, Osbern, and his sister's son and numbers of his housecarls as well as those of the king (Edward the Confessor), were slain there on the festival of the Seven Sleepers (27 July).

The casualty figures are given only by the *Annals of Ulster*, ed. W.M. Hennessy (1887–1901).

4. Anderson, *Early Sources*.
5. Fordun, *Chronica Gentis Scotorum*.
6. Wyntoun, *Orygynale Cronykil*, ii.
7. *New Statistical Account*, xiii, *Banff-Elgin-Moray* (Edinburgh, 1845), 318.
8. Cited in S.R.J. Erskine, *Macbeth* (Inverness, 1930) who attributes the passage to Macbeth in 1057.
9. Eric Talbot, personal communication. See *Scottish Archaeological Forum*, 14 (1981).
10. Macbeth's burial on Iona is cited in the *Chronicle of the Kings of Scotland*, Anderson, *Early Sources*.
11. Recent revisionist tendencies in fiction e.g. Nigel Tranter's *Macbeth the King* (London, 1978) reinstate Macbeth as a hero. The daring thesis of Dorothy Dunnett's *King Hereafter* (London, 1982) is that Macbeth and Thorfinn were one and the same person.
12. *Lufnaut* (Chronicle of Melrose); *Wode of Lunfanan* (Wyntoun); *Lunfannaine* (Holinshed). Lumphanan is probably derived from the Gaelic *Llan*, a church or enclosure, coupled with the name of St *Finan*, one of the disciples of St Kentigern. Irreverent local gossip has it that the village was named after the accidental death of a cottager whose 'lum fa'n in' on top of him during a windy night!
13. Lulach's Stone: W. Douglas Simpson, *PSAS*, 60 (1926), 273–8. Luath's Stone: Coles, *PSAS*, 37 (1903), 87–8. Lulach's Stone is a scheduled ancient monument.

PART II. BATTLEFIELDS OF THE MIDDLE AGES: REFERENCES

1. For coloured paintings of Scottish soldiers of the period see C. Rothero, *The Scottish and Welsh Wars 1250-1400* (Men-at-arms series, Osprey Publications, London).
2. Froissart's Chronicle, translated by Lord Berners in Whitelock, *English Historical Documents, 500–1042*.

CHAPTER 5. ROBERT BRUCE'S CAMPAIGNS IN THE NORTH EAST: SOURCES

The most important narrative source for these battles is J. Barbour, *The Brus* (Spalding Club, 1856), which was composed in about 1375. Fordun's *Scotichronicon*, which originates from the same period, also mentions Slioch and Barra but lacks Barbour's wealth of circumstantial detail and adds little of substance. Barbour was a prominent member of the Aberdeen clergy and hence may have had some first-hand knowledge of this campaign. He presents his Bruce as a hero king and champion of liberty, and tends to attribute feats of arms carried out by his supporters to the king personally. He has proved a generally reliable source although he appears to have reduced the interval between the battles of Slioch and Barra, perhaps for dramatic effect—see G.W.S. Barrow and P.M. Barnes, 'The movements of Robert Bruce between September 1307 and May 1308', *Scottish Historical Review*, 49 (1970), 46–59.

Surviving documentary evidence provides precious scraps of information on the war in the north and there is probably much unpublished evidence of this type which has not yet been used by historians. A.J. Lilburn, for example, has used unpublished accounts in the Public Record Office to throw light on the occupation of Coull Castle during the wars of liberation 'The Castle of Coull', *Aboyne Highland Games Programme* (1984), 27–9.

English chroniclers either knew little about Bruce's days 'in the heather' or found it inexpedient to write about them. The contemporary author of the *Life of Edward II* was tempted to relate the Scottish king's famous deeds but checked himself by reminding his readers that Bruce was officially a sacrilegious traitor. The most detailed modern history is E.M. Barron's *The Scottish War of Independence* (Inverness, 1934). G.W.S. Barrow's biography, *Robert Bruce and the Community of the Realm of Scotland* (2nd edn., Edinburgh, 1976) incorporates the author's recent research on Bruce's itinery between 1307 and 1308, and Ranald Nicholson, *Scotland: The Later Middle Ages* (Edinburgh, 1974), treats the wars of independence in depth. *An Historical Atlas of Scotland c.400–c.1600* (St Andrews, 1975) provides excellent maps and short articles on the political state of the North East at this time. E. Meldrum provides an article on the battles of Slioch and Barra in 'Bruce's Buchan Campaign', *Deeside Field* (1966), 20–6.

CHAPTER 5. ROBERT BRUCE'S CAMPAIGNS IN THE NORTH EAST: REFERENCES

1. According to Barbour, Comyn had made a pact of blood against Bruce, desiring

   Vengeans on yhou, schir king, to tak
   For Schir Johne the Cumynis sak
   That quhilom in Dumfres was slane.

2. The main sources for the course of these events are an almost illegible letter from the sheriff of Banff, partially deciphered recently, and a letter from the earl of Ross. See Barrow, *Robert Bruce and the Community of the Realm*, 249. Elgin Castle had been destroyed during the Moray rebellion in 1297, but had presumably been repaired in the interim.

3. Barbour, *The Brus*. Barbour supplies the weather report for the campaign:

   This was eftir the Martymes [Martinmas: 11 November]
   Quhen snow had helit all the land.

4. Ibid.

5. Fordun, *Scotichronicon*. See Barron, *The Scottish War*.

6. For the dating of the battle of Slioch and the still more problematic battle of Barra, see Barnes and Barrow, 'The movements of Robert Bruce', 46–59.

7. Meldrum 'Bruce's Buchan Campaign', 20.

8. An anonymous verse chronicle inserted in the chronicle of Bower, dates the battle of Barra to Ascension, 1308:

   Anno milleno trecenteno dabis octo,
   In festo Domini, quo scandit sidera coeli...

   The assignation of both Slioch and Barra to major dates in the Christian calendar seems somewhat suspicious, but we have no better evidence.

9. Details derived by Barrow and Barnes, 'Movements', from the letter of the sheriff of Banff.

10. Existence of a settlement in the vicinity of modern day Old Meldrum is implied by several passages in Barbour, although Meldrum, 'Bruce's Buchan Campaign', has pointed out that Barbour's *'Ald Meldrom'* probably refers to a stream Allt Meldrum (now the Lochter burn), and not to a settlement of that name. The present town dates from the seventeenth century.
11. Fordun, *Scotichronicon*.
12. Meldrum, 'Bruce's Buchan Campaign'.
13. Barron, *Scottish War*.
14. *Records of Aboyne*, ed. Charles Gordon, marquis of Huntly (New Spalding Club, 1891).
15. A.J. Lilburn, 'The Castle of Coull', 26–9. For an imaginary reconstruction of the slighting of Coull, see Simpson *Earldom of Mar*.
16. Lilburn, 'Coull'. For traditional story, see Alexander Keith *A Thousand Years of Aberdeen* (Aberdeen, 1972), 27–8.
17. Grampian Regional Council register of archaeological sites.

CHAPTER 6. CULBLEAN: SOURCES

Nearly all of what we think we know about the battle of Culblean rests on a single source, Andrew Wyntoun's *Orygynale Cronykil of Scotland*, ed. D. Laing, (Edinburgh, 1872), composed in the early fifteenth century. The earlier books of Wyntoun's chronicle are fictitious, but he is well-informed on events between 1330 and 1340 and, like Barbour, provides circumstantial evidence and a sound knowledge of local geography to buttress his story. A cautious and discriminating approach is suggested by his use of qualifying phrases like 'thai say' and 'men sayd'. Otherwise the only other contemporary source is the *Scotichronicon* of Fordun, which is briefer and blander.

The site of the battle of Culblean has long been a subject of controversy. Victorian antiquaries placed the battlefield east of the Dinnet lochs. J. Michie's description of the battle in his *History of Loch Kinnord* (revised edn., Aberdeen, 1910) is little more than a paraphrase of Wyntoun. W. Douglas Simpson's study of the battle, the 'Campaign and Battle of Culblean', *PSAS*, 64 (1930), 205 and subsequently in his *Earldom of Mar* (Aberdeen, 1948) is still regarded by many as canonical. Fenton Wyness suggests an alternative reconstruction in his *Royal Valley* (Aberdeen, 1968). Ranald Nicholson brought to the Culblean episode the fruits of his research on the Scottish wars of the 1330s, published in his *Edward III and the Scots* (London, 1965). His painstaking reconstruction of the battle is more faithful to the military tactics of the period and to Wyntoun's description than any of the foregoing accounts. Best of all, it tends to reaffirm Wyntoun's reliability as a witness.

CHAPTER 6. CULBLEAN: REFERENCES

1. The military and political events of 1330–5 were much neglected by historians until Nicholson's seminal work, *Edward III and the Scots*. His subsequent volume *Scotland. The Later Middle Ages* covers the period in greater depth and assurance than previous Scottish histories.
2. Wyntoun, *Orygynale Cronykil*, from which the quotations in this chapter are taken.
3. This recalls the battle of Bannockburn, which was provoked by the English need to relieve Stirling Castle before its agreed surrender date.
4. Earl Patrick of Dunbar was a former adherent of the English king, but, tiring of the incessant English border raids on his estates, had rejoined the Bruce party. Sir Alexander would owe feudal dues to his kinsman, earl Patrick, and was

presumably one of his knights. Sir Alexander had inherited the forfeited Strath-bogie lands and hence had a strong motive in opposing David of Strathbogie. The leading roles given to Gordon and his kin in the Culblean campaign are probably the product of later Gordon legend. Sir Alexander was a comparatively junior figure at that time.

5. Identification made by G.M. Fraser in 1925 and accepted by Simpson and Nicholson. The site has not been excavated.
6. Nicholson, *Edward III and the Scots*.
7. Ibid. For the meaning of 'Umast' and 'Tothir', I have followed A. Watson and B. Allen, *Placenames of Upper Deeside* (Aberdeen, 1981).
8. As I discovered by experiment.
9. Sir Walter Scott, *The Lady of the Lake*, Canto V, x.
10. The Wyntoun reference to the bearing down of bushes, probably those of juniper which still grows here, is a good example of the type of circumstantial evidence which gives credence to Wyntoun.
11. W.D. Simpson, 'The campaign and battle of Culblean', 205.
12. Fenton Wyness, *Royal Valley*, 68–74.
13. Sir Alexander Ogston's *Antiquities of Cromar* (Third Spalding Club, 1931) covers the prehistoric remains of this area in detail. A general account of the history and wildlife of the nature reserve is given by P. Marren, *Muir of Dinnet, portrait of a National Nature Reserve* (Nature Conservancy Council, 1979). The description of the battle of Culblean therein is based on Simpson.

CHAPTER 7. HARLAW: SOURCES

Harlaw suffers from a lack of contemporary sources and from too many dubious later accounts based on the Harlaw ballads. The earliest sources are the Aberdeen Council minute, which gives no details, the MacDonald battle song in *Highland Papers*, i (Scottish History Society, 1914), and the Latin chronicle of Walter Bower, published as *Liber Pluscardensis*, ed. F.J.H. Skene (Edinburgh, 1877–80). Better than any of these is John Major's *History of Greater Britain*, written over a century later in 1521 (Scottish History Society, 1892). The anonymous poem, *Battel of Hayrlaw*, may be a near-contemporary source although it first surfaces in print as late as 1548. The Harlaw ballads are of still later provenance but incorporate material not found elsewhere and some of this may have been based on fact.

Nineteenth century views on the battle of Harlaw, such as the *New Statistical Account*, xii, *Aberdeenshire* (Edinburgh, 1845), are mainly uncritical, whilst that in J. Davidson, *Inverurie and the Earldom of the Garioch* (Edinburgh, 1878) makes improbable assertions without citing evidence. A useful corrective to Lowland tradition is the chapter in W. MacKay's *Sidelights in Highland History* (Inverness, 1925), 281–302. W. Douglas Simpson's *Earldom of Mar* (Aberdeen, 1949) includes a carefully reasoned section on the battle. A detailed account based primarily on the MacDonald version of events is given by I.F. Grant in her *Lordship of the Isles* (Edinburgh, 1982) whilst Ranald Nicholson's *Scotland. The Later Middle Ages* (Edinburgh, 1974) contains interesting comments on the significance of the episode. Another recent account is in Ronald Williams' *The Lords of the Isles* (London, 1984).

CHAPTER 7. HARLAW: REFERENCES

1. Major, *History of Greater Britain*.
2. Hugh MacDonald: 'History of the MacDonalds', *Highland Papers*, i.
3. *Liber Pluscardensis*.
4. Grant, *Lordship of the Isles*.

5.   Fordun, *Chronica Gentis Scotorum.*
6.   Major, *History.*
7.   Nicholson, *Scotland. The Later Middle Ages,* 234.
8.   Wyntoun, *Orygynale Cronykil.* It is frustrating, to say the least, that Wyntoun gives us page after hero-worshipping page of Mar's exploits without ever mentioning the greatest of them all—Harlaw.
9.   Simpson, *Earldom of Mar,* which cites a witness list to a charter granted by the earl on 26 December 1410.
10. Wyntoun, *Orygynale Cronykil.*
11. 'He was a man brave and bold, who prospered in all things, and died in the battle of Harlaw, and with him many praiseworthy burgesses, staunch and steadfast, rooted in honest principles and inured in all probity (whose names, for lack of time, and because of errors as to names, cannot now be set down as it were fitting), in defence of the town, and for the liberty of their fatherland, under the banner of Alexander Stewart, Earl of Mar. And the said Robert was buried before the altar of St Ann, in the foresaid parish Church. On whose soul may God have mercy.' From the roll of benefactors in St Nicholas Church, cited by Simpson, *Earldom of Mar.*
12. Ibid.
13. *Macfarlane's Geographical Collections* (Scottish History Society, 1906–8), i, 6, 17.
14. W. Simpson, *The Province of Mar* (Aberdeen, 1943).
15. Williams, *Lords of the Isles.*
16. Traditional, but there seems no reason to doubt it, viz. J.F. Leslie, *The Irvines of Drum and collateral branches* (Aberdeen, 1909).
17. Nicholson, *Later Middle Ages,* 237.
18. *New Statistical Account,* xii, *Aberdeenshire* (Edinburgh, 1845), 566–70.
19. Ibid.
20. A. Keith, *A Thousand Years of Aberdeen* (Aberdeen 1972), 53–4.
21. Simpson, *Earldom of Mar.*

CHAPTER 8. CORRICHIE: SOURCES

With the battle of Corrichie one passes at last out of the murk of the chronicles and epic romances and into the sunlit world of eye-witness reports and letters. Two letters contained in the *Calendar of State Papers relating to Scotland,* i, ed. J. Bain (1900), pp.662–3, by Randolph, the English ambassador, provide not only the most reliable account of the battle but also an informed commentary on the political events leading up to it. Another source, the *Diurnal of Remarkable Occurrents* (Bannatyne and Maitland Clubs, 1833) was probably sufficiently close to events to be reliable. John Knox's lengthy description in his *History of the Reformation in Scotland,* ed. W. Croft Dickinson (Edinburgh, 1949) is tendentious and coloured by his hostile attitude to Queen Mary. Later accounts, notably Buchanan's *Rerum Scoticarum Historia,* ed. J. Aikman (Edinburgh, 1827) and David Calderwood's *History of the Kirk of Scotland* (Wodrow Society, 1842–9) follow Knox and have little of substance to add. We do not have a contemporary account written from the Gordon point of view, although the *House of Gordon,* ed. J.M. Bulloch (New Spalding Club, 1903–12) contains biographical details of some of the leading participants and their forfeitures, based on the late sixteenth-century Balbithan manuscript.

Modern histories and biographies generally pass quickly over the Corrichie episode. Antonia Fraser gives a concise account in her well-known biography, *Mary Queen of Scots* (London,1969). W.D. Simpson provides the most detail in his *Earldom of*

Mar (Aberdeen, 1948) and Fenton Wyness another of his reconstructions in *Royal Valley* (Aberdeen, 1968). The latter is marred by over-reliance on the largely fictitious ballad of Corrichie, attributed to William Forbes (1772). G. Donaldson, *All the Queens Men: Power and Politics in Mary Stewart's Scotland* (London, 1983) places the Corrichie episode in its contemporary context of political power-struggles. Nigel Tranter gives prominent place to a dramatised account of the battle in his novel, *The Queen's Grace* (London, 1953).

CHAPTER 8. CORRICHIE: REFERENCES

1. Fraser, *Mary, Queen of Scots.*
2. Keith, *A Thousand Years of Aberdeen*, 154.
3. *Calendar of State Papers relating to Scotland*, i. This is the best primary source for the events of the rebellion and battle, and is quoted freely in this chapter.
4. *The House of Gordon.*
5. Donaldson, *All the Queens Men*, includes a list of Huntly's known active supporters.
6. The *Diurnal* states that Huntly's army numbered 800 although Randolph says that his 'whole company was not above 500'. Conceivably, desertions might have depleted the army between the camp at Garlogie and the battle on the following afternoon. In *A History of the Scottish People* (London, 1969) 41, T.C. Smout cites an instance of Huntly's ineffective attempts to call out his feudal tenants to oppose Mary. His Mackintosh tenants were intercepted en route to Huntly's standard by the chief of Clan Mackintosh, who, as their clan chief, successfully called them out to fight *against* Huntly.
7. Knox, *History of the Reformation.*
8. Fenton Wyness, *Royal Valley*, 108, states that the Hill o' Fare was forest in 1562. This is very unlikely. There appears to have been a severe timber shortage in Scotland by the sixteenth century and the early map of the North East by Gordon of Straloch (1654) shows no woodland on or near the Hill o' Fare. Moreover, contemporary accounts plainly state that the battle was fought on the open hillside.
9. Robert Lindsay of Pitscottie, *Historie and Cronicles of Scotland*, ed. A.J.G. Mackay (Scottish Text Society, 1899–1911).
10. Simpson, *Earldom of Mar.*
11. Fenton Wyness, *Royal Valley*, 108–9.
12. Ibid.
13. Knox, *History of the Reformation.*
14. The defeat of the Gordon horse presumably took place before the main foot engagement although this is not clearly stated in the sources.
15. Buchanan, *Rerum Scoticarum Historia.*
16. Cuthbert Graham, 'What Really Happened at Corrichie?', *Leopard Magazine*, June 1979.
17. The best estimate of losses is that of Randolph: 'eleven score' Gordons slain; of Moray's force none, 'but divers hurt and many horses slain'. According to Holinshed's Chronicle, 120 of Huntly's men were slain and 100 taken prisoner.
18. *House of Gordon.*
19. From the 'Chronicle of Aberdeen', cited by Fenton Wyness in *Royal Valley*, 109.
20. Simpson, *Earldom of Mar.*

CHAPTER 9. BLOOD FEUDS: SOURCES

The battles of Tillyangus and the Craibstane share similar contemporary sources. Robert Lindsay of Pitscottie was present in Aberdeen on the day after the Craibstane fight and provides the most detail, *Historie and Cronicles of Scotland*, ed. A.J.G. Mackay (Scottish Text Society, 1899–1911), although unravelling his tortured prose is a painful business. He mentions Tillyangus only briefly. *The Diurnal of Remarkable Occurrents* is reticent on both battles, as is 'The Chronicle of Aberdeen 1491–1595', *Miscellany of the Spalding Club*, ii (1842). Fairly detailed accounts of Tillyangus were written by the participant houses of Gordon and Forbes and are contained in the compilations *The House of Gordon*, and *The House of Forbes*, ed. A. and H. Taylor (Third Spalding Club, 1937). A good but later account is that of Sir Robert Gordon in his *Genealogical History of the Earldom of Sutherland* (Edinburgh, 1813). The Scottish continuation of Holinshed's *Chronicles of England, Scotland and Ireland*, v (London, 1808), quoted in *The House of Gordon*, is well-informed on the Craibstane fight. The Aberdeen burgh archives, on the other hand, pass softly and silently over the matter.

Simpson is good on the battle of Tillyangus in his evergreen *Earldom of Mar*, but neither it nor the Craibstane fight figure prominently in recent histories. The best known episode of this private war is romanticised in the ballad of Edom o' Gordon. The recent K.M. Brown, *Bloodfeud in Scotland, 1573–1625* (Edinburgh, 1986) is essential reading for trying to understand these conflicts.

CHAPTER 9. BLOOD FEUDS: REFERENCES

1. Quoted in *The House of Forbes*.
2. Ibid., citing *History of the Feuds and Conflicts among the Clans* (Glasgow, 1764), 88–9.
3. Gordon of Straloch, *Origo et Progressus Familiae Gordoniorum de Huntly in Scotia*, cited in *The House of Gordon*.
4. *House of Forbes*.
5. Richard Bannatyne (Bellenden), *Memorials of Transactions in Scotland* 1549–73 (Bannatyne Club, 1836).
6. *House of Forbes*.
7. *Diurnal of Remarkable Occurrents*.
8. Buchanan, *Rerum Scoticarum Historia*.
9. *House of Forbes*.
10. Grampian Regional Council, register of archaeological sites.
11. Simpson, *The Earldom of Mar*.
12. Simpson gives a full account of the historical controversies over the burning of Corgarff in *PSAS*, 61, and in the *Earldom of Mar*.
13. *Diurnal*.
14. Letter from Forbes to Lords of the Articles, 1578, cited in Simpson, *Earldom of Mar*.
15. *Diurnal*.
16. Lindsay of Pitscottie, *Historie and Chronicles of Scotland*.
17. Ibid.
18. Continuation of Holinshed's *Chronicles of England, Scotland and Ireland*, v, (London, 1808).
19. Pitscottie, *Historie*.
20. Ibid.

CHAPTER 10. GLENLIVET: SOURCES

The battle of Glenlivet took place after the spate of early Scottish histories, which are the main narrative sources for the events of the 1560s and 1570s, had diminished to a trickle. This loss is more than compensated for, however, by the correspondence between the English ambassador to the Scottish court, Thomas Bowes, and the secretary of state to Queen Elizabeth, Robert Cecil. With the Virgin Queen's advancing age, Scottish affairs and the career of the heir presumptive, James VI, were followed in England with more than the usual amount of interest. Bowes' letters on the campaign and battle have been preserved, and published in the *Calender of State Papers relating to Scotland*, xi (1936). This sequence of letters makes fascinating reading: it begins with gloomy predictions on the likely outcome of Argyll's expedition, cites the testimony of eye-witnesses at the battle and finally, when sufficient reliable information had been obtained, provides a detailed and balanced report sent to Cecil on 12 October. Bowes was kept very well-informed throughout the campaign, probably, like Randolph at Corrichie, by servants attached to Argyll's force. He also obtained an eye-witness account from the other side, in the form of a dispatch based on the testimony of a servant boy in Huntly's company.

Bowes' account can be supplemented by two anonymous letters, cited in David Calderwood's *History of the Kirk of Scotland* (Wodrow Society, 1842–9), which were evidently written by a person or persons close to Argyll. This provides additional information, notably on the heroic behaviour of the MacLean chief and on the alleged treachery of Lochnell, although the writer is clearly less impartial than Bowes. Taken together, this series of letters provides excellent contemporary evidence for the events of the battle. *The Ballad of Glenlivet* (first printed in 1681) is early in date and, it has been suggested, incorporates an unpublished eye-witness testimony (*House of Gordon*). If so, it is much the most valuable of the north eastern battle ballads. Perhaps because the battle of Glenlivet was an isolated incident which led to no new political developments, there are very few modern reconstructions and even King James' most recent biographer passes quickly over it. An exception was Andrew Lang, *History of Scotland* (Edinburgh, 1900–7), who had a taste for the drama of the battlefield, but he attached too much credence to the Calderwood letters and was apparently unaware of the Bowes correspondence. See also K.M. Brown, *The Bloodfeud in Scotland*.

CHAPTER 10. GLENLIVET: REFERENCES

1. Moray was the son-in-law of the earl who had triumphed over Huntly's grandfather at Corrichie. The murder of the 'bonny earl' was denounced from every pulpit in the land, although he had brought retribution on his own head by suborning Huntly's dependents and provoking disorder in the north. The ballad makers followed the example of the ministers of the kirk by representing the earl as a well-intentioned innocent.

2. Letter from the English ambassador, Thomas Bowes, to Secretary Cecil, dated 24 September 1594, *Calendar of State Papers relating to Scotland*, xi.

3. Ibid., letter, based on eye-witness reports, from Bowes to Cecil dated 12 October, correcting an earlier estimate of 4,000 horse and foot on 3 October.

4. Ibid., Bowes-Cecil correspondence, dated 24 September.

5. Ibid., dated 12 October.

6. Ibid., dated 7 October.

7. Ibid., dated 28 September.

8. Ibid., dated 12 October etc.

9. Anonymous letter cited in Calderwood, *History of the Kirk of Scotland*.

10. Ibid. Huntly's force assembled 'on a faire green field'. 'At last the parties drawing

neere (each) other within a shott, Huntlie's forces marched forward with a sober pace, in respect the enemie was on the hight of a hill rough and high'.

11. Ibid. 'Macklaine ... having a jacke upon him, two habergiouns with a murrion, and a Danish axe, he perceiving Huntlie's standard, played so valientlie with the axe, that he slue foure or five, untill the time he came to Huntlie's standard, and sticked the horse whereupon the bearer raid, and nixt cutted himself in two at the waste, and brought the standard away'.

12. *Calendar of State papers relating to Scotland*, xi, Bowes-Cecil correspondence, 12 October.

13. Ibid., Bowes to Cecil, 8 October: Argyll lost Lochnell and 300–400 'of the common sort'; Huntly lost 14 'landed gentlemen of good quality', but there was 'great difference' in the report of persons slain, 'some say under 100'.

     Bowes to Cecil, 12 October: Argyll lost 500 men killed according to one account; 'Maclean slain and others to the number of 200' by another. Calderwood: Huntly lost 460 men, mostly 'in the beginning'.

14. *House of Gordon.*

15. *Calendar of State Papers relating to Scotland*, ii, Bowes to Cecil, 12 October.

16. Ibid.

17. G. Donaldson, *Scotland. James V–James VII* (Edinburgh, 1965), 194.

18. *Calendar of State Papers relating to Scotland*, ii, Bowes to Cecil, both descriptions by eye-witnesses.

CHAPTERS 11–14. THE CIVIL WARS: SOURCES

The battles of the Civil War in the North East tend to share common narrative sources. Four of these stand head and shoulders above the rest, and provide a continuous and often colourful narrative of the unfolding events as contemporaries saw them. These are:

John Spalding, *Memorialls of the Troubles in Scotland and England 1624–1645* (Spalding Club, 1850–1).

James Gordon, Minister of Rothiemay, *A History of Scots Affairs 1637–1641* (Spalding Club, 1841).

Patrick Gordon of Ruthven, *A Short Abridgement of Britane's Distemper 1639–1649* (Spalding Club, 1844).

George Wishart, *The Memoirs of James, Marquis of Montrose*, ed. A.D. Murdoch and H.F.M. Simpson (London, 1893). All four accounts are partial to varying degrees, and none are sympathetic to the covenanters. Wishart and Gordon of Ruthven cover all the north eastern battles, whereas Spalding's account ceases shortly before Alford, and James Gordon covers the First Bishops' War only. Spalding is arguably the liveliest and most immediate of the four, and his all too brief depictions of the sack of Aberdeen and the battle for the Brig o' Dee are among the highlights of contemporary Scottish histories. Gordon of Ruthven is the most important source for the battles of Aberdeen and Alford. As some counterweight to the Montrose/Gordon faction, there is the 'Book of Clanranald' in *Reliquiae Celticae*, ed. A. MacBain and J. Kennedy (Inverness, 1892–4) which gives a Highlander's point of view of the battle of Alford.

The Covenanters were understandably reticent about their defeats, but William Baillie's version of events at Alford is printed in Robert Baillie, *Letters and Journals*, ed. D. Laing (Bannatyne Club, 1841–2). This is the first time we have first-hand tactical details from one of the commanders-in-chief in a battle. If only we had as much from Montrose. The earl of Lothian also has a few words to say about his part in the battle of Fyvie, printed in *Correspondence of ... Earl of Ancram, and ... Earl of Lothian*, ed. D. Laing (Edinburgh, 1875), i, 178.

The ballads are unusually reticent about the Civil War, but there are several versions of the Battle of the Brig o' Dee. One of these, printed in *A Book of Scottish Pasquils*, ed. J. Maidment (Edinburgh, 1868), is strongly covenanting in tone, whilst the *Bonnie John o' Pitmeddin* seems to incorporate local royalist sentiment. The ballad of the Battle of Alford hero-worships Lord Gordon at the expense of Montrose, who is not mentioned at all.

Modern histories of the Civil War are numerous. Montrose earned no less than three biographies within two years (Ronald Williams, 1975; Max Hastings, 1977; Edward J. Cowan, 1977). All contain detailed accounts of his battles although Cowan's documentation is more thorough than the others. A useful corrective to the domination of Montrose is David Stevenson's *Alasdair MacColla and the Highland Problem* (Edinburgh, 1980). The First Bishops' War of 1639 is covered in the same author's *The Scottish Revolution, 1637–44* (Newton Abbott, 1973). Alexander Keith provides two interesting chapters on the impact of the war from the standpoint of the burgh of Aberdeen in *A Thousand Years of Aberdeen* (Aberdeen, 1972).

The battle of Alford is one of the few north eastern battles of which an adequate account exists in publications which are specifically about British battlefields. H.C.B. Roger's *Battles and Generals of the Civil Wars* (London, 1968) and W. Seymour's *Battles in Britain*, ii (London, 1975) provide maps and aerial photographs. The battle of Fyvie is one of the set pieces in A.M.W. Stirling's *Fyvie Castle: its lairds and times* (London, 1928).

The most important book on the military organisation, tactics and campaigns of the Civil War is P. Young and R. Holmes, *The English Civil War* (London, 1974). To date, we await a comparable work covering the Civil War in Scotland.

CHAPTER 11. THE FIRST BISHOPS' WAR: REFERENCES

1. Spalding, *Memorialls*.
2. Huntly's written complaint about the 'unfair meenes' which had led to his incarceration at Edinburgh still survives. It concludes with his famous affirmation of loyalty 'you may tak my heid from my schuderis but not my hairt from my sovereigne'. No one, however, had suggested removing his head at this stage.
3. According to Gordon of Ruthven he was only thirteen at this time.
4. Spalding, *Memorialls*.
5. P. Gordon of Ruthven, *A Short Abridgement*.
6. J. Gordon, *History of Scots Affairs*.
7. The last recorded use of the longbow on the battlefield was by a party of Camerons and Farquharsons at a skirmish near the Pass of Ballater in 1654, after they had been intercepted by a detachment of Cromwell's Roundheads under Colonel Morgan. In the rocky confines of the pass, the archers proved surprisingly effective.
8. The covenanters consistently showed a marked absence of any sense of humour. The incident is eloquent of the Aberdonians feelings towards them.
9. Stevenson, *The Scottish Revolution*.
10. J. Gordon, *History of Scots Affairs*.
11. There were 'severall feeld peeces tacken off of Dunotyre for that purpose... (and) two brasse battering pieces, half canone, which served them to great pourpose', Spalding, *Memorialls*.
12. P. Gordon, *A Short Abridgement*.

13. Spalding, *Memorialls*.
14. J. Gordon and Spalding both give lively accounts of the battle, with a wealth of circumstantial detail. I have attempted to conflate these sources which, although in agreement about the general drift of events, differ in their reporting of detail and in their apportionment of blame.
15. Spalding, *Memorialls*.
16. *The ballad of Bonnie John o' Pitmeddin*:

> He rode on, and further on,
> unto the Twa Mile Cross;
> and there, the Covenanters' shot
> it flung him frae his horse.
> Some rode upon the black and grey,
> some rode upon the broon;
> but bonnie John o' Pitmeddin
> lay gaspin' on the grun.

The unfortunate Pitmedden had been 'dung in three' by Colonel Henderson's shot, and was thereupon stripped of his clothing by Forbes of Craigievar: 'they left him nae a flee'.
17. Spalding names the townsfolk killed as John Forbes, Patrick Grey, David Johnston and Thomas Davidson; the covenanter was a Ramsay, brother to the laird of Balmain. David Stevenson has pointed out that Spalding was only concerned with recording the names of his fellow Aberdonians. There may well have been other casualties about which we know nothing.
18. This time, the fine was paid. The account still survives in the burgh records: 'Item, 21st June: Deburst to the Erles of Mersheall and Montrose, sojours, at command of the Baillies and with adwyse of the whole toune, for saving the toune from ploundering at the intaking of the Brig o' Dee, £4,000'.
19. *Calendar of State Papers, Domestic, 1639* (1873), 386.

CHAPTER 12. JUSTICE MILLS (OR ABERDEEN): REFERENCES

1. Spalding, *Memorialls*, ii, 406.
2. M. Hastings, *Montrose. The King's Champion* (London, 1977), 180.
3. Spalding, *Memorialls*: 'The nicht befoir this feild wes fought oure people saw the moone ryss as reid as blood tuo houris befoir hir tyme ... Quhairu pone follouit blood and hairschip bothe, and many honest men brocht to their grave'.
4. The most detailed sources of the battle disagree over the deployment of the royalist wings. Gordon of Ruthven places Nat Gordon and Hay on the left and Rollo on the right. His version of the battle commands more credence than that of Wishart, since the latter is plainly in error on a number of points. Spalding has little to say on the subject.
5. Gordon of Ruthven, *A Short Abridgement*, 80–4.
6. Suggested by Keith in *Aberdeen*, 195.
7. Gordon of Ruthven, *A Short Abridgement*.
8. Spalding, *Memorialls*: 'The fight contynewis hotlie during the space of two houris. At last we tak the flight'.
9. Ruthven, *A Short Abridgement*.
10. Wishart, *Memoirs*, 66–9. Spalding also mentions that some of the Fife regiment died in the battle.
11. Spalding, *Memorialls*.
12. Aberdeen Council records, cited in Keith, *Aberdeen*, 196.

13. E.J. Cowan, *Montrose, For Covenant and King* (London, 1977), 167.
14. Hastings, *Montrose*, 188.
15. See, for instance, '*Walkin' the Mat, Past Impressions of Aberdeen*' (Aberdeen, 1980), 101.
16. Keith, *Aberdeen*, 196.

CHAPTER 13. FYVIE: REFERENCES
1. The well-known story of the Fyvie chamberpots is related by Wishart, who rejoiced in this form of backs-to-the-wall heroism.
2. Wishart, *Memoirs*.
3. Gordon of Ruthven, *A Short Abridgement*. There is little dispute over these figures.
4. *Correspondence of ... Earl of Ancram.*
5. Wishart says Magnus O'Cahan; Ruthven, Donald Farquharson. The same discrepancy arises with their respective accounts of the battle of Alford.
6. *Correspondence of ... Earl of Ancram.*

CHAPTER 14. ALFORD: REFERENCES
1. The ballad of the battle asserts that the royalist camped at Asloun. If so, it is probable that Montrose spent the night at Asloun Castle; he usually accepted comfort whenever it was offered, and one is reminded of the fatal battle of Philiphaugh, where his Irish soldiers were attacked in their camp while Montrose was tucking into a hearty breakfast at Selkirk.
2. The battlefield is described by Wishart, *Memoirs*, 108–11. For modern reconstructions of the battle of Alford, see Rogers, *Battles and Generals of the Civil War*, Seymour, *Battles in Britain*, ii, and J. Kinross, *The Battlefields of Britain* (Newton Abbot, 1979).
3. The sources are at odds as to the precise number, and reconstructions therefore differ eg. *c*.2,500 foot, 600 horse (Williams), 2,000 foot, 600 horse (Hastings), 1,200 foot, 500 horse (Kinross). General Baillie, of course, maintained that he was greatly outnumbered.
4. Wishart, *Memoirs*: these figures are accepted by most modern reconstructions.
5. Or, according to Gordon of Ruthven, *A Short Abridgement*, by James Farquharson of Inverey, who was acceptable both to the Highlanders, 'for he had their language', and to the Gordons, for he was a dependent of the house of Huntly. George Drummond of Balloch also commanded a company but, we are told, 'his command could not be much, since he wanted the (Gaelic) language'. Cowan, *Montrose*, points out that such a man, with estates in Perthshire, would almost certainly have spoken Gaelic.
6. Wishart, *Memoirs*, corroborated by Baillie, *Letters and Journals*, ii, 417–8.
7. Wishart, *Memoirs*.
8. Baillie, *Letters and Journals*.
9. Gordon of Ruthven, *A Short Abridgement*, 128–31.
10. *Reliquiae Celticae*, ii, 195.
11. Gordon of Ruthven, *A Short Abridgement*.
12. Ibid. Ruthven's three pages of praise underline his purpose in writing. He was a Gordon, concerned principally in recording the doings of the great name of Gordon. He was not much interested in anybody else. Much the same could be said of the balladeer of the battle who fails to mention Montrose even once!
13. Cowan, *Montrose*, 211.
14. Gordon of Ruthven, *A Short Abridgement*.

15. S.R. Gardiner, *History of the Great Civil War* (London, 1893–4).
16. An example is the battle of Auldearn. Gardiner's 'classic' account of the battle has been repeated time and again, and only very recently have serious doubts been cast on its accuracy, Stevenson, *Alasdair MacColla*.
17. W. Douglas Simpson (1919), 'The Topographical Problem of the Battle of Alford', *Aberdeen University Review*, 6 (1919).
18. Williams, *Montrose*.

CHAPTER 15. INVERURIE AND THE '45: SOURCES

The Inverury fight was a relatively minor episode in the eyes of contemporaries and was overshadowed by great events elsewhere during the winter and spring of 1746. The *Scots Magazine* for December 1745 devotes only a paragraph to it, and the *Gentleman's Magazine* of January 1746 is scarcely less reticent. The episode was of special interest to Aberdeen, however, and some attempt at accurate reportage of the affair was made in the following years. An anonymous report, probably written at the end of 1746 or early 1747 by a local minister and entitled 'Memoirs of the rebellion in 1745 and 1746 so far as it concerned he Counties of Aberdeen and Banff' is a well-informed and very readable local account of these turbulent months and by far the best version of the Inverury skirmish that we have. W.B. Blaikie did a service to local history by publishing it in *Origins of the Forty Five* (Scottish History Society, 1916). Another contemporary source, which supplements the anonymous 'Memoirs', is a letter to the bishop of Aberdeen by John Daunies, contained in *The Lyon in Mourning*, ed. H. Paton (Scottish History Society, 1895–6), ii. The MacBean Collection, housed in the University of Aberdeen, is one of the finest historical treasuries of the Jacobite era in existence and contains most or all of the principal sources. See M.D. Allardyce, *Aberdeen University Library. MacBean Collection. A Catalogue* (Aberdeen, 1949).

General histories of Jacobite activities in the North East during the '45 include C.S. Terry, *The Rising of 1745*, (London, 1900), which provides excellent bibliographic coverage, and A. and H. Taylor, *Jacobites of Aberdeenshire and Banffshire in the Forty Five* (Aberdeen, 1928). Alexander Keith, *A Thousand Years of Aberdeen* (Aberdeen, 1972) devotes a brief chapter to Aberdeen's unhappy experience of occupation by Jacobite and government troops. The best modern account of Jacobitism is B. Lenman, *The Jacobite Risings in Britain, 1689–1745* (London, 1980).

CHAPTER 15. INVERURIE AND THE '45: REFERENCES

1. 'Memoirs' in *Origins of the Forty-Five*. This source is quoted extensively; indeed it could almost stand by itself, without further comment.
2. 'Memoirs'.
3. Mr Horn of Westhall, for instance, who, realising that arms were likely to be in short supply, dutifully equipped all of his tenants with home-made spears. He later had second thoughts and decided against taking any further action.
4. 'Memoirs'.
5. Ibid.
6. Letter, dated 1749, from papers of Robert Forbes, published in *The Lyon in Mourning*, ii, 344.
7. 'Memoirs'.
8. Ibid.
9. *Lyon in Mourning*.
10. 'A few were killed on either side. The rebels took 41 prisoners; among whom are Mess. Gordon of Ardoch jnr., Forbes of Echt and John Chalmers, one of the Regents in the University of Aberdeen'—*Scots Magazine* (December 1745).

'Upon the Macleods side was taken Gordon of Ardoch and 60 private men; on both sides 14 killed and 20 wounded'—John Daunies.

11. The 'Memoirs' author is the only source to mention the capture of Mac-Crimmon.

12. 'Memoirs'.

13. For this, and like episodes elsewhere, See John Prebble, *Culloden* (Harmondsworth, 1961).

INDEX